ABOUT THE AUTHOR

James Morrison is a Reader in Journalism in the School of Creative and Cultural Business at Robert Gordon University, Aberdeen. He specializes in moral panics and media-political discourses around stigmatized groups, including benefit claimants, immigrants and teenagers, and how the public responds and contributes to these narratives through interpersonal communication and social media. Before becoming an academic, he was a full-time journalist, working for a succession of newspapers, including *The Independent on Sunday*, before going freelance. He has since written for numerous papers and magazines, including *Guardian Society*, *The Times*, *Telegraph Magazine* and *The Ecologist*. He is a senior examiner and member of the National Council for the Training of Journalists' Public Affairs Board and the author of *Essential Public Affairs for Journalists*. Other recent academic publications include the monograph *Familiar Strangers, Juvenile Panic and the British Press: The Decline of Social Trust* and articles in *Digital Journalism* and the *Journal of Applied Journalism and Media Studies*.

SCROUNGERS

MORAL PANICS AND MEDIA MYTHS

JAMES MORRISON

ZED

Scroungers: Moral Panics and Media Myths was first published in 2019
by Zed Books Ltd, The Foundry, 17 Oval Way, London SE11 5RR, UK.

www.zedbooks.net

Copyright © James Morrison 2019

The right of James Morrison to be identified as the author
of this work has been asserted by him in accordance with
the Copyright, Designs and Patents Act, 1988.

Typeset in Haarlemmer MT by seagulls.net
Index by James Morrison
Cover design by Steven Marsden

A catalogue record for this book is available from the British Library

ISBN 978-1-78699-214-7 hb
ISBN 978-1-78699-213-0 pb
ISBN 978-1-78699-215-4 pdf
ISBN 978-1-78699-216-1 epub
ISBN 978-1-78699-217-8 mobi

MIX
Paper from
responsible sources
FSC
www.fsc.org   FSC® C013604

Printed and bound by CPI Group (UK) Ltd, Croydon, CR0 4YY

CONTENTS

LIST OF TABLES

LIST OF ACRONYMS AND ABBREVIATIONS

ASB	antisocial behaviour
ASBO	antisocial behaviour order
BSA	British Social Attitudes
DCLG	Department for Communities and Local Government
DfES	Department for Education and Skills
DLA	Disability Living Allowance
DHSS	Department of Health and Social Security
DSS	Department of Social Security
DWP	Department for Work and Pensions
ESA	Employment and Support Allowance
EU	European Union
HB	Housing Benefit
IB	Incapacity Benefit
IDS	Iain Duncan Smith
IFS	Institute for Fiscal Studies
IMF	International Monetary Fund
IPSO	Independent Press Standards Organisation
IRA	Irish Republican Army
IS	Income Support
JAM	just about managing
JSA	Jobseekers' Allowance
LGBT	lesbian, gay, bisexual, transgender
LHA	Local Housing Allowance
LLAKES	Centre for Research on Learning and Life Chances

MP	Member of Parliament
MEP	Member of the European Parliament
NAO	National Audit Office
NEET	young person not in education, employment or training
NHS	National Health Service
NSPCC	National Society for the Prevention of Cruelty to Children
OAP	old age pensioner
OECD	Organisation for Economic Co-operation and Development
ONS	Office for National Statistics
OPEC	Organization of the Petroleum Exporting Countries
PCS	Public and Commercial Services Union
PIP	Personal Independence Payment
UC	Universal Credit
WCA	Work Capability Assessment

ACKNOWLEDGEMENTS

I am heavily indebted to Professor Peter Golding and Sue Middleton for *Images of Welfare*, their ground-breaking, multi-faceted anatomy of an earlier 'scrounger' panic, against which all other works on this subject should be judged. As Peter observed in a recent email exchange, the 'enduring relevance' of the 'scrounger' folk-devil is enough to leave one 'perennially depressed' (though that is not my aim!). Thanks are also due for the sage advice and feedback I received from other academics (and editors) in relation to the various conference papers, articles and proposal drafts involved in this book's gestation. Chief among these have been my editor at Zed Books, Ken Barlow; my erstwhile PhD supervisor, Professor James Curran, at Goldsmiths; Dr Justin Schlosberg, at Birkbeck; Jakob Horstmann, at Transcript Verlag; Professor Chas Critcher, at Sheffield Hallam; Dr Stuart Waiton, at Abertay; Professor Bob Franklin, at Cardiff; Staffordshire University's inestimable, irrepressible Professor Mick Temple; and Samira Ahmed (surely Britain's most cerebral journalist).

I also want to thank the family, friends and colleagues who have encouraged and emboldened me by repeatedly reassuring me that this was a project (and cause) worth pursuing – despite all the competing commitments and pressures that consistently threatened to derail it. Of friends and colleagues, my thanks go out especially to my political soulmate and fellow traveller, Justin McKeating, and to Dr Fiona Smith and Dr Elizabeth Tait at Robert Gordon University. Endless thanks, also, to my beautiful wife, Annalise, and three children, who have tolerated my 'working holidays' (and evenings and weekends) over the past two years. I also owe everything to my father, Andrew, who endured years of involuntary unemployment and poverty during the 1980s, and my late mother, Helen, who stood at his side throughout, loving and resolute to the end. Above all, though, I want to thank my brother, Alan Morrison: a gifted and passionate poet, polemicist and campaigner who, aside from his inspiring verse and calls to arms in defence of the Welfare State, has had more experience than most of the unforgiving harshness of 21st century social (in)security. In summing up the disturbing levels of satisfaction the Great British public is assumed to derive from today's media diet of poverty porn and shirker-bashing news stories, the wording of his recent poem '"St. Jude" and the Welfare Jew' could hardly be more apt:

> ... it's permanent open season for press-
> Persecution of the unemployed as
> '*Parasites*' – fleas of unearned leisure;
> Calling strugglers '*scroungers*' is
> England's guiltless pleasure ...
> (*Shabby-Gentile*, Culture Matters, 2018)

Beyond this, I want to acknowledge the unnecessary, often brutal, suffering inflicted on the numerous people for whom I wrote this book: the unsung casualties put through the wringer by the relentless onward march of 'welfare reform' and its invidious enabling and accompanying discourses. This book aims to do everything within its power (however modest) to expose and contest these injustices for what they are – and point the way towards a *genuinely* 'fair', compassionate, more socially secure future. The fightback has begun.

INTRODUCTION

SCROUNGERPHOBIA REVISITED

SHIRKER-BASHING AND FERAL FREAK-SHOWS

SCROUNGER

NOUN

Informal, derogatory

A person who borrows from or lives off others.

[with modifier] 'welfare scroungers' (Oxford Dictionaries 2017b)

When Jeremy Corbyn launched his 2016 campaign to be re-elected leader of the Labour Party, declaring he had 'helped change the debate on welfare' and that no 'frontbench politician' would ever again use 'disgraceful, divisive terms like "scrounger", "shirker" or "skiver"' to dismiss claimants, his comments marked something deeper than a statement of personal principle (Corbyn 2016). They signalled a public repudiation of 40 years of mainstream political consensus (upheld as much by Labour as the Conservatives) around the framing of benefit recipients as feckless, workshy and largely responsible for their own poverty. In going on to explicitly link Britain's mistreatment of its poorest citizens with the disenfranchisement felt by a much wider constituency, the 'left-behind', including voters in one-time Labour heartlands who had recently voted to leave the European Union, he hinted at something more profound. At last a national party leader was grappling with the shared sense of dislocation felt by millions for whom decades of neoliberalism had failed to bear fruit. Eschewing divide-and-rule discourses often used to deflect attention from the structural forces responsible for working-age poverty, he instead floated a now more widely accepted thesis: that the zero-hours contract, payday loan, low-rent economy of post-industrial Britain enriches few and, ultimately, impoverishes all.

While Corbyn's sentiments represented the most direct expression to date by an establishment political figure of an emerging counter-discourse against the problematization of social security, the ground for his full-throated remarks had been laid in surprising quarters. Though more measured in tone, exactly four months earlier Conservative Stephen Crabb had used his maiden House of Commons speech as Work and Pensions Secretary to call time on years of cuts to the Welfare State under his predecessor, Iain Duncan Smith. In a striking break with the rhetorical tone struck by Tory frontbenchers since at least the 1990s, Crabb – the son of a single mother who had raised him, for a time, on benefits – acknowledged that 'behind every statistic' was 'a human being' and that governments sometimes 'forget that' (Crabb 2016). Equally remarkably (if disingenuously), Duncan Smith had also disowned the continuing 'attack on working-age benefits' the day before, in a resignation letter condemning then Chancellor George Osborne's determination to cut disability benefits further (quoted in McCann 2016).

A more strident assault on anti-welfare discourse came during the 2017 general election campaign, in a calibrated pincer-movement from ex-Prime Minister Gordon Brown, combining a stump speech in his former constituency, Kirkaldy, with an angry comment piece in the *Guardian* (Brown 2017). In his article, Brown predicted that five more years of Conservative rule would induce an 'epidemic of poverty' worse than the 'darkest days of Thatcher–Major rule'. Condemning the 'rancid Tory talk of "skivers" and "shirkers"', he accused the incumbent government of wanting a 'free hand to wage war on the poor' (Brown 2017). This was the same Brown, lest we forget, whose Labour Work and Pensions Secretary, James Purnell, had presided over stringent new levels of conditionality for unemployed claimants; part-privatization of welfare services; and (most notoriously) the introduction of Work Capability Assessments to test the 'fitness for work' of people on sickness and disability-related benefits.

What, then, lay behind this apparent sea-change in the political framing of the unemployed and those too sick to work – and how rapidly had it come about? In the months preceding Crabb's tacit *mea culpa* and Brown's double-speak appeal to voters' compassion, a groundswell of resistance had been brewing. One manifestation of this was the acclaim heaped on socialist filmmaker Ken Loach's then latest offering, *I, Daniel Blake*, whose eponymous protagonist is a middle-aged carpenter fighting to retain his disability benefits after suffering a heart attack. The film's depiction of contemporary poverty not only generated more mainstream media attention than any number of Loach's earlier works, but won the Palme d'Or at Cannes and, importantly, catalysed a fierce national debate about the brutality of welfare cuts. Like his seminal 1966 masterpiece *Cathy Come Home*, it landed at precisely the right moment: galvanizing an already simmering counter-discourse mounted by a vague and informal, but increasingly audible, alliance of grassroots claims-makers, ranging from issue-specific groups representing the disabled, such as the Black Triangle Campaign, through homelessness charities like Shelter to e-petition keyboard warriors to writers and painters, from poetry imprint Caparison to the disabled artist Vince Laws.

For all these countervailing forces, though, it would be folly to pretend that the battle against the stigmatization of people experiencing poverty is won. On the contrary, this book argues that the discourse of distrust and suspicion about the nature and motivations of people claiming benefits remains deeply engrained. How could it not be, after two generations of neoliberal hegemony, during which small government, individualized prescriptions for complex societal problems have been evangelically pursued over any concerted efforts to promote more redistributive or community-oriented approaches – let alone a recognition that the *problems themselves* are systemic, rather than the result of individuals' personal failings? The inevitable backlash against the meanest, most invidious discourses masks the fact that deep-rooted suspicions and resentments, fuelled by politicians and much of the media, continue to divide many of those whose collective best interests would be better served by uniting to demand a new, more equitable, settlement.

This is not to downplay significant recent strides made to counteract long-running received wisdom about the (false) distinction between 'deserving' and 'undeserving poor'. One heartening finding of the 2017 British Social Attitudes survey was that the proportion of respondents agreeing that 'most dole claimants' were 'fiddling' was 'at its lowest level since 1986', showing 'a sudden drop in the perceived prevalence of benefit manipulation, which, if sustained, indicates a major shift in attitudes towards benefit claimants' (Baumberg Geiger et al. 2017). For all such progress, though, the extent to which attitudes towards the economically poorest have become more tolerant and trusting has been overstated. While the number of survey respondents who judged 'fiddling' endemic decreased significantly between 2014 and 2016 (from 35 to 22 per cent), this still left almost one in four members of the public buying into the scrounger discourse. By contrast, 'a double standard' (to quote the survey's authors) continued to apply towards 'tax avoidance and benefit manipulation', with respondents judging welfare recipients 'more harshly' than those guilty of 'what might be considered similar "offences"' relating to taxation (Baumberg Geiger et al. 2017). For this reason alone, interrogating the discourse of distrust that poisons debates about British poverty remains as urgent as ever.

This book's purpose is not to explore what it *means* or *feels like* to suffer poverty in twenty-first century Britain. Nor does it offer a policy prospectus for how the UK might be transformed into a more economically equal society, or even a detailed debunking of the many bogus claims made about the *cost* of social security or routinely exaggerated pronouncements about benefit fraud. Others have already tackled these themes admirably. For nuanced, moving ethnographic accounts of the reality of life for those subsisting on meagre wages and benefit top-ups, look no further than the work of sociologists Tracy Shildrick, Robert MacDonald and Colin Webster (2012) or Kayleigh Garthwaite (2014, 2016). For a systematic treatise on the structural causes of today's wide-scale deprivation and how politics might usefully address these, social scientist Joanna Mack and economist Stewart Lansley (Lansley & Mack 2015) mount an impressively counter-discursive case based on an in-depth survey of its drivers. Development studies professor Guy Standing (2014, 2016) on the post-working-class 'precariat' is equally essential.

Though the concerns of all these studies – inequality, labour market insecurity, and political misdiagnoses and misrepresentations of their causes – are inherently relevant to *Scroungers*, its ambit is distinct in several respects. Primarily, it is not so much an exploration of the nature, causes or symptoms of poverty, but the popular *portrayals* (and, by inference, *perceptions*) of groups in society who are socioeconomically 'poor'. Inverted commas are used here advisedly, as several academics (e.g. Lister 2004a and 2004b) have rightly decried the depersonalizing, patronizing ways in which people are categorized as poor (often by well-intentioned agencies, scholars and commentators), and how this term, like more pejorative labels, acts as a disempowering identity-marker that casts people as one-dimensional victims; as 'different or "other"' to we 'non-poor' (Welshman 2007: 231). In so doing, this discourse both obscures the more complex (often positive) realities of people's lives, while failing to acknowledge the key obstacle preventing them using their agency as social actors to lift themselves out of poverty: 'access to resources' (Lister, as cited in Welshman 2007: 231). In a book concerned with contesting the objectification of people experiencing poverty it seems wise to proceed with this note of semantic caution. The presence of inverted commas should therefore be assumed wherever terms like 'the poor' appear.

One of this book's key arguments is that the discursive (re)construction of 'scroungers' by definers both primary (politicians and state agencies) and secondary (news media) has been deliberate and calculated. In recent decades these discourses have consistently been mobilized to achieve two aims, pursued with varying degrees of ideological and utilitarian vigour. The first has been the drive, by governments nominally of Left *and*

Right, to legitimize successive policy projects involving the marketization and rollback of the Welfare State, and retrenchment in public spending generally: most recently the austerity policies pursued since the 2007–8 financial crash. By portraying the unemployed and other claimants as workshy and undeserving, and Britain's economic resources as overstretched, Ministers and their ideologically aligned media acolytes have repeatedly sought to justify and win public support for ever harsher cutbacks, conditions and sanctions. The second aim has been to distract attention from the true underlying *causes* of economic and social issues the nation has faced, from the 1976 International Monetary Fund (IMF) crisis to 1980s deindustrialization to the crash, using divide-and-rule tactics to deflect blame from money markets, mean employers, landlords and governments themselves, by scapegoating more proximate and (notionally) recognizable social archetypes: 'abject figures' like 'the chav' (Tyler 2013: 9) living over the road, on the next street or a neighbouring estate, and other suspicious-looking 'familiar strangers' (Morrison 2016b) we encounter in passing as we troop to work, pile onto the bus or queue in the supermarket. Reproduction of such scapegoats is, as sociologist Imogen Tyler (2013: 9) argues, integral to the success of 'neoliberal governmentality': they are 'ideological conductors mobilized to do the dirty work'; 'mediating agencies through which the social decomposition effected by market deregulation and welfare retrenchment are legitimized'. Throughout this book, we revisit these key concepts – abject figures and familiar strangers – to consider how such endlessly adaptable projections of our fears and suspicions underpin scrounger myths, facilitating their repeated revival as 'sensational' hegemonic confections tasked with 'hiding and mystifying the deeper causes' of society's problems (Hall et al. 1978: vii).

What, then, is the book's empirical purview? Rather than focusing on the connotations of political speeches, policy announcements or manifestoes (though all feature), its primary concern is the process by which popular discourses about people experiencing poverty, particularly benefit claimants, are negotiated, manifested and reproduced in day-to-day narratives promoted through the mainstream news media. The use of the term 'through' (rather than 'by') is as deliberate as that of 'popular'. While the primary focus of *Scroungers* is the framing of *newspaper* discourses about claimants and the discursive interplay between press narratives and those who inform and respond to them, the overarching 'public sphere' (Habermas 1996) of which all these are but layers is much deeper, richer and more 'intertextual' in nature (Fairclough 1992). Reflecting this, the book touches on the inter-discursivity of representations of poor people not only across different sections of the print and online press (national and local) but between news narratives, political rhetoric and realms of popular culture embracing everything from reality TV to drama. In other words, the overall canvas on which its findings are painted is that of *popular* discourse(s): not news frames alone.

What, though, do we mean by the term '*through* the media'? In analysing how normative portrayals of (and assumptions about) claimants and other groups are mediated and (re)constructed in the public sphere, the aim is to consider this as a dynamic, *multidirectional* process. In focusing on the print and online press, *Scroungers* sets out to unpack the dynamics of how dominant frames used to construct ideas about poverty are (re)produced through an increasingly fluid interplay between journalists, their sources (politicians, campaign groups and other claims-makers) and audiences (the public): one which, up to a point, has become as bottom-up as it is top-down. It combines analysis of the way news articles frame those living in poverty with detailed consideration of how below-the-line audience comment threads accompanying them online not only *respond* to these texts but *extend* them. A central argument is that the increasing permeability of boundaries between journalists and their publics online, as shown by the ability of audience members to post testimony *contributing* to news narratives, not just comments *reacting* to them, means the authority and authorship of professional news-makers is increasingly contested. The book builds on arguments proposed by this author elsewhere (Morrison 2016a and 2018) that, taken together, news articles and threads represent a more 'complete' account of a story than the article alone could ever be. In contributing to these meta-narratives, audience members bringing their own *evidence* to the table are embellishing, consolidating and/or modifying otherwise 'unfinished' stories (Morrison 2016a and 2018). More than ever before, then, media frames that seek to define our consensus views of reality are constructed *through* the news (and sources informing it), rather than *by* it. We also see extensions of this process in the wider virtual space of social media, in which other (self-selecting) publics collaborate in constructing ideas about our social world. For this reason, as in the case of sampled comment threads, analysis extends to Twitter dialogue around key 'discursive events' (Wodak 2001: 48): stories in our overall press sample that attracted especially widespread coverage.

In addressing all these dimensions, *Scroungers* aims to build on classic studies of the analogue media era, particularly sociologists Peter Golding and Sue Middleton's *Images of Welfare* (1982), and recent histories of the evolution of notions of 'deserving' versus 'undeserving' poor (e.g. Macnicol 1999; Welshman 2013; Skeggs 2004), to examine the dynamics of how such oppositions are reproduced in today's socially mediated age. In doing so, it draws on theoretical literature ranging from seminal writings on 'moral panics' (Cohen 1972; Hall et al. 1978) to conceptualizations specific to portrayals of economically marginalized groups, such as social 'abjection' (Skeggs 2004; Tyler 2013), class 'disgust' (Jensen 2013, 2014) and 'wasted humans' (Bauman 2004), to reach tentative conclusions about how and why deserving/undeserving media-political archetypes, and the popular perceptions they reflect and promote, remain so durable in late capitalist Britain.

Chapter 1 surveys changes and continuities in representations of poverty through history, identifying key contextual pinch-points when stars aligned to construct crystallizing moments problematizing the 'dangerous classes' (Pearson 1983). Chapters 2 and 3 switch to the present and, specifically, how false oppositions between those who 'play by the rules' (Brown 1999; Cameron 2013) and 'play the system' (Purnell 2008a) – 'workers' and 'shirkers' – have been constructed and consolidated in neoliberal Britain. Later chapters explore the nature and effects of public contributions to these discursive frames, through comment threads and Twitter, and how discourses of deservingness have become so embedded that they now insinuate themselves into news narratives ostensibly not even *about* poverty or welfare (e.g. stories about crime or children).

'WE'RE ALL IN THIS TOGETHER': REFRAMING 'FAIRNESS'

The immediate politico-economic context for this book is the period of sustained 'fiscal consolidation' (Osborne 2010a), or austerity, initiated by the Conservative–Liberal Democrat Coalition government formed in 2010 and continued by the Tory-led administrations succeeding it. Austerity was ostensibly motivated by Ministers' determination to eradicate an annual UK budget deficit which by March 2010 (shortly before the then Labour government left office) had risen to 70.3 per cent of gross domestic product (GDP) (ONS 2017b), largely due to the global financial crash. In framing their case for cutting public spending to reduce Britain's debt, the Coalition made concerted efforts to redefine 'fairness'. One of the earliest articulations of this reframing of the word 'fair' in the context of policy decisions taken with the asserted aim of balancing the nation's books was then Chancellor of the Exchequer George Osborne's October 2010 Commons statement heralding what became an era-defining Comprehensive Spending Review (Osborne 2010b). Arguing that there was 'nothing fair' about 'burdening future generations with the debts we ourselves are not prepared to pay', he declared his 'guiding principle' would be a concept of 'fairness' both intergenerational and, crucially, society-wide (Osborne 2010b).

In illustrating how he might achieve this 'fairer' settlement between young and old, rich and poor, at a time of looming budgetary restraint, Osborne began discursively reinventing the principles underpinning Britain's longstanding (if increasingly contested) post-war consensus around social security or, as he derisorily labelled it, 'welfare'. Reframing fairness as the idea that 'we are all in this together' and must all 'make a contribution', he transformed a model of social glue that had long rewarded affluent pensioners and mothers as much as low-earners and the unemployed into a divisive entity: a set of oppositions, and asymmetric transactions, which meant 'working families who pay for it from their taxes' had every right to feel short-changed and ripped off (Osborne 2010b).

As it transpired, this was to be the gentlest, least brazenly anti-welfare speech of Osborne's six years as Chancellor: a tenure in which he orchestrated an alignment between rhetoric and policy his predecessors ultimately dubbed his 'war against the poor' (Brown 2017). Indeed, his rhetorical reframing of fairness was initially careful to encompass a recognition of 'the vulnerable': a studiedly ill-defined passive noun that, accompanied by repeated invocations of the virtues of an *active* one ('hardworking families'), spoke less of compassion than thinly veiled disdain towards a helpless and 'abject' mass (Haylett 2001; Tyler 2013). Incantations about 'fairness' would be repeatedly revived by Tory, Lib Dem and, indeed, Labour politicians to draw similarly simplistic counterpoints between *contributors* (taxpayers) and *non-contributors* (claimants and immigrants). In his 2013 leader's speech to the Conservative Party Conference, Prime Minister David Cameron spoke of the 'enduring principle, seared in our hearts' that his government's 'new economy' and 'welfare system' would reward those who 'work hard, save, play by the rules' and do their 'fair share' (Cameron 2013). By repeating the term 'hardworking' six times in this single speech, and scrupulously aligning it with Conservative values in opposition to (Labour) 'welfare' for those who 'reject work', Cameron crystallized a binary distinction between 'workers' and 'shirkers', 'strivers' and 'skivers' (Jensen 2014): archetypes honed by Osborne, the Department for Work and Pensions (DWP) and their press cheerleaders as distinctly twenty-first century twists on the decades-old scrounger myth (Garthwaite 2011, 2012). Most explicit was the section headlined 'Welfare', which conflated three enduring straw-man enemies in calculated opposition to the hallowed Tory tenets of thrift and hard graft: 'people who could work, but don't' (the unemployed); 'those who live in homes that hardworking people could never afford' (big families claiming Housing Benefit); and those with 'no right to be here in the first place' (immigrants lured by Britain's 'soft-touch' welfare state – Ross 2013).

That the number of people falling into any of these categories of Britain's latter-day 'undeserving poor' was minimal to non-existent, as abundant research demonstrated (e.g. Sinfield 1981; Shildrick et al. 2012), was just one reason for regarding these claims as pernicious. The other was that Cameron's attempt to starkly juxtapose those who 'choose the dole' with the deserving ranks of the 'hardworking', in a caricatured sequence of instrumentalist decisions reeled out as 'leave school, sign on, find a flat, start claiming housing benefit and opt for a life on benefits', was couched as justification for 'sorting out' an 'unfair' system (Cameron 2013). As social policy scholar Jay Wiggan's masterful dissection of Coalition 'welfare reform' discourse shows, this determination to 'sort out' the system was presented in draft legislation as restoring the 'balance in favour of the "rights of taxpayers"' who were 'being abused'; with 'social protection' reframed as a 'generous gift from "us" to "them"' and 'fairness' transformed from 'being about the rights of those in need to access material goods or employment' to 'a justification for strengthening' that 'old principle of less eligibility' for those contributing less to the pot (Wiggan 2012: 390). As the coming chapters show, Coalition rhetoric was rooted in numerous earlier attempts to reframe/reform social security. In the immediate ministerial context, 'ownership' of Acts passed to achieve these goals fell, as Wiggan (2012: 386) emphasizes, to Iain Duncan Smith: the moralizing Work and Pensions Secretary whose public 2007 epiphany, on a visit to Glasgow's deprived Easterhouse estate, had spurred him to set up the Centre for Social Justice think-tank to heal a supposedly cancerous problem he and Cameron subsequently framed as, variously, the 'broken society' and 'broken Britain' (Slater 2014). This powerful discursive construct, with its connotations of 'broken' communities, families and, by extension, welfare, represented the Coalition's iteration of the 'underclass' concept repeatedly adopted and adapted by previous governments to problematize a supposedly ever-present mass of disenfranchised, deviant anti-citizens who invited, at best, pity and, at worst, 'disgust' (Jensen 2013). Paired with the Tories' parallel, interwoven discourse around Britain's fractured social contract, specifically the disconnect between people who 'put in' and 'take out', the 'broken society' offered a vivid, commercially attractive frame for the media to exploit, in both news coverage and popular entertainment.

Not that the discursive reframing of fairness was confined to ministerial statements, policy documents or media. In the end, the Osborne–Cameron–Duncan Smith discourse proved so successful it was adopted (if uncomfortably) by both Lib Dems and Labour's Opposition. As titular 'Deputy Prime Minister', then Lib Dem leader Nick Clegg felt obliged to pay lip service to his bedfellows' more hard-line anti-welfare discourse. Sure enough, in an October 2010 announcement foreshadowing Osborne's spending review, he justified benefit cuts by arguing there was 'nothing intrinsically good' or 'fair' about high welfare spending (Clegg 2010). In truth, the short section of Clegg's speech devoted to this subject was qualified by an overall emphasis on a principle he dubbed the 'fairness premium': one designed (unlike most spending review outcomes) to help 'disadvantaged' children and young people through a range of measures from free school meals to financial assistance for those who might otherwise be deterred from going to university following his government's decision to treble tuition fees (Clegg 2010). Nonetheless, Clegg would echo Osborne's mantra more closely in a later article for the benefit-bashing *Sun*, praising the 'millions of people' in 'Alarm Clock Britain' who 'get up every morning and work hard to get on in life', rather than 'rely on state handouts' (Clegg 2011).

In its desperate efforts to find a voice casting it as a fiscally credible government-in-waiting, Labour was even fuller-throated than the junior Coalition partners in endorsing a more conditional approach to social security. A choreographed June 2013 speech from Newham Dockside, east London, by its then leader, Ed Miliband – framed, in language long associated with pre-Thatcher Tory governments, as a 'One Nation plan for social security reform' – was peppered with rhetoric straight out of the Coalition hymnbook. Though Miliband's pink-hued iteration of 'fair' embraced criticism of the 'nasty, brutish and unfair' reality of work for those reliant on 'zero-hours contracts' and exploitative employers' use of agency workers to 'unfairly avoid giving people the pay and conditions offered to permanent staff', he echoed Osborne's intergenerational definition of 'fairness' by proffering sticks rather than carrots: in headline terms, a 'compulsory jobs guarantee' for young people, to 'pass on a fair and sustainable [welfare] system to the next generation' (Miliband, E. 2013). Moreover, Miliband later directly responded to Cameron's push for curbs to EU economic migrants' rights to receive benefits on entering Britain by committing Labour to halting such claims until they had paid sufficiently into the system (a promise included in his party's 2015 election manifesto). This was a direct extension of the underlying 'contributor/non-contributor' opposition promoted by Coalition Ministers: a pernicious, misleading disjunction Miliband happily described as enshrining principles of 'contribution, responsibility' and, crucially, 'fairness' (Helm 2014).

'SKIVERS' AND 'SHIRKERS': CONSTRUCTING A NEW 'SCROUNGERPHOBIA'

Osborne's reframing of 'fairness' as a discursive justification for cutting working-age benefits reached its zenith in 2013. It was during this year that a toxic discourse pitting 'workers' against 'shirkers' reached such a febrile pitch in Britain's public sphere that it erupted into full-blown 'moral panic' (Cohen 1972). If there could be any lingering doubt about how far to the reactionary right media (mis)representations of 'welfare', and unemployed households particularly, had shifted by 2013, consider this edited extract from a comment piece by ex-Conservative and future United Kingdom Independence Party (UKIP) Member of the European Parliament (MEP) Janice Atkinson, published in the *Daily Express* on 8 March 2013. Head-lined 'Our welfare state is just rewarding feckless behaviour', it was accompanied by a landscape shot of a quintessentially abject 'problem family': single mother Heather Frost and 'her brood of 11 children', vilified by the tabloids for reducing a neighbour's life to 'a living hell' through 'cruel taunting and tormenting'. Atkinson wrote:

> Most people cannot afford more than two children and choose to limit their families. When the state funds feckless families there is no limit to the children they can have as they are guaranteed funding. Child benefit should be restricted to three children. A larger family is a lifestyle choice. Those like Heather Frost should not be paid to have children and the taxpayers should not be funding the houses they then go on to 'need'. If you start to withdraw benefits and instead channel the money into schemes that directly benefit the children then that is a first step to weaning them off the taxpayer. That's why the 'pupil premium' that pays schools more for every student they have from a deprived background is an excellent idea. You cannot imagine many deadbeat parents using benefits to buy a book to help their children read before they start school. The welfare system is deeply rotten and has to be changed. (Atkinson 2013)

Though paired with a championing of one of the Coalition's more progressive policies (the Lib Dem-inspired 'pupil premium') and carefully couched as a *defence* of what Atkinson asserted to have been the (more conditional and contributory) founding principles underpinning William Beveridge's social security template, she ended by accusing today's Welfare State of breeding 'parasites and persecutors' and casually conflating 'these families' with antisocial behaviour and criminality. While avoiding the term 'scrounger' itself – or either of its then fashionable, but equally objectifying synonyms, 'shirker' and 'skiver' – Atkinson's diatribe invoked numerous other stigmatizing tropes, from repeated use of the adjective 'feckless' to ventriloquized Coalition phrases. Most symbolic was her casual framing of 'welfare' as a 'lifestyle choice' and recipe for a 'culture' of 'something for nothing'. Viewed alongside 2013's multiple pronouncements by Osborne and Duncan Smith, Miliband's conflicted, but implicitly compliant, responses, and Cameron's October conference speech, this was chillingly redolent of the late 1970s 'scroungerphobia' discourse anatomized by Golding and Middleton in *Images of Welfare* (1982).

That 2013 was the year 'shirkerphobia' came of age is illustrated by hard data demonstrating its escalating prevalence in newspapers. Table 0.1 gives figures for the occurrence of the nouns 'skiver', 'shirker' and 'scrounger' and other pejorative terms commonly applied to working-age claimants in the national and regional press for each year in the decade up to and including 2016. As column 5 illustrates, 2013 witnessed an extraordinary spike in the use of stigmatizing terminology, with the word 'shirker' more than doubling in usage from the previous year (from 229 to 593); 'skiver' more than tripling (from 163 to 570); and significant increases for almost all other synonyms, from 'benefit tourism' to 'something for nothing': phrases repeatedly used in government discourses about EU migrants claiming working-age benefits in Britain and non-working claimants generally (UK or foreign). Most striking was the resurgence of the invective 'scrounger', which insistently outnumbered each other term ('skiver' and 'shirker') by nearly four to one.

TABLE 0.1 OCCURRENCES OF PEJORATIVE LABELS FOR CLAIMANTS IN UK PRESS ARTICLES, 2007–16

	2016	2015	2014	2013	2012	2011	2010	2009	2008	2007
'Scrounger'	605	1187	1622	2103	1468	1099	1214	481	647	406
'Shirker'	264	267	243	593	229	147	173	119	153	112
'Sponger'	151	210	287	308	294	351	414	249	230	165
'Skiver'	127	177	130	570	163	125	136	126	105	120
'Workshy' or 'work-shy'	563	466	436	775	760	719	874	404	538	446
'Something for nothing'	370	406	506	850	730	500	288	308	403	218
'Underclass'	344	399	450	521	663	1,053	552	613	657	663
'Benefit tourism'	186	230	596	450	150	164	105	121	108	86
'Benefit tourist'	75	93	153	229	59	102	63	43	55	37
'Welfare tourism'	18	34	73	69	6	11	16	9	2	5
'Welfare tourist'	13	20	12	41	14	14	14	8	5	12

Source: Lexis Library.

In so doing, it suggested that the legacy of 1970s 'scrounger-phobia' remained as historically hardwired as ever in media (and public) consciousness. Of all associated terms, only 'sponger' and 'work-shy'/'workshy' peaked at an earlier pinch-point: 2010. This was the year in which Cameron's Conservatives were first elected, with a headline-grabbing promise to introduce a 'three-strikes-and-you're-out' ban on benefits for unemployed people persistently refusing to take work (Shipman 2010) or repeatedly convicted of welfare fraud (Hall 2010).

The measure of how entrenched and socially *accepted* elite-powered scrounger discourse had become by 2013 is perhaps best illustrated by the most objective barometer of public opinion: the British Social Attitudes survey. The 2014 BSA (the first after 2013's sustained rhetorical assault on the unemployed) showed that, after a slow rise in support for more social security spending, from 27 per cent in 2009 (shortly after the crash) to 36 per cent in 2013, the proportion of respondents favouring this had plummeted back to 30 per cent: a drop of 6 per cent in a single year (Taylor-Gooby & Taylor 2015: 6). More telling was the longer-term trend in attitudes towards the unemployed under the Coalition. Though there had been 'a slight increase' in the proportion saying 'benefits for the unemployed' were 'too low and caused hardship' between 2013 and 2014 (from 22 to 27 per cent), the overall picture since 2010 had 'changed little', with 'most people' (52 per cent in 2014) still believing 'benefits for the unemployed' were 'too high and discourage work' (Taylor-Gooby & Taylor 2015: 9). More dramatic had been the historical trend observed by BSA researchers in response to a specific 'statement' about the unemployed. While only 27 per cent of people agreed that 'around here, most unemployed people could find a job if they really wanted one' in 1993, this had soared to 68 per cent by the year of the crash (2008), and though attitudes became slightly more sympathetic as 'unemployment rose' in its wake, the upward trend in public scepticism about the job-hunting efforts of the unemployed climbed sharply again between 2013 and 2014, from 56 to 59 per cent. The authors concluded that public opinion remained 'far more inclined to view unemployment as an individual responsibility' than in the late 1980s and early 1990s (Taylor-Gooby & Taylor 2015).

What was it, then, about 2013 that motivated Ministers and media to stage such a full-throated assault on the unemployed and other working-age claimants? Why were the circumstances of that year so conducive to rendering these simplistic, divisive descriptors so narratively attractive? In short, why should 2013 have been a crystallizing moment for the latest manifestation of Britain's simmering scrounger discourse: a toxic melting-pot containing all the ingredients needed to revive and reinvigorate a moral panic?

To begin answering this question, we must consider three related sub-questions. Firstly, what aspects of the politico-economic context of 2013 Britain were conducive to stigmatizing this social group? Put another way, why was it considered politically or socially justifiable, and expedient, to do so? Secondly, what contextual factors (if any) did 2013 and the years running up to it share with earlier periods of scroungerphobia? Thirdly, how did the distinctive 2013 rebranding of this discourse (the construction of 'skivers' and 'shirkers') take shape, both under the Coalition and beforehand?

SALIENT 'SCROUNGERS': TIMING A MORAL PANIC

According to Paul Johnson, director of the Institute for Fiscal Studies (IFS), by 2013 Britain had suffered a 'deeper' slump than in any comparable five-year period (including during the Great Depression of the 1930s), with 'household incomes and spending' dropping further and staying lower for longer (quoted in Allen 2013). For the millions whose incomes pegged them just above the benefits threshold, or whose single status rendered them ineligible for working tax credits (themselves being reduced), this translated into wage caps, nominal pay rises well below the rising cost of living and cuts to the public services on which they depended. All of this sharpened the need for Ministers to harness every weapon in their armoury to maintain popular support for their chosen measure to drive down Britain's deficit: austerity. Not coincidentally, 2013 was also the year in which the Coalition's most punitive changes to the package of support available for unemployed people would either be announced or implemented. These included the introduction of a £26,000-a-year household 'benefit cap' (Kennedy et al. 2016) and the start of a three-year, 1 per cent freeze on annual rises in working-age benefits, replacing the annual uprating in line with prices which (based on one index or other) had survived since 1987 (Kennedy 2011). Most significantly, 2013 would see the introduction of the Coalition's long-touted all-in-one flagship benefit: Universal Credit (UC). Designed to replace a byzantine tangle of working-age benefits for the unemployed and low earners, including Jobseeker's Allowance (JSA), Housing Benefit (HB) and Employment and Support Allowance (ESA) (the main payment for out-of-work sick and disabled people), UC was conceived as a way of both rationalizing welfare and incentivizing employment by withdrawing it more gradually than before from those moving into work. In truth, it was as much a tool for slashing social protection as streamlining benefits and improving 'fairness'. As various studies have shown (e.g. Dean 2012; Fletcher 2015), UC ushered in a system of US-style 'Workfare' (in Britain, 'Mandatory Work Activity') and continual Kafkaesque monitoring by job advisors, backed by brutal sanctions.

With Osborne's second Spending Review also due in 2013, the sheer number of changes pending that year made the political imperative for Ministers to ramp up the rhetoric around their brand of 'scroungerphobia' more acute than ever: there were simply so many cuts (implemented and impending) to legitimize. Cue a months-long campaign to frame claimants as justified targets for the necessary economies, with Cameron himself firing the opening salvo during a theatrical July 2012 exchange at Prime Minister's Questions. In a scarcely noticed steal from a 1974 Margaret Thatcher speech, he jabbed an accusatory finger at Miliband's Labour benches, declaring, 'we back the workers, they back the shirkers' (quoted in Douieb 2012). Three months later, in a crafted soundbite symbolizing all that was most invidious about the Coalition's welfare policies, Osborne used his annual Tory conference speech to juxtapose the image of a 'shift-worker, leaving home in the dark hours of the early morning', beneath 'the closed blinds of their next-door neighbour, sleeping off a life on benefits' (Osborne 2012).

As to how and why 2013-style 'shirkerphobia' came to echo the 1970s 'scroungerphobia' panic so strongly, we can begin to understand this parallel by unpacking the comparative politico-economic contexts in which each phenomenon flourished. As with numerous other moral panics (e.g. Cohen 1972; Hall et al. 1978), the main reason these comparable discourses successfully embedded themselves at particular junctures was that the concepts of 'scroungers' or 'shirkers' had come to represent salient scapegoats on which to offload blame for society's ills: in these cases, stagnating wages, insecure employment and rising living costs. The context for 1970s 'scroungerphobia' had been one of sudden, dramatic economic decline leading to rising unemployment, coupled with periodic spikes in inflation and spiralling wage demands from those in work. During the early to mid-1970s, mounting economic tensions between the West and the Organization of the Petroleum Exporting Countries (OPEC) had coincided with (and fuelled) a series of industrial disputes in the still largely nationalized energy and manufacturing sectors. Successive crisis-points included the 1974 miners' strike, which abruptly curtailed Edward Heath's Conservative administration, to the 1976 downturn that spurred then Labour Chancellor Denis Healey to seek a politically embarrassing bailout from the

IMF. Against this backdrop began the slow but steady onward march of neoliberalism. This embryonic 'Thatcher–Reagan consensus' favoured privatization of industry and the utilities and deregulation and liberalization of markets for everything from heavy goods to high finance, as well as the underlying engine for production and consumption: labour itself. Set against this disruptive politico-economic context, it was hardly surprising that politicians (and media) sought to mobilize support for, at first incremental but ultimately seismic, market reforms using a classic divide-and-rule displacement tactic: pitting hardworking, wage-controlled, taxpaying workers against a welfare-reliant, *tax-subsidized* unemployed. Golding and Middleton's analysis of press coverage in 1976, a 'year of the cuts' (1982: 59) and 'dismantling' of the 'welfare consensus' (1982: 77) long predating the sustained attacks on claimants engineered by the Coalition, showed how inflationary annual up-ratings for the unemployed were effortlessly framed as the 'good life' or (in the *Daily Telegraph*'s words) 'a featherbed for every hard luck case around' (Golding & Middleton 1982: 104), at least compared to the woes of low-waged workers.

Fast-forward to 2013 and analogous dynamics were at play, amid the ongoing politico-economic fallout from the 2007–8 crash and ensuing UK recession. In the teeth of a public-sector wage freeze, with all workers facing soaring fuel and housing costs, cuts to working tax credits and (in many cases) a Darwinian fight for secure employment, it is easy to understand how millions of hardworking families could be sensitized to images of jobless claimants living off their taxes. It was against this backdrop of (government-instigated) falling real-terms living standards for the employed majority that Osborne and his Treasury colleagues commenced their 'war against the poor' (Brown 2017). This full-frontal assault involved normalizing a carefully constructed discourse embodying all the tropes of 1970s 'scroungerphobia' in a concerted effort to win public support for relentless cuts to working-age benefits which would slash the welfare safety-net and, more crucially, existentially threaten the 'cradle-to-the-grave' principles underpinning the Beveridge Report that conceived it (Beveridge 1942). For a Chancellor whose austerity rallying cry was the oft-repeated platitude 'we're all in this together', loosening the bonds of solidarity underpinning Britain's post-war social security settlement was audacious. Yet far from identifying this hypocrisy, let alone challenging it, most of the mainstream media served as Osborne's unswerving acolytes, reeling out tale after tale about workshy and/or bogus claimants and feckless families: a non-stop rogues' gallery of folk-devils characterized as much by their general moral deviancy and (in some cases) outright criminality as their asserted welfare dependency. To this disgusting, malodorous mass could be attached any number of labels, from 'skiver' or 'shirker' to other recently coined pejoratives, like 'chav' (Jones 2011). In turn, these infinitely malleable labels could be projected onto various recognizable archetypes: an odious cast of overweight, pallid, tobacco-voiced malingerers that the struggling ranks of overworked, underpaid, pound shop-frequenting 'Alarm Clock Britain' might easily associate with the abject figures and familiar strangers with whom they daily crossed paths.

As to the origins of the *iteration* of 'scroungers' that the Coalition years crystallized as 'shirkers', ironically the groundwork had been laid under (New) Labour. To return to Table 0.1, before its 2013 peak there were two earlier spikes in post-millennial 'scrounger discourse': in 2008 and 2010 respectively, when the term 'sponger' also enjoyed a renaissance after years of disuse. What was it, then, about the politico-economic contexts of these two earlier points that contributed to the revival of scrounger stereotypes? One clue lies in the initially dramatic, then slower-burn, rise to prominence of the twin terms 'broken society' and 'broken Britain' (Slater 2014): slogans patented by Duncan Smith, but weaponized repeatedly by Cameron following the financial crisis and during the 2010 election campaign. As at other times of widespread economic insecurity, then Labour premier Gordon Brown set the scene for some of what was to come in a now-notorious 2007 conference speech, by implicitly pitting insecure working-class communities in the party's former industrial heartlands against job-poaching immigrants with his promise to create 'British jobs for British workers' (Brown 2007). Rattled by a then-resurgent Conservative Party, his Ministers also became increasingly embroiled in a rhetorical arms race over who would demand the most from (and award the least to) claimants: one that would continue to play out under successive welfare spokesmen when Labour returned to Opposition (e.g. Byrne 2012). Amid these discursive skirmishes, the threat supposedly posed by immigrants was repeatedly conflated with that represented by a wider rump of those content to 'play the system' (Purnell 2008a), rather than 'play by the rules' (Brown 2008): notably the long-term unemployed. Meanwhile, the Tories fanned the flames of this emerging, twin-pronged moral panic by co-opting the longstanding Labour notion of 'hardworking families' (Brown 1999) to champion the cause of the deserving masses, as they doggedly soldiered on amid stagnating wages, overstretched public services and rising living costs bequeathed by Labour's alleged 'economic mismanagement' (quoted in Porter 2008) – and, of course, 'soft-touch' immigration and welfare policies (Cameron 2011).

As Chapter 2 demonstrates, though, New Labour's approach to welfare had been anything but lenient. Under successive Ministers, it had experimented with increasingly punitive approaches to benefit entitlement for the unemployed, long-term sick and disabled, paired with a moralistic, quasi-Victorian association of 'antisocial behaviour' with claimants described by criminologists Barry Goldson and Janet Jamieson (2002: 91) as the 'criminalization of welfare need'. Like the Coalition, Tony Blair and Gordon Brown's governments had sought to mobilize consent for their reforms by constructing a discourse: one with deep-rooted historical antecedents tapping into a centuries-old continuum of oppositions between the 'deserving' and 'undeserving poor'. In so doing, their long-running emphasis on conditionality for working-age claimants, as manifested in successive waves of 'welfare reform' (itself a rhetorical construct), opened the floodgates to much harsher measures to come.

Beyond the above, if there was one other force instrumental in pump-priming the shirker panic that took full flight in 2013 it was the arrival of a new dynamic in the construction of popular discourses: social media. The contribution made to the discursive melting-pot by this new, virtual, public sphere is explored in more detail in Chapter 4, but for now it is worth noting that the early stages of 'shirkerphobia' coincided with the period during which social media use came of age. By 2013, 57 per cent of UK citizens were regularly using Facebook, YouTube, LinkedIn and (of specific relevance here) Twitter (ONS 2013). The latter had been registered as a company in 2007: significantly, the year the longitudinal content analysis data shown in Table 0.1 begins. It was later buoyed in popularity by the profile it gained during the 2011 'Arab Spring' (Bruns et al. 2013). Meanwhile, the other principal forum for public participation in constructing news discourse, online comment threads, began proliferating even earlier, with three-quarters of all US online media outlets already incorporating them by 2008 (Johnson 2008) and most national (and many regional) UK papers swiftly doing likewise. By the time shirker discourse had gained momentum, in the early Coalition years, a variety of active audience communities existed in the social media sphere, with users regularly posting comments, sharing news with friends online, tweeting reactions to stories – and even contributing additional information to 'journalist-led narratives' to consolidate, embellish and (occasionally) contest them (Morrison 2016a).

Resurgent scrounger discourse in the former of the abject figure of the 'shirker' was, then, the product of a collision of circumstances: a perfect storm of factors part-accidental, part-evolutionary and part-deliberate. All those minded to weaponize this discourse needed to do to embed images of shirkers in the public imagination was harness a steady stream of real-world examples demonstrating the prevalence of the problem. As these last sections illustrate, there was to be no shortage of such morality tales, courtesy of two strands of the media: reality TV and the tabloid press.

SYMBOLIC SCROUNGERS: GENERALIZING EXCEPTIONS

Of all 'scrounger' (or 'shirker') stories to capture the editorial and public imagination in 2013, none was more emblematic of this divisive discourse than the baleful tale of unemployed Mick

Philpott. Already a notorious sometime television personality –
following a 2007 interview with daytime talk-show host Jeremy
Kyle, in which he defended his demand for a bigger council
house to cater for his ever-multiplying offspring – in April 2013
Philpott was jailed for starting a fire that killed six of his 15
sleeping children at his Derby home. That Philpott's 'crocodile
tears' in the dock dominated front-page headlines (e.g. Lazzeri
2013; Tomlinson & Dolan 2013) in the very same month that
Osborne mounted his biggest assault yet on the social security
budget can only be a coincidence. Nonetheless, the accident
of timing of this exceptional tragedy with the launch of a long-
planned timetable of iniquitous welfare cutbacks was all too
convenient for a government eager to exploit any high-profile
example of moral degeneracy by claimants as justification for
tackling what they blithely dismissed as 'dependency culture'
(Osborne 2008).

Sure enough, the tabloids swiftly seized on this grisly happen-
stance, mobilizing all the discursive tropes of 'episodic framing'
(Iyengar 1991) to present the Philpotts' case as symptomatic of
an endemic moral malaise among welfare recipients. Some of
the most unrestrained invective appeared in the *Daily Express*,
which branded Philpott 'Britain's most evil scrounger', and *The
Sun*, which accompanied its coverage of his conviction with an
editorial arguing that a 'central lesson' of this extreme case was
that an overgenerous benefits system can 'debase humanity'
(The Sun 2013). Equally vociferous was the *Daily Mail*, which
ran a huge front-page picture of Philpott surrounded by his
progeny beneath the screaming headline: 'VILE PRODUCT
OF WELFARE UK'. In the same edition, historian A.N. Wilson
used the story as a pretext to elide wider lessons about the 'bleak

and often grotesque world of the welfare benefit scroungers' – hysterically asserting that there were 'not dozens, not hundreds, but tens of thousands in our country' (Wilson 2013). So vicious was the paper's overall coverage that, even at a time of normalized claimant-bashing, it provoked several complaints to then newspaper regulator the Press Complaints Commission (Moseley 2013), and condemnation from prominent Labour politicians, notably ex-Deputy Prime Minister John Prescott and Dame Margaret Beckett (a Derby MP).

Those of a different political persuasion wasted no time, however, in exploiting the wave of tabloid disgust to align themselves with Wilson's view that the family typified benefit-claiming households. Most brazenly, Osborne used a visit to Derby on the day of Philpott's sentence to suggest his case raised 'a question for government and for society about the welfare state, and the taxpayers who pay for the welfare state, subsidising lifestyles like that': a re-tread of his oft-repeated mantra about benefits being 'a lifestyle choice' (Osborne 2013). Asked two days later if he endorsed this view, Cameron was similarly content to link Philpott's deviancy to problems fostered by the 'welfare system'. Despite insisting both he and Osborne recognized that Philpott (not the system as a whole) was 'responsible' for his crime, he seized the opportunity to reiterate the well-worn message that 'welfare is there to help people who want to work hard', while again decrying those who saw it as 'a lifestyle choice' (quoted in Helm 2013). In mobilizing such imagery to diagnose the nature of a culture Philpott supposedly epitomized, such pronouncements had the discursive effect of generalizing most, if not *all*, claimants as lazy, possibly even criminal, non-contributors: in essence, scroungers.

Given how *normalized* scrounger discourse had become by 2013, it is hardly surprising that, at the time of writing, Google Trends data quantifying levels of 'interest over time' in the search term 'scrounger', measured relative to its historical high-point (in March 2005), identified the period between January 2012 and June 2014 as one of renewed and sustained interest among UK internet users (Google Trends 2018a). Intriguingly, January 2012 (when it reached 92) was a significant month during the prolonged policy battle over the Coalition's welfare cuts programme, with household benefit cap proposals temporarily derailed through defeats and amendments in the House of Lords. A notable surge in the number and frequency of searches, meanwhile, occurred in the two months from March to May 2013: a period during which the unfolding Philpott case was consistently in the national media spotlight. Though it would be naïve to interpret a correlation between high levels of newspaper coverage of an issue and increased online searches using the same terminology as any kind of *causal* relationship, it is hard to dispel the suspicion that ever-heightening demonization of 'scroungers' in the media-political sphere (whether cast in those terms or as 'skivers' or 'shirkers') helped pump-prime public interest in these terms at this particular time. Put differently, the power of media-political discourse to *sensitize* the public to issues of (constructed) societal concern appears to have been hard at work, as demonstrated by its conspicuous curiosity about a term that had barely figured in searches as recently as March 2010 (the last time 'scrounger' had scored a value of zero).[1] A focus of this book are the agenda-setting factors that conspire to renormalize scrounger discourse in this way – invoking what Tracy Jensen (2014) calls (after Pierre Bourdieu) 'doxa', or 'that which goes without saying because it comes without saying', and Ruth Patrick (2017) terms the 'machine of welfare commonsense', trampling 'alternative portrayals in its wake'.

THE POOR AS MEDIA SPECTACLE: FREAK-SHOW TV AND THE RISE OF 'POVERTY PORN'

The discursive (re)construction of scrounger myths peaking in 2013 was, then, far from the product of conventional primary and secondary definition alone. While the touch-paper was undoubtedly lit by Ministers keen to legitimize a radical programme of Welfare State shrinkage, the short-term success of their project was assured by a pincer-movement of popular narratives trading on lazy stereotypes peddled as much by tabloid television as the downmarket press.

Though it would be early the following year before reality TV perfected the formula for objectifying claimants for the purposes of popular entertainment, in the guise of now-seminal Channel 4 docusoap *Benefits Street*, not for nothing has Jensen described 2013 as 'the year when public debate about the welfare state exploded' in the guise of a 'new genre' of 'factual' programme-making (Jensen 2014). In truth, though, *Benefits Street's* antecedents, the series itself and the numerous copycats they spawned merely represented the latest stage in a continuum of programming which had had the effect (if not always the intention) of sensationalizing and demeaning the lives of claimants: problematizing them as, at best, outlandish dropouts and, at worst, behaviourally deviant sub-humans. Of all supposedly factual programmes to promote what is today known as 'poverty porn' (Jensen 2013, 2014), none courts controversy more gleefully than *The Jeremy Kyle Show*: the lurid, outrageous daytime talk show in which the eponymous host habitually mocks and provokes guests lured into playing out family grudges and custody battles in front of a studio audience. It was with good justification that, in 2007, a Manchester district judge condemned the show for indulging in 'human bear-baiting', as he sentenced a security guard embroiled in one such skirmish: making him the first person to be convicted of assault on a British television programme (Dowell 2007). It is also apt, if ironic, that Kyle was a principal architect of Mick Philpott's earlier infamy. The high-profile media exposure Philpott enjoyed from his appearance on the programme led to an almost postmodern turn of events, as he conspired in his own construction as a scrounger poster-boy, even volunteering to regale a famously moralistic ex-Conservative Minister about his delight in playing the system in the unsubtly titled documentary *Ann Widdecombe Versus the Benefits Culture*. Indeed, the concept of Philpott as a media bogeyman – an anti-icon constructed more through the small screen, and ensuing tabloid coverage, than by a dysfunctional, failing Welfare State – was directly addressed by criminologist David Wilson in a *Daily Mail* article published in the wake of his conviction. The piece was headlined 'How Jeremy Kyle helped create Shameless Mick', in an implied intertextual reference to Channel 4 comedy-drama *Shameless* and Philpott's equally workshy (if more benign) fictional counterpart, Frank Gallagher (Wilson 2013). As later chapters show, this pop-cultural allusion reflected the mainstream media's widespread use of references to *Shameless* and other TV shows invoking popular stereotypes about claimants, such as BBC comedy *Little Britain* – typically as shorthand signifiers of scrounger culture. What the rolling 'Mick Philpott

Show' came to represent, then, was the reduction of serious (if flawed) debates about the future of social security; the tension between 'fairness' to taxpayers versus the unemployed; and the balance between contributory and non-contributory welfare, to the level of a cynically manipulative, day-glo shell-suit-wearing, circus freak-show or 'media spectacle' (Debord 1967).

A growing TV preoccupation with feral family freak-shows, often involving 'racialized' (Skeggs 2013: 90) invocations of 'class-based disgust' directed against abject, dysfunctional 'white trash chav culture' (Tyler 2013: 31), had therefore become progressively more pronounced long before the rash of shows ushered in by the popularity of *Benefits Street*. In the end, though, the rise of poverty porn to the mass pop-cultural phenomenon it became probably owes more to the fact that *political* discourse around 'skivers' and 'shirkers' was (by then) fully established than the discourse itself owes to poverty porn. That said, the fact that TV programme-makers were busily conceiving, producing and scheduling shows like this during the period when this discourse was asserting its dominance in the wider public sphere is signif-icant: a testament to their cynical faith in viewers' appetite for these objectifying narratives during a period of sustained assault on the Welfare State. Perhaps more importantly, the subsequent explosion of poverty porn into peak-time entertainment on mainstream channels, including BBC1, undoubtedly played a key role in reproducing and *legitimizing* scrounger discourse. While press and politicians may have constructed this discourse, then, commercially driven TV programmers were heavily complicit in stoking and prolonging it.

EVERYDAY SCROUNGERS: 'ABJECT FIGURES' AND 'FAMILIAR STRANGERS' AS FOLK-DEVILS

A central contradiction of scrounger discourse is that its power and potency rests on two paradoxical positionings of claimants. On the one hand they are conceived of as outlandish circus animals or depraved 'abject figures' (Tyler 2013), inhabiting a liminal state beyond the bounds of normal human decency. On the other, they are cast as undesirable but all too identifiable (even everyday) archetypes. In other words, for expedient media-political discourses juxtaposing 'shirkers' with 'workers' to have the desired effect on public opinion they must be both salient and plausible – and this salience and plausibility depends on the *recognizability* of the stereotypes they evoke.

A common tactic for squaring such circles, well-rehearsed from the construction of numerous earlier moral panics, is to present exceptions as norms: *generalizing* from the particular to portray behaviours that appear 'revolting' (Tyler 2013) and reprehensible to civilized folk (a notional 'us') as typical of or endemic to an abject mass of insurgent savages ('them'). Thus, Philpott was transformed from the exception he doubtless was – a callous, avaricious opportunist whose criminal conduct had little to do with the fact he claimed benefits – into the *epitome* of the dehumanizing, antisocial effects of spending life on the dole: a morally bereft enemy within typical of 'Welfare UK' (Dolan and Bentley 2013). To achieve the discursive somersault necessary to paint the Philpotts (individuals judged newsworthy *because* they are exceptional) as typical, problem-definers must find ways of aligning them with more commonplace, socially proximate images of fecklessness and indolence. It is into this discursive space that everyday, recognizable 'abject figures' (Tyler 2013) are herded: the chubby, tracksuit-wearing 'chav mum' (Tyler 2008); faceless, shuffling teenager in hoodie or baseball cap; cussing dad leading his brood of sullen offspring; or idle 'next-door neighbour', peacefully 'sleeping off a life on benefits' (Osborne 2012). These scrounger types are all 'familiar strangers' (Morrison 2016b): chalk outlines onto which any dress code, value system, shade of morality or behavioural characteristic can be projected by those intent on exploiting our distrust and suspicion of others for political and/or commercial gain. They are 'strange' to us, in that they are not of our kind: they dress, speak and act differently; they mix in different circles; and our twin worlds rarely, if ever, fully collide. Yet they are all too familiar, not just from their routine appearances in TV docu-soaps and sitcoms, or news stories about sink estates, street crime and obesity, but from the marginal interfaces of our daily lives. They may not live next door or on our street, but familiar strangers inhabit our shopping centres, parks and playgrounds. We glimpse them in GP waiting-rooms, shops, pubs and cafes, even at the school gates. We can imagine their disgusting lives, even if we never experience them.

It is the infinite malleability of the familiar stranger template that allows politicians and media to tug it this way and that, filling it with whatever features and faults fit their moral missions of the moment. An argument of this book is that this template has proved crucial to the successful construction, and reinven-tion, of 'scrounger' folk-devils in contemporary UK discourse. 'Scroungers' have become such an enduring locus for our resent-ments and frustrations at least partly because familiar stranger frames – alongside more extreme freak-show spectacles – have *normalized* them, suggesting they are all around us, all of the time; that *anyone* could be on the make, from our neighbours and those on the peripheries of our social circles to people we see on the bus, queue behind in the supermarket, pass in the street. Yet no popular discourse appears overnight or from nowhere, so we begin by considering the 'scrounger' in historical context. In short, how and why has this phantom figure repeatedly rematerialized over time?

CHAPTER 1

MORAL PANICS, SCAPEGOATING AND THE PERSISTENCE OF PAUPER FOLK-DEVILS

If the poor are always with us, so too are the prejudices, precon-
ceptions and panics that consistently typify the way societies
conceptualize them. 'How to deal with the poor', as Golding and
Middleton (1982: 6) put it, 'has always been the central policy
issue for the state, and before the state for the church and feudal
authorities'. This was as much the case for early kings and ecclesiasts calibrating the balance between control and compassion
as it is for latter-day politicians and bureaucrats obsessing over
distinctions between rights and responsibilities and optimum
levels for pitching social protection.

While this book's purview primarily concerns the question
of how we think and talk about poverty in today's Britain, there
is considerable evidence (patchy in places, firmer in others) to
suggest that persistent distinctions between the more and less
'deserving' – long emblematic of British discourses around
'the poor' – have close comparisons, even parallels, elsewhere.
They can be glimpsed in the slow-burn migration of 'underclass'
rhetoric in the late twentieth century from the United States (via
Britain) to Germany, the Netherlands, Brazil, Nicaragua and
even India (Mann 1994). More recently, they have leeched their
way further abroad, thanks to an ever more globalized public
sphere, entering the cultural vocabularies of societies that used
to have little truck with stigmatizing those living in poverty. Such
lexical incursions include the appropriation and reinvention of

the arcane term 'bludger', nineteenth century British slang for pimp (Oxford Dictionaries 2017a), as an Antipodean variant of 'scrounger'. This development is especially incongruous in Australia, where historical resistance to recognizing the *existence* of an underclass used to fascinate academics, who blamed it on everything from blue-collar inverted snobbery and 'suspicion of "tall poppies" and social climbing' (Turner, quoted in Mann 1994: 91) to ancestral memories of 'the stain' of deportation as a 'dangerous class' that must be 'kept thousands of miles away for fear it would contaminate the morals of those around them' (Mann 1994: 91).

Why, then, have these intergenerational, and increasingly *international*, discursive distinctions between people thrust into poverty through no fault of their own and those judged to have brought their misfortunes on themselves repeatedly resurfaced through time? How have ideas about 'deserving' versus 'undeserving' poverty evolved down the centuries, and what *aspects* of them have proved most resilient and enduring? What forces have conspired at specific points in history to send simmering suspicions of less productive, less able, less *contributing* familiar strangers in our midst boiling over into full-blown moral panics about 'the residuum', 'scroungers', 'shirkers' and any number of other stigmatizing shorthand terms for the unemployed, disabled and destitute? Are there particular confluences of factors that render such discourses salient at analogous points in time: crystallizing moments conducive to scandalizing public opinion about morally deviant enemies within and mobilizing support for scapegoating measures designed to distract from the underlying causes of society's ills? In short, there are lessons to be learnt from our past about the *roots* of today's ideology of deservingness and its *nature*; what it shows us about the ways such discourses have been contested historically; and how this knowledge might be harnessed to confront and overcome contemporary scrounger myths.

This chapter begins the process of addressing the above questions, by unpacking a series of related ambivalences about 'the poor' that have manifested themselves through time. On our way, we will encounter a colourful cast of characters: from the 'mobile poor' and 'sturdy beggars' of Medieval folklore to the 'idlers', 'vagabonds' and 'problem families' of later epochs. These culturally constructed anti-citizens were the abject figures and familiar strangers of their day: recognizable (if fanciful) archetypes who provided convenient scapegoats for, or freak-show exemplars of, invariably more complex social problems. In considering these contextually specific manifestations of recurring oppositions, the chapter offers a broad interpretive framework for the rest of the book, in which our focus switches to polarities that characterize conceptions of poverty today.

'VOLUNTARY' VERSUS 'INVOLUNTARY POVERTY'

According to a long historical tradition, people living in poverty were once treated with unbridled charity. Though stripped of dignity and agency and infantilized by their reliance on 'the comprehensive ecclesiastical altruism of feudal religious charity, alms-giving and monastic hospitality' (Golding & Middleton 1982: 7), early Medieval paupers could at least rest safe in the knowledge that no one had yet devised a rationale to blame them for their own plight. Indeed, considerable academic literature, including empirical studies of parish records (McIntosh 2011), supports the notion that early Christian attitudes towards the poor displayed a degree of non-judgemental (if patronizing) benevolence that would shame later turns towards more selective, sometimes punitive, welfare regimes. Driven by unswervingly literal interpretations of the gospels, early 'canon law' generally emphasized 'the innocence of poverty', avoiding any 'easy equation between destitution and moral inadequacy' (Tierney 1959: 11–12). Such compassion was intimately bound up with other doctrinal virtues upheld not just by Christianity but also other religions, often related as much to the faithful's (self-interested) pursuit of godliness as their determination to deliver the needy from want. 'Pious endowments', 'good works' and other conspicuous displays of beneficence offered routes to spiritual salvation (by way of worldly renown), for both early Christians and Muslims (Jones 1980), while monastic teaching venerated those who voluntarily eschewed worldly possessions. This was the basis for the 'Rule' set down in AD 520 by St Benedict (Artz 1953: 185), requiring his monastic order to uphold a 'tria substantialis of obedience, celibacy, and poverty' (Butler 1919, cited in White 1971: 15). And compassion towards the poor was not confined to the Church: as historian Marjorie McIntosh's meticulous compilation of a database of 1,005 alms-houses and hospitals established between 1350 and 1599 illustrates, early forms of organized poor relief were as likely to emanate from philanthropists espousing continental-style 'civic humanism' or its 'Christian or Northern' variant, who held that 'well-ordered' states had 'responsibilities' to 'promote the well-being of the entire community' (McIntosh 2011: 21).

Yet only the most superficial reading of history could deny that, even in the early centuries of Christianity, there were exceptions to such unalloyed charity. By the later Medieval period, a combination of conflicted ideologies and increasingly urgent economic pressures had led to a marked retrenchment in the culture of giving. A 'more likely' story, as Golding and Middleton (1982: 7) argue, is that medievalist Brian Tierney (1959: 11–12) was right to offer a revisionist view of the early Church's position as one which had long scorned 'voluntary poverty' (at least by anyone other than monks) as an 'identifiable malaise', with 'idleness' pointedly 'condemned'. If correct, this judgement casts doubt on suggestions there was ever widespread belief that poverty 'equated with virtue' (Tierney 1959: 11–12).

In England, the decades encompassing the Black Death and the reign of Elizabeth I respectively have long been identified as periods during which economic imperatives, driven first by crisis, then incipient capitalist ideology, swept aside any lingering precedents favouring unconditional altruism. Golding and Middleton (1982: 8) chart the reconceptualization of the (able-bodied) poor as a potential economic asset in the fourteenth century, singling out the 1349–57 Statute of Labourers and ensuing 'vagrancy laws' criminalizing 'the mobile poor' (itinerant vagabonds) as measures designed to contain and exploit them to address a 'crisis in the feudal economy'. By commodifying hobos (albeit for reasons more pragmatic than purely ideological), successive laws legitimized using their forced labour to help address a dire situation in which food production no longer met 'the subsistence needs of the peasants', let alone 'surplus needs of the land owners' – especially during a plague that ultimately decimated half the population (Golding & Middleton 1982: 8). Yet however effective conscripting the poor might have been in the short term, disruption wrought by the Black Death would have long-lasting consequences both for agricultural output and associated issues around the maintenance of both 'work discipline' and 'social order' among those 'outside the labour force': non-serfs or (in today's terms) the unemployed (Golding & Middleton 1982: 8). The epidemic's aftermath, argues McIntosh (2011: 17), saw an exodus from many manors of peasants seeking 'better opportunities elsewhere', in turn undermining landowners' control over their 'remaining tenants', who might 'gradually acquire more property' and become parish leaders. This incipient social mobility conspired with such acute labour shortages that it *empowered* unbonded workers-for-hire 'who chose not to work regularly' to 'find enough casual employment to get by' (an early twist on today's feted flexible labour markets). the later, explosive, rejection of feudalism symbolized by 1381's Peasants' Revolt, meanwhile, 'heightened fear' among elites that 'all forms of hierarchy were at risk' (McIntosh 2011: 17).

The time was ripe for concerted efforts to harden hearts and minds against the poor, especially those who threatened 'the maintenance of work discipline' and 'good order of the work force' (Golding & Middleton 1982: 6–7). 'These two central issues', as Golding and Middleton (1982: 6–7) observed, would 'weave their way through the centuries of society's dealings with poverty', with the othering and vilification of paupers who 'exploit systems of income maintenance or subsistence provided by society for an impoverished minority' (forerunners of today's 'shirkers' and fraudsters) central to defining the acceptable limits of compassion. Thus, as early as 1349 an ordinance condemned to prison any '"reaper, mower, or other servant"' who left employment 'before the end of the term of service agreed upon' (Middleton 1997: 227), and by 1357 the then Archbishop of Armagh was preaching that beggars and others reliant on poor relief should be 'hated by their neighbours', based on God's teachings about the 'merits of labour' and legitimate wealth accumulation (cited in McIntosh 2011: 17). At a time when the labouring poor were battling bubonic plague and ever more parlous living and working conditions, it is easy to understand how such scapegoating rhetoric, directed at those judged to be shirking their duty to contribute to the common weal, touched raw nerves. Building on this theme of *non-labouring* poor, successive early vagrancy acts passed between 1349 and 1388 to conscript vagabonds would pave the way for the construction of 'a pre-industrial, property-less [sic] and disciplined working class' heralding the 'much tighter controls of later decades' (Golding & Middleton 1982: 9).

Of the various antecedents of the 'undeserving' poor discursively constructed through the propaganda pincer-movement of state regulation and Christian sermon, no figure was more emblematic of hardening attitudes towards paupers than the 'idle' or 'sturdy beggar'. Though physically able, this itinerant phantom, first identified in the 1388 Statute of Cambridge (Middleton 1997: 208), spent his life wandering between parishes, scavenging from those who toiled for a living. He therefore epitomized morally repellent malingering, starkly opposed to the idealized virtues of the similar 'discursive invention' who was his antithesis: the 'worker' or 'good subject' defined in the 1349 Ordinance and refined and embellished throughout the 1350s and 1360s (Middleton 1997: 230). This legalistic distinction between 'good' and (by implication) 'bad' subjects represents one of the first symbolic expressions of elite-directed disdain towards the able-bodied unemployed. It is easy to see the legacy of this tradition in contemporary discourses about scroungers and shirkers: idle recipients of state 'handouts' who *could* work but don't; wastrels content to remain 'voluntarily' poor by refusing to provide for themselves. Indeed, the sturdy beggar construct is more pernicious than this, foreshadowing wider vistas of suspicion about the deservingness of everyone from rough-sleepers to Romani 'gypsies' to severely disabled claimants that today we subject to disability 'hate crime' (Disability News Service 2017) or force to prove their incapacity in fitness-for-work tests. Once 'rogues, vagabonds and sturdy beggars had entered the scene', to quote Golding and Middleton (1982: 9), they would 'personify wilful poverty for decades, indeed centuries'.

In weeding out from the property-less mass sub-classes of malingerers against whom public support could be mobilized to impose punishment and servitude, fourteenth century elites arguably conspired to engineer Britain's first moral panic against scroungers. Widely defined as 'a threat or supposed threat from deviants or "folk-devils"' (Goode & Ben-Yehuda 2009: 2), the late sociologist Stanley Cohen's (1972: 50) definition of the 'moral panic' conceived it as a hegemonic tool used by a dominant 'control culture' to (re)assert social order by constructing plausible (if largely fictive) bogeymen on to whom deviant characteristics could be projected, often to deflect blame or attention from more complex social problems. What more clearly defined control culture could there be than that which prevailed in a deeply religious Medieval age when most of the populace were illiterate and definitions of acceptable moral boundaries were comprehensively dictated by clergy and Crown?

Talk of panics aside, if the 14th century did witness a decisive break with more charitable attitudes towards poverty, this was at least partly spurred by perceived economic necessity: something elites could *assert* (if only as a pretext) given the manifest devastation wrought by the Black Death. That the ensuing agrarian crisis gave them an excuse to dispense with charity and contain and commodify the previously mobile poor demonstrates how even such calamitous acts of God could be transformed into fortuitous ideological tools to drive political and economic reform. Is it so far-fetched to draw analogies between the opportunistic actions of an already insecure feudal elite in exploiting the effects of this plague on food production, environment and public health to assert the immutability of the status quo – and the duty of good subjects (the 'hardworking families' of their day) to fall into line – and the similarly repressive actions that typified responses from neoliberal elites to more recent crises, such as the 2007–8 crash? In the event, the post-Black Death period ushered in a centuries-long continuum of measures to degrade and persecute the poor, though it would take 'a further shift of gear into full-blown mercantilism' to 'sharpen more clearly the discrimination between "god's poor and the devil's"' – the 'poor and the paupers' – which was to form 'the crux of later legislation' (Golding & Middleton 1982: 9).

The process of *embedding* distinctions between 'deserving' and 'undeserving' poverty (based, principally, on people's willingness to work) unfolded rapidly during British history's second decisive break with the supposed unconditional charity of the earlier Christian period: that accompanying the sustained economic reforms of Henrys VII and VIII and, especially, Elizabeth I. There is much to support the view that this 'Tudor revolution in government' represented a rapid acceleration of earlier, more evolutionary, trends: perhaps even the first truly hegemonic attempt to construct a framework for long-term 'social control' (Golding & Middleton 1982: 9). Indeed, few words better describe the sustained, comprehensive nature of the Tudor reforms than control and centralization. Among its myriad expressions was a 'further secularisation of charity', which it coded into 'systematic and compulsory form' (in 1536) and, finally, a 1553 law formally distinguishing between three sub-divisions of the poor: 'the impotent (chronic sick, orphans, the aged); casualty (war-wounded); and thriftless (rioters, vaga-bonds, the idle)', with 'the last group' pointedly singled out as 'the problem' (Golding & Middleton 1982: 10). As at so many points in history, though, this state-directed hegemonic project to construct a durable ideological discourse, by reviving earlier problematizations of the 'voluntary' poor, would not have succeeded without Church collusion. As discussed at length else-where (including by this author), 'elite-engineered panics' fail to catch fire if 'different branches of the establishment disagree with one another' (Morrison 2016a: 23). In Tudor times, no such divi-sions existed: evangelical reinterpretations of biblical morality happily adopted a 'Puritan-influenced certainty that effort was duly rewarded and idleness the mark of the sinner' (Golding & Middleton 1982: 11). This discursive alignment occurred against a backdrop of spiralling poverty, caused by (among other factors) the 'fluctuating fortunes of the cloth industry, the enclosure of common lands and conversion of arable land to pasture' and an 'ending of monastic hospitality and monastery-gate "doles"', that would ultimately provoke 'food riots and recurrent unrest' – but not before the Tudors had fostered a growing societal 'obsession' with wanton idleness undermining the newly capitalized 'free market' and growing 'labour shortage' (Golding & Middleton 1982: 10–11).

A brief (pragmatically driven) hiatus in the dominance of discourses vilifying idlers in opposition to an emerging Protestant work ethic saw 'the rich' persuaded to reintroduce the 'machinery of parish relief and public charity', if only to quell the increasing 'disposition to riot' in some quarters (Coats 1976: 110). But it was not long before equilibrium was restored, backed by the largely hegemonic musings of influential thinkers, including John Locke and Daniel Defoe. Henry Fielding's 1751 investigation into highway robberies digressed into statements generalizing 'those who are able to work and not willing' as 'much the most numerous class of poor' (quoted in Golding & Middleton 1982: 17): un-evidenced assertions redolent of today's sweeping tabloid rants. If one statutory measure crystallized the divide-and-rule positioning of this 19th century distinction between 'workers' and 'shirkers', though, it was the 1834 Poor Law Amendment Act. Inspired by the thinking of leading moralists (chiefly utilitarian social reformer Jeremy Bentham and Thomas Malthus, whose writings on population control continue to colour debates about intergenerational poverty even today), the Act sought to address the toxic mix of rising destitution and insecurity among the propertied classes that characterized the post-Napoleonic depression: a period during which the 'creaking machinery of the Elizabethan poor law' neither met 'the needs of the industrial poor' nor quelled 'the fears of the urban bourgeoisie' (Golding & Middleton 1982: 14–15). It did so by supplanting the existing system of outdoor relief (donations of food, clothing and/or money to the destitute dating back to Elizabethan times) with a principle of 'less eligibility', underpinned by a catch-22 question for would-be claimants chillingly echoed in today's mandatory work activities:

the 'workhouse test'. The 'test' was brutally simple: in all but the most extreme cases, a precondition for anyone's ongoing receipt of poor relief was their willingness to enter a factory-style work-house, earning their keep as unpaid drones in the service of rebuilding Britain's war-ravaged economy.

As at almost all turns in policy-making towards the poor, the imperatives behind the 1834 Act had to be scrupulously legiti-mized in the public sphere, and consent mobilized through an alliance of State, leading intellectuals and that other enduring arbiter of public morality and (supposed) economic necessity: the Church. In this case, beyond being endorsed by ecclesiasts like Malthus, the Act introduced another long-lasting innovation, by weaving discourse laced with Christian sentiment into the wording of the report on which it was based. Running through this document was a rich vein of proselytizing about Protestant mores: its authors framing themselves as pursuers of a 'missionary task' to diffuse '"the right principles and habits"', paired with a rejection of degenerate behaviours such as 'excessive breeding' or 'dependence on the ale-house and indolence' (Golding & Middleton 1982: 16). In crafting what E.P. Thompson described as a 'sustained attempt to impose an ideological dogma', twinned with 'the comforting thesis that poverty was both inevitable and morally culpable' (1968: 295), how removed was this approach, in substance, from the moralizing entreaties of latter-day Christian reformer Iain Duncan Smith, as he condescendingly coaxed the unemployed into demonstrating 'purpose, responsi-bility, and role models for children' by yielding to 'work' as the 'best route out of poverty' (Duncan Smith 2015)? Perhaps the ultimate fusion of 'the secularised Calvinism of the work ethic' and the moral framework of late Victorian hegemony, however, came with the inclusion of the passive, objectifying term 'unemployed' in the *Oxford English Dictionary* for the first time in 1882 (Golding & Middleton 1982: 295).

Beyond their ultimate historical expression in the workhouse test, echoes of successive elite-engineered panics about the 'voluntary poor', 'vagabonds' and 'sturdy beggars' continued into the early 20th century. Almost as soon as society had finally recognized the existence of structural unemployment, with the introduction of the first state-backed out-of-work benefits, this fledgling advance was qualified by a 'search for the scrounger': the on-the-take chancer who must inevitably accompany any display of public generosity (Deacon 1978). Against the backdrop of post-war austerity, falling wages for those who *had* retained work, and the global ripple-effect of the Great Depression, familiar scapegoats swiftly reappeared in popular discourse: non-working able-bodied men relying on the hard graft of their toiling (yet similarly impecunious) fellow citizens. This increasingly crystallized suspicion of the unemployed also found expression in early writings by the architect of the Welfare State, William Beveridge. Commenting in 1904 on proposals for 'work colonies' outlined in William Booth's 1890 *In Darkest England and the Way Out* – a tract that 'Orientalized' the English poor every bit as much as anthropological writings have consistently othered natives of the Indian sub-continent (Said 1978) – Beveridge condemned 'the mass of idlers and dependants' minded 'to reap an easy harvest' from 'relief funds', but who 'ceased to apply' when 'they found that work was demanded' (quoted in Golding & Middleton 1982: 29). He would, of course, obliquely revisit the concept of 'idlers' years later, in his template for the Attlee government's welfare reforms, the *Report on Social Insurance and*

Allied Services, declaring war against five 'Giant Evils': 'Want, Disease, Ignorance, Squalor and Idleness' (Beveridge 1942).

Discourses informed by the 'workhouse test' still taint the way we propose solutions to poverty to this day: their ultimate expression being in narratives that go beyond stigmatizing people, to *criminalize* them. It is to these that we now turn.

'LAW-ABIDING' VERSUS 'CRIMINAL POOR'

From vagabonds to vagrants, 'sturdy' to 'aggressive' beggars, poor relief 'fraudsters' to modern-day 'benefit cheats', 'hooligans' to 'hoodies', those on the lowest rungs of the social ladder have consistently been cast as deviant and *anti*social, if not outright criminal. Diagnosing the dynamics of how and why this creeping criminalization first emerged returns us to the conundrum of governance by centralizing Medieval authorities: the desire to balance the 'set of problems related to labour control' with 'the problem of social order outside the labour force' (Golding & Middleton 1982: 6–7). To maintain loyalty and morale among the working poor – initially *pragmatic* goals which morphed into proto-capitalist ideology – it was judged necessary to discourage, and ultimately outlaw, handouts for the 'pejorative figure of the alms-seeking able-bodied vagrant' (Middleton 1997: 229). At the same time, a 'related' concern emerged about the need to 'discipline' the unemployed, to maintain wider 'social order' (Golding & Middleton 1982: 7): a mode of early law-and-order thinking infused with Magna Carta sentiment.

What emerged from this web of early social policy was a 'criminalisation of certain forms of pauperism', and specifically those seeking to exploit the system (Golding & Middleton 1982:

7). As early as the 14th century, then, statutory seeds of suspicion were sown about both the *honesty* of those pleading poverty, disability or inability to find work and their methods of salving their needs: specifically, their willingness to fraudulently abuse the generosity of others. Subsequent Statutes of Labourers and vagrancy laws were therefore about more than merely ostracizing the wilfully idle. They discursively pathologized paupers' behaviour as a threat to both social and moral order: ultimately reframing them as criminals. This discourse can be glimpsed as early as the identification of 'the fraudulent nonworker' in the 1349 Ordinance (Middleton 1997: 230), which effectively outlawed unemployment through the pincer-movement of a 'contract clause' threatening idlers with prison and an 'enforced labour' clause ordering any unemployed person, 'servile or free', to 'serve him who shall require him' at the 'specified customary rate' (Middleton 1997: 227, citing Putnam). As Medievalist Anne Middleton argues, this might be viewed less as an *ideological* line in the sand than an emergency response to the sudden, drastic labour shortages wrought by the rampaging Black Death. Unlike later measures unambiguously designed to prosecute idleness, the ordinance only 'applied to a defined spectrum of persons': namely 'agrarian landless labourers or those whose holdings were insufficient to support them without wage labor'. And only when 'a wandering worker in search of day labor refused service' with due '"regard to his rank"' did he become legally 'culpable' (Middleton 1997: 227–8). Though a third clause of 1349's ordinance explicitly prohibited charitable giving to 'sturdy beggars', it took the 34 Ed 3 (1360) to impose a tangible punishment for idlers generally: 15 days' imprisonment for any able-bodied person minded to 'serve the summer' without work, outside the town where they 'dwelled in the winter' (Chambliss 1964: 68). But not until the 1388 Statute of Cambridge – by which time 'sturdy beggars' had come to be known by a range of stigmatizing colloquialisms, from *'mendinantz* [begging friars] and *vagerantz'* to *'stafstrikers, faitours* [swindlers]' and *'lolleres* [a derogatory term for the evangelical ascetic poor popularized in Chaucer's *The Canterbury Tales*]' – was this category of scrounger, one which would 'have an enduring existence in political action and ideology', sharpened into a solid 'political *bête noire*', through its 'earliest shadowy appearance' in formal legislation (Middleton 1997: 229).

By the time of Henry VII's wholesale 'suppression of vagrancy', the criminalization of idleness had entered a punitive new phase: crystallized in a 1547 Act ventriloquizing the voice of God to preach that 'Idleness and Vaganondrye is the mother and roote of all thefts' and any vagabond or sturdy beggar 'given to loytringe' for three days would be 'marked with an whott iron in the brest and the marke of V' (quoted in Golding & Middleton 1982: 9–10). In these and other vagrancy laws emphasizing the 'divers and subtle crafty and unlawful games and plays' of those 'whole and mighty in body, and able to labour' but still given to 'begging', late sociologist William Chambliss (1964: 71) notes a paradigm shift away from earlier drives to convert idlers into 'laborers' to a pointed 'concern with *criminal* activities'. As the first law with this focus, the 1530 statute began the gradual process of redefining vagrancy less as wilful economic inactivity than as an *intrinsically criminal* condition, characterized by such deviant traits as cunning, duplicity and (reflecting colourful superstitions of the time) 'crafty sciences' (Chambliss 1964: 71). The 1530 Act was, then, a symbolic milestone: paving the

way for a long-term trend towards extending the criminalization of certain (poor-related) *behaviours* (pick-pocketing, benefit
fraud, 'aggressive begging' – Waiton 2009) to *poverty itself*. This
qualitative discursive shift would ultimately normalize narratives bracketing poverty and crime together: an association
which (as coming chapters demonstrate) continues to poison
media-political rhetoric around everything from benefit fraud
to 'problem parenting'.

After the epochal 1530 shift, the 16th century offered still
more criminalizing sentiments, with punishments for vagrants
'clearly engaged in "criminal" activities', like 'loitering' or
'playing the vagabond', rapidly ramped up from mere removal
of an ear's 'gristle' to 'gaol', and repeat offenders suffering the
'pains and execution of death' as 'a felon' and 'enemy of the
commonwealth' (27 H 8.c.25 1535, quoted in Chambliss 1964:
72). Ever more degrading and brutalizing crackdowns followed:
from the use of hot irons to publicly brand idlers caught 'lurking',
'loitering' or 'idle wandering by the highway side' with a letter
V (for 'vagabond') or S ('slave') to the construction (by the
1700s) of the 'rogue' as an even more 'disorderly and dangerous
person' (Chambliss 1964: 74). Just as the '"criminalistic" aspect'
of legal definitions of vagrancy moved from being 'relatively
unimportant', when the priority had been to deter begging and
conscript all able-bodied people into work, to one 'of paramount
importance' when it suited elites to reframe unemployment
as a law-and-order issue (Chambliss 1964: 75), so too did the
scroungers of their day come to embrace a more encyclopaedic
range of 'vices'. Elizabethan definitions of the 'licentious', 'disso-
lute' and 'wicked behavior' of vagrants encompassed everything
from manifestly criminal acts far from confined to the poor

(specifically forgery and counterfeiting) to 'juglers, pedlars, tinkers', 'common players in interludes, and minstrels': forerunners, in essence, of today's unlicensed buskers (14 El c.5, quoted in Chambliss 1964: 73). By 1743 the net had extended further, to embrace ever more specific variants of 'vagrant' inimical to political imperatives of the time, including clear antecedents of modern-day scroungers. These ranged from a distinctly Georgian iteration of today's absent father – defined as 'all persons who run away and leave their wives and children' – to 'persons going about as patent gatherers, or gatherers of alms, under pretense of loss by fire or other casualty' foreshadowing contemporary ideas about bogus beggars and benefit fraudsters (quoted in Chambliss 1964: 73).

Within a little over a century, moreover, renewed impetus would be given to these stigmatizing discourses through the (by then) 'burgeoning newspaper press', which delighted in both reflecting and reproducing 'the slogans, mythologies, passion and debate surrounding society's continuing bewilderment about what to do with the poor' (Golding & Middleton 1982: 29). Initially finding voice in *The Times*' resurrection of centuries-old archetypes of 'idlers and imposters', this 'zeal for classification and moral exhortation of the poor' was accompanied by the 'investigatory urges of a new journalism, released from political patronage and corruption by the expansion of the mid-century' (Golding & Middleton 1982: 21). Although some such reporting made notable early attempts to advance counter-discourses, among them Henry Mayhew's socially analytical writings in the *Morning Chronicle*, George Sims' commercially opportunistic *How the Poor Live* was coloured by demeaning language every bit as Orientalizing as William Booth's: describing his entry into 'a dark continent' as 'interesting as any of those newly explored lands which engage the attention of the Royal Geographical Society' (Sims 1883: 5). Meanwhile, W.T. Stead's *Pall Mall Gazette* adopted a salacious, circulation-driven approach to explore 'the sordid life of London's lower orders' that foreshadowed the poverty porn of today (Golding & Middleton 1982: 23).

In the realms of law-and-order policy-making, meanwhile, criminalizing rhetoric had been adopted as a pliant discursive framework to first problematize then justify authoritarian clampdowns on multifarious unruly behaviours and outbreaks of 'hooliganism' attributed to the lower orders (Pearson 1983). This marauding deviancy involved everyone from the 'dangerous classes' threatening to invade from 19th century Paris to 'wild and incorrigible' street children (Cunningham 1991: 105) to those responsible for the sensational, widely reported London 'garrotting panics' of 1856 and 1862 (Sindall 1987). It would resurface again, periodically, throughout the 20th century and into the 21st: in the supposed 1970s 'mugging' epidemic by black youths imported from urban America (Hall et al. 1978); a near-contemporaneous US 'wave' of 'crimes against the elderly' by similarly imagined feral delinquents (Fishman 1978); and England's 2011 urban riots, widely blamed on a sub-stratum of rootless, savage tearaways (Kelsey 2015).

Such manifold associations of criminal or antisocial activity with vagrancy and unemployment have been continually redefined over time to consolidate distinctions between a virtuous poor – those providing for their families and contributing to society (in today's parlance, 'playing by the rules') – and a venal poor. In the earlier 19th century, the Poor Law Amendment Act's authors had strained to 'distinguish the small minority'

of 'blamelessly indigent' from a 'larger group of the "vicious"
and indolent': separating 'pauperism from poverty' as both
'the object' of the new law and 'its empirical presupposition'
(Golding & Middleton 1982: 17). In defining pauperism as 'a
qualitatively different condition' that both derived from and led
to deviant 'attitudes, behaviour and morality', they were laying
the foundations for various theories about pathological poverty
that would dictate the direction of discourse in the next century.

Before we turn to examining the evolution of this early
underclass thinking, though, no overview of the creeping criminalization of the destitute would be complete without considering
the other defining trend in 20th century poverty discourse(s):
the interlacing of the (new) rhetoric of social security policy
with the reimagined spectre of the idler. No sooner had a
prototype state pension been introduced by Herbert Asquith's
Liberal government than the press were clamouring to expose
the 'cunning exploitativeness of beneficiaries', with the *News
of the World* hailing the 'First Conviction' for fraud (Golding &
Middleton 1982: 36). Meanwhile, the very wording of the fledgling social insurance system introduced in David Lloyd George's
'People's Budget' carried the scent of suspicion: emphasizing
the 'conditional and supervisory' nature of proposed unemployment benefits, and numerous qualifications to preserve 'less
eligibility' and deter 'malingering' by 'the "shirkers and shams"'
(Hansard, Vol 24, 4 May 1911, Col 635; Vol 26, 24 May 1911,
Col 331). And scarcely had this embryonic state-backed relief
been rolled out than resentment began swirling around those
it was meant to help, with (as always) periods of austerity and
economic turbulence transforming them into a lightning-rod for
public opprobrium. Thus, introducing the Second Reading of a

1924 Unemployment Insurance Bill predicated on the 'mockery' of telling 'an unemployed man to look for work' at a time when 'we know that there is no work', Labour's Earl de la Warr still saw fit to remark that discouraging 'the shirker' was a 'very desirable object' (Sackville 1924), while the earliest throes of the Depression saw the party's first Prime Minister, James Ramsay Macdonald, regale the Trades Union Congress with reference to letters he had received from supporters (symbolically termed 'our people') complaining about 'neighbours or fellow-workmen' who were 'abusing' the system (quoted in Deacon 1978: 78). Once again, these othering us-and-them terms were trained on empirically recognizable archetypes, in this case early incarnations of fraudulent claimants: a discourse of distrust with all the tropes of familiar stranger narratives on which today's scrounger rhetoric rests.

'WORKING-CLASS POOR' VERSUS 'UNDERCLASS POOR'

Discrimination between the deserving and undeserving poor would finally come of age with the emergence of underclass thinking. Here was a theoretical paradigm which simultaneously redefined poverty as a miserable condition that stained society's conscience and *pathologized* it as a cultural/behavioural state that was native to those experiencing it. Early convictions that such pathologies existed rested on the identification of a colourful array of dysfunctional vices: idleness, irresponsibility and all manner of scrounging behaviours, from begging to fraud. What made this culture disturbing was the imagined threat it posed to the prevailing moral order, based on the premise that it could be passed, like a faulty gene, from one generation to another. Rather

than being a *symptom* of wider factors at least partly the responsibility of politicians and society at large (for example, structural
economic inequality) such behaviours were conceived as *endemic
to*, and *characteristic of*, a certain breed of person. The underlying
conceit of more judgemental underclass thinking was, then, that
such problem behaviours were *causes*, rather than consequences,
of poverty.

There were many problems (ethical and intellectual) with
this thinking. While more liberal adherents of early underclass
theses at least recognized that behavioural traits displayed by
certain sub-classes were largely the product of *socialization* in
deprived circumstances, those inclined towards fashionable
scientific theories, such as evolutionism, cast society's excluded
as irredeemable moral degenerates; a sub-species of human,
an *untermensch*, whose deviant characteristics were inscribed
genetically. Even more confused was the tangled middle path
paradoxically portraying the dysfunctional norms of the underclass as both socially *and* biologically inscribed: the outcome
of an unholy, dehumanizing conspiracy between nurture and
nature. It was these modes of thinking that recast poverty as a
kind of hereditary disease, whether physical, mental or a toxic
combination of both. This set the scene for disturbing turns in
ecclesiastical, charitable and political ideas about how to deal
with an abject rump wallowing at the bottom who might be
beyond help, let alone conscription into gainful employment.
Indeed, if there was a single defining feature of the underclass
paradigm that went further than numerous earlier demonizing
discourses, it was the sense that some people were not *worth*
helping, employing or even punishing; that society was better off
without them.

Though it took until the late Victorian period for patholog-ical poverty thinking to gain popular traction by acquiring its own language, its roots can be traced back to centuries before the earliest articulation of terms like 'residuum', let alone 'underclass'. Early hints emerged in the Tudor objectification of children reared in households in which 'idleness' was 'so rooted' 'that hardelie theie maye be brought after to good twifte and labour' (1 Edward VII c.3, cited in Golding & Middleton 1982: 8) and Locke's observations the following century that poverty stemmed from 'relaxation of discipline and corruption of manners' (cited in Golding & Middleton 1982: 12). Not until the 1880s did these piecemeal, underdeveloped ideas crystallize into a full-fledged concept. Once established, though, the notion it enshrined – that of a stubborn rump of unchangeable anti-cit-izens defined as much by poverty of character and aspiration as material want – would continue simmering beneath future debates about intractable hardship, occasionally exploding into full-blown panic. As social policy theorist John Macnicol (1987: 296) notes in his critique of the repeated (but largely futile) 'pursuit of the underclass' by social researchers, 'the concept of an inter-generational underclass displaying a high concentra-tion of social problems' and 'remaining out-with the boundaries of citizenship, alienated from cultural norms and stubbornly impervious to the normal incentives of the market, social work intervention or state welfare' has been 'reconstructed periodi-cally', displaying 'striking continuities', while also undergoing 'important shifts of emphasis'.

In his comprehensive chronological survey of the concept's evolution, historian John Welshman (2013) frames his narra-tive around 'six phases' identified by Macnicol: post-1880s

ideas about a 'social residuum'; its 1930s reconceptualization as a 'social problem group'; the 1950s construction of the
first 'problem family' paradigm; and successive, intertwined
pathologizing paradigms evolving since the 1990s, as latter-day
politicians and agencies edged away from *overtly* dehumanizing
discourses towards devising strategies to (re)integrate those
reared in a 'culture' or 'cycle' of poverty (Welshman 2013: xix).
If any common underlying discourse is shared by these wavering
definitions of what Welshman terms 'the excluded' – a disadvantaged, objectified social minority at times more notional than real
– it is the inference that they exist *outside* or *beyond* the bounds
of normal civil society. Specifically, they are consistently characterized as qualitatively different from a superior *working* class: a
sub-working class that needs to 'reconnect' to the hardworking
communities of which it was once part (BBC News 1997). Clear
oppositions are, then, repeatedly constructed between twin
but antithetical *classes*: a self-respecting, participating working
class and a disreputable, self-segregating 'workless class' (BBC
News 1997).

In these diametrically opposed social constructs we glimpse
the apotheosis of the deserving/undeserving antinomy: an overarching classification of 'good' and 'bad' poor people that both
distils and amalgamates key elements of earlier discourses to
redefine the poorest as a breed apart. Nowhere was the template
for this disjunction more starkly set out than in the observations
of Salvation Army founder William Booth and fellow Victorian
'social explorers', like his namesake Charles, who 'held up at
arm's length' the 'strange and faintly disgusting morality of life
in darkest England' to 'reaffirm the need for clear distinctions
between the casual and respectable poor'; 'the "residuum"' and

the 'true working classes' (Golding & Middleton 1982: 25). Of vital importance to this early manifestation of underclass thinking was William Booth's *moralistic* conviction (shaped by his Nonconformist beliefs) that, if left untreated, residual deviancy would contaminate the wider ranks of the urban poor. By contrast, Charles Booth's more sociological analysis of 4,000 individual cases of poverty in Hackney, east London, was more merciful: while he identified 'a handful' of 'barbarians', to him they constituted 'a very small and decreasing percentage' (Booth 1888: 305). Yet, despite concluding that earlier fears about 'hordes ... coming forth from their slums' destroying 'modern civilisation' had proved unfounded, his exhaustive taxonomy of eight 'classes' of pauper found room for five whose assorted deviancies 'constituted the real problem of poverty'. Of heads of families included in classes A and B (the first defined as agents of 'disorder', in terms foreshadowing recent antisocial behaviour debates), he dismissed 4 per cent as 'loafers' and one in seven as impoverished through 'drink' or 'obvious want of thrift' (quoted in Welshman 2013: 14–15).

Central to the residuum's conceptualization as a sub-human contagion was the suggestion that, contrary to later iterations of underclass which problematized its cultural *separateness*, late Victorian paupers were considered not nearly separate *enough*. In one sense, then, the overriding mission became less a quest to *reform* this hopeless rump, by coercing them into the ranks of the (true) working class, than to *insulate* everyone else from them. In wrestling with how to protect the 'respectable poor' from their would-be corrupters, policy-makers eyed the report of the 1884–5 Royal Commission on the Housing of the Working Classes and the Poor, which warned that allowing the 'better sort of lodgers' to live beside 'the worse' risked 'contamination' (Kaufman 1907). Even well-meaning reformers feared that the 'constant association' of 'criminal classes' with 'the poor' would corrode the latter's 'sense of right and wrong' (Golding & Middleton 1982: 25).

Amid the smouldering *fin-de-siecle* panic about creeping corruption of the God-fearing masses by a virulent residuum, various policy prescriptions were conceived. Some (though often couched in compassionate rhetoric) now seem disturbingly extreme. No movement was so conflicted as the Eugenics Society, whose members advocated everything from cruel-to-be-kind initiatives to limit the poor's suffering, such as birth control, to brutal methods, including forced sterilization, to preserve the purity of the national gene pool by slowly extinguishing the ranks of the congenitally deprived. Well over a century after Malthus had condemned poor relief as a recipe for 'overpopulation' that was 'sapping the will to work and encouraging imprudent breeding habits' (quoted in Golding & Middleton 1982: 14), influential contributions to the society's canon included a September 1929 comment to its secretary by David Caradog Jones that was chillingly redolent of the language of Nazi racial purists. In it, he spoke of a need to target the 'abnormal', ranging from those 'born blind, the very deaf, the epileptic' and 'the mentally deficient' to people 'persistently addicted to drink, crime or vice' (quoted in Welshman 2013: 61). Others advocated the splendidly contradictory goal of simultaneously *removing* the residuum from society and *reintegrating* them into it: by conscripting its 'troublesome unemployed' into labour colonies strongly redolent of workhouses (quoted in Welshman 2013: 26).

And, while there would be at least one significant interruption to the continuum of conceptions about an unsalvageable underclass – 'the advent of full employment during the First World War' exposing the residuum as 'a social rather than a biological creation'; its 'lifestyle' caused less by 'hereditary taint' than 'poor housing, inadequate wages and irregular work' (Welshman 2013: 3) – the underlying ideology of pathological poverty would prove remarkably resilient, repeatedly renewing itself throughout the 20th century. Far from being the preserve of reactionaries or religious zealots, in its implicit recognition of its conceptual opposite – the put-upon, exploited respectable poor – the notion of underclass even found favour with the most unlikely political adherents. It was Karl Marx and Friedrich Engels (1977: 92), after all, who distinguished between the enslaved working-class masses ripe for revolution (the proletariat) and the 'lumpenproletariat' or '"dangerous class"' they dismissed as a 'passively rotting mass thrown off by the lowest layers of old society': a sub-stratum whose desperate, economically disconnected 'conditions of life' rendered it more likely to become a 'bribed tool of reactionary intrigue' than a force for progressive change. Even Sidney and Beatrice Webb, socialist activists and co-authors of the Labour Party's 1918 'new constitution', would buy into the reasoning that some people were 'unemployable', though they conceded that this condition was curable through a redistributive programme to introduce 'a national minimum of education, sanitation, leisure and wages' (Welshman 2013: 22). More prosaically, one of Britain's most influential social reformers, Seebohm Rowntree, put his name to a 1913 report into the condition of the unemployed of York which devoted a whole chapter to the 'work-shy': emphasizing the 'importance' of ceasing to 'manufacture shirkers' in terms that have reverberated down the decades to infuse the latter-day scrounger myths on which this book focuses (Rowntree & Lasker 1911: 173). At the time, this derogatory label drew on a contextually specific association with a different kind of malingering: that of conscientious objectors refusing to fight in the Great War, as deplored in a 1925 letter from Rudyard Kipling to fellow novelist H. Rider Haggard, pronouncing himself 'sick' of seeing 'good men' volunteer 'for the benefit of the shirkers' (quoted in Pinney 2004: 226). Yet, in appropriating this term, Rowntree evoked images of pathological poverty as unforgiving as any: objectifying men who lost their jobs because they were 'drinkers'; social casualties often of 'poor stock' and 'growing up amid a degraded environment, with a slum street for an unguarded playground', and 'receiving the legal minimum of education' with 'no encouragement from their parents' (Rowntree & Lasker 1911: 173).

The essence of subsequent underclass thinking has rested on repeated diagnoses of cultures of poverty. Put simply, this concept rests on a belief that children born into poverty are not only denied the socioeconomic advantages of those from middle-class families, but that, crucially, the experience of being brought up in such households leads them to *stay* poor: by failing to gain an adequate education, becoming unemployed or otherwise benefit-reliant in adulthood, and lapsing into inherited 'cycles' of behaviour they then pass on to their own offspring. The essence of this thinking is that children are inculcated with normative 'poor' attitudes and behaviours though a toxic combination of dysfunctional parenting, lack of opportunity and social marginalization. What renders such ideas about intergenerational poverty so intriguing in the context of evolving conceptualizations of the underclass is that (unlike many earlier paradigms) they incorporate a discourse which both blames *and* absolves people for their deficiencies. In the 'medicalisation of the residuum' observable in the late Victorian 'social problem group' thesis, successive surveys pathologizing vagrancy and rootless, antisocial poverty had the (ironic) discursive side effect of letting truly 'deviant families off the hook', by suggesting they were *doomed* to poverty, whether they attempted to escape it or not (Welshman 2013: 45–6). Wind forward, and post-1960s 'culture of poverty' debates saw an early recognition that, far from being attributable to innate *genetic* faults, transmitted poverty was largely caused by external factors, including ones only governments potentially had the power to ameliorate. In his 1964 address to the US Congress, Sargent Shriver, special assistant to President Lyndon B. Johnson for the federal poverty programme, lamented the 'rigid way of life' of many poor Americans: a 'cycle of inadequate education, inadequate homes, inadequate jobs and stunted ambitions' (quoted in Welshman 2013: 87).

Yet however compassionate such rhetoric may sound, the durability of culture of poverty ideas rests, in part, on a far less altruistic mode of thinking: the 'comforting discovery' for 'the middle-class' that such (sub)cultures are 'small and concentrated enough' to be 'helped or contained', and the attention they redirect 'away from income inequality and the class structure' towards 'culture and behaviour' (Welshman 2013: 154). As historian E.P. Thompson observed in 1968, 'the sleep of the rich' is 'made easy' by 'the comforting thesis' that poverty is 'both inevitable and morally culpable' (cited in Golding & Middleton 1982: 15). But there is also that lingering flipside to this perspective, visible

even in the musings of reactionary thinkers who might otherwise cheerfully dismiss the congenitally poor as unsalvageable:
a wider establishment concern with maintaining social control.
Just as Thompson warned that the 'somnolence' of 'the rich' was
'disturbed only by the fear that this view might not be shared
among the poor' (cited in Golding & Middleton 1982: 15), so
too leading purveyors of family pathology theories (in Britain,
the likes of Keith Joseph, a principal architect of Thatcherism)
have concerned themselves with finding a 'cure'; if nothing else,
to preserve society's delicate overall equilibrium. Decades after
the drastic prescriptions of eugenics won support from intellectuals, for many at the forefront of New Right thinking – and the
insurgent Thatcher–Reagan economic project – the 'cultural'
problem of transmitted poverty could *not* be ignored, for fear it
would fuel rebellion and curtail incipient neoliberalism. Their
conflation of ideas about intergenerational poverty with broader
conceptions of behavioural and/or congenital deviancy has
continued to inform recent debates about poverty that are the
focus of the next chapter.

'POOR PEOPLE LIKE US' VERSUS 'THE OTHER POOR'

For the construction of moral panics, demonizing discourses and
ideologies of poverty to succeed, they must acquire the complicity
of society *generally*. In other words, a corollary, even prerequisite,
for the plausible scapegoating of a deviant and dangerous 'them'
first requires the identification and mobilization of a collective 'us': one seen to represent the normative, socially accepted
values and behaviours binding the majority together. Moreover,
the most successful and enduring scrounger discourses are those

that co-opt not only the middle or moneyed classes but also those whose financial and material means are much closer to the conditions of the minority being othered: the wider 'working classes' who often also rely (wholly or partly) on social protection.

With this in mind, if there was ever an object lesson in how naturalized such discourses can become, it was crystallized in these despairing words from Sarah Teather, one of only four Lib-Dem MPs to vote against a 2013 Bill capping annual benefit rises:

> People who come to my constituency office these days for help with some kind of error in their benefits often spend the first few minutes trying to justify their worth. They usually begin by trying to explain their history of working and that they have paid tax. They are desperate to get over the point that they are not like other benefit claimants – they are not a scrounger. It is perhaps a feature of the way in which the term 'scroungers' has become so pervasive in social consciousness that even those on benefits do not attempt to debunk the entire category, only to excuse themselves from the label. (Quoted in Williams 2013)

What Teather identified was a perception (and *self*-perception) among many people living in poverty that goes beyond *echoing* normalized discourse about benefit claimants: to *internalize* the stain of the scrounger as one that might easily be applied to *them*. Disjunctions between 'claimants like us' and 'scroungers' – deserving and undeserving welfare recipients – is at its most invidious when it moves those enduring poverty to continually question (and justify) *their own* conduct; to avoid being accused of the same feckless behaviours, and tarred with the same stig-matizing brush, as their neighbours.

As with all other discursive oppositions, this ultimate expression of the perniciousness of scrounger discourse – attaching a badge of shame to the unemployed and fomenting heterogeneous, internalized tensions between confected *sub-groups* of claimants – has historical precedents. There is a long tradition of othering narratives being used to promote suspicions between various iterations of the working and non-working poor, with Church, State and policy-makers at times fuelling sub-divisions even within the ranks of the unemployed. In words chillingly evocative of rhetoric used by modern-day politicians to pit the noble, striving 'shift-worker' against the shirking 'next-door neighbour, sleeping off a life on benefits' (Osborne 2012), C.O. Stallybrass, Liverpool deputy medical officer for health, responded to the seminal 1943 *Our Towns* report into the 'hygiene' of urban communities by condemning instances when 'the whole family' may 'be discovered in bed at an hour when children should be in school' (quoted in Welshman 2013: 74). And, at a lay level, interviewed for Golding and Middleton's anatomy of 1970s 'scroungerphobia', a 37-year-old single parent on supplementary benefit claimed to 'know quite a few of them [scroungers] personally', while a 50-something slaughterhouse worker estimated six out of ten claimants were scrounging, based on seeing '40 or 50 of them in the pub' (Golding & Middleton 1982: 172). So naturalized was scrounger discourse that one of the fiercest proponents quoted was unemployed himself. Viewing scrounging through the prism of a decade of industrial unrest, this 55-year-old conflated people *without* work with those *refusing* to work (strikers), complaining 'we spend too much supplementing the families of strikers' and 'more pressure' was needed to force 'people to get work' (Golding & Middleton 1982: 177).

As well as the various us-and-them identifiers already explored in this chapter – bonded versus mobile poor; 'good subjects' versus 'sturdy beggars'; 'respectable' versus 'criminal' poor; 'working class' versus 'underclass' – two other linking threads connect the numerous historical manifestations of scroungers. These are the feelings of 'disgust' directed at claimants, particularly the unemployed, and their longstanding association with 'failure' (Dean 1991: 39). In the words of social policy scholar Kirk Mann (1994: 79–80), 'there is always something unsavoury about the underclass', whether framed as 'the residuum, the dangerous class, the relatively stagnant population, the lumpen-proletariat' or whatever else is 'the fashion of the day': all such labels denote 'a class of failures'.

A recurring symbolic expression of these twin discourses of failure and disgust has been the repeated determination of elites to *physically* remove or separate the underclass from wider society: whether by overtly criminalizing them and confining them to workhouses or labour colonies; using more clinical, Darwinian prescriptions to 'control and cleanse' them, such as sterilization and other forms of eugenics; or spatially segregating their neighbourhoods and communities (Mann 1994: 86). In the post-war period of the 20th century, such geographical separations were often well-intentioned: from the construction of sprawling estates of 'homes fit for heroes' and the soaring tower blocks that replaced them to Harold Wilson's 1960s Community Development Projects; later Conservative Minister Michael Heseltine's inner-city regeneration schemes; and, ultimately, the 'action zones' used by Tony Blair's first administration to address health, education and family welfare inequalities in disadvantaged areas. One unintentional *discursive* effect of such policies, though, was to fuel these communities' alienation, as they were, first, *relocated* to the peripheries and, once there, *targeted* for (equally othering) policy interventions.

The 'social exclusion' many such neighbourhoods went on to suffer in material terms, having failed to benefit from rising living standards experienced by the general population in the 1980s, would (in the eyes of many, broadly liberal, commentators) translate into a further hardening of social attitudes towards the abject mass they were seen to represent. In his 1989 book *Losing Out? The Emergence of Britain's Underclass*, former Social Security Minister Frank Field laid bare what Welshman (2013: 167) paraphrases as 'a significant change' in the attitudes of 'mainstream society' towards 'those who had failed to "make it"', whom they widely regarded as social 'failures'. Describing 'the very poor' as inhabiting a 'political, social and economic apartheid', set apart from 'the working-class', Field argued their 'failure' was symbolized by the introduction of 'Invalidity Benefit': a payment nominally aimed at those too sick or disabled to work, which had the discursive effect of branding many former workers in deindustrialized areas 'invalid'.

But, whatever the causes and drivers of such exclusion, how much hard *evidence* is there for the existence and persistence of culturally distinct sub-classes in modern times?

PATHOLOGICAL POVERTY: MYTH OR REALITY?

It is beyond this book's ambit to detail the empirical basis (or otherwise) for the various theses advanced about pathological poverty. However, a brief consideration of such evidence as exists is wise, if only because of the impact such ideas continue to have on how people experiencing poverty are framed in popular discourse. That these research findings have themselves been distorted (or used selectively) by politicians, media and other actors is an important caveat to consider as we attempt to unpack the ideological, commercial and other agendas underpinning the ways in which narratives about those experiencing poverty are repeatedly (re)constructed in the present. In the end, it is by *testing* the veracity of disputed truth-claims (and discourses they promote) against the best data, and calling out bias, omission and inaccuracy where it exists, that viable counter-discourses against enduring 'scrounger' myths might be constructed.

The advantage we have in critiquing recent theories is that, since the late 20th century, there has been a steady build-up of academic research to test their substance. That much of this endeavour has been led by social scientists, not politicians, campaigners or journalists with more obvious agendas, gives us some grounds for asserting that, while *elements* of under-class thinking might be sound, overriding suggestions that there exists a social sub-stratum locked in an unbreakable dependency culture is false (Dean & Taylor-Gooby 1992). Moreover, the idea that those living in deprived communities are a breed apart or a threat to the moral order – and their poverty somehow socially and/or biologically inscribed – has been roundly debunked by findings demonstrating that, where 'cultures' of poverty exist, they are often highly *functional*, not dysfunctional: displaying rational responses to externally imposed conditions, rather than pathological predispositions to problem behaviours.

To illustrate, ethnographic studies designed to address the 'fundamental question' of whether people are poor 'because they behave differently' or whether 'they behave differently because they are poor' (Welshman 2013: 87–8) have repeatedly failed to find firm evidence of oft-cited badges of pathological poverty: intergenerational unemployment and cultures of dependency. In his US-based study *La Vida* (1966), the late social anthropologist Oscar Lewis identified a 'culture of poverty' among 100 low-income Puerto Rican families from four slums and their New York equivalents, but argued this was 'not just a matter of economic deprivation': he also witnessed entrepreneurial spirit a world away from abject, apathetic underclass representations consistently conveyed by politicians and media (quoted in Welshman 2013: 89). Examples included the communities' development of 'a cash economy' and a dominant value system stressing aspirational goals that would gladden the hearts of neoliberals, including 'the accumulation of wealth and property, upward mobility and thrift' (quoted in Welshman 2013: 89). Four years earlier, in *The Urban Villagers* (1962), sociologist Herbert Gans had identified a working-class sub-culture distinct from those of the middle classes in a deprived Boston neighbourhood, largely typified by 'lower-class female-based' family units, yet with behavioural norms representing rational '*responses* that people make to the *opportunities* and the *deprivations* that they encounter'. Foreshadowing Lewis' observations, he noted that, 'when opportunities were available, individuals and families responded by attempting to put into practice their hopes for a better life' (Gans 1962: 95). In a leading British sociological study, meanwhile, Ken Coates and Richard Silburn (1970: 166–7) implicitly accepted the existence of the 'problem family' but went on to argue that poorer households were not 'culturally distinct from the richer', as they 'appeared to respond to the same values, to share the same basic assumptions, to accept similar restraints'.

As the next chapter demonstrates, later researchers would similarly fail to identify clear-cut evidence for wide-scale cultures of poverty, transmitted deprivation or intergenerational unemployment. For now, though, let us simply quote the key findings of two seminal studies. In exploring the question of whether 'cycles of disadvantage' exist at a time when the UK was on the cusp of its 1970s 'scroungerphobia' panic, psychiatrist Michael Rutter and developmental psychologist Nicola Madge (1976: 5–6) concluded that 'the culture of poverty concept' was 'inadequate for an analysis of British society'. Similarly dismissive was Kirk Mann and Sasha Roseneil's (1994: 329) damning conclusion nearly two decades later about the risk to social cohesion posed by divisive media-political discourses about pathological poverty: namely that any 'threat' to society arose not from 'supposed constituents and reproducers of the underclass', but from 'those who propagate the concept of a dangerous class'.

CHAPTER 2

PROBLEM FAMILIES AND 'THE WORKLESS'

THE RHETORICAL ROOTS OF SHIRKERPHOBIA

SHIRK

VERB

[with object]

Avoid or neglect (a duty or responsibility)

(Oxford Dictionaries 2017c)

'I believe the person who is prepared to work hardest should get the greatest rewards and keep them after tax. That we should back the workers and not the shirkers.'
(Margaret Thatcher, speech to the Young Conservative Conference, 9 February 1975)

If the term 'scroungerphobia' captured the essence of 1970s claimant-bashing discourses, a speech delivered by Margaret Thatcher half-way through that decade offered an early flavour of more recent incarnations of the scrounger myth. Two days before being elected Leader of the Opposition, the future prime minister set out her typically individualistic vision of Methodism-tinged meritocracy to a boisterous audience at the 1975 Young Conservative Conference. In a pitch for social mobility ostensibly targeting cultures of entitlement at the *top* of Britain's class structure as much as the bottom, she argued that 'we should judge people on merit' rather than 'background' (Thatcher 1975). Yet scarcely had she uttered a mantra with which few on the Left could wholly disagree than it was reframed not as a championing of equal opportunities or redistributive social policies, but the Protestant work ethic: in Thatcher's terms, the conviction that those 'prepared to work hardest should get the greatest rewards and keep them after tax'. In going on to contend that it was 'praiseworthy' to 'want to benefit your own family by your own efforts', she crystallized a moralizing vision of economic self-reliance prioritizing kin over community, self over society: explicitly championing 'workers' over 'shirkers' (Thatcher 1975). Fast-forward 37 years and it was David Cameron's use of a near-identical phrase during a heated exchange with Ed Miliband in the Commons that exposed the hollowness of his previous claims to espouse 'compassionate Conservatism' (Cameron 2006).

Though newspapers continue to favour the historically hardwired term 'scrounger' to scapegoat the supposedly indolent mass which Thatcher derided as 'shirkers', in many ways it is the latter term (denoting avoidance of duty and responsibility) that has been mobilized most effectively as a rhetorical engine for hegemonic political control. Like her heroes, John Wesley and William Gladstone, Thatcher was an evangelistic champion of 'self-help and thrift' (Gladstone 1890, quoted in Wrigley 2016: 60). The daughter of a God-fearing self-made man (a grocer and lay preacher), the reverence for hard work and self-advancement underpinning her free-market ideology was framed in language as redolent of chapel pulpit as political podium. And she was not alone in drawing inspiration for her beliefs from religious teachings: the twin values of 'duty' and 'responsibility' underscored policy discourses promoted by a stream of moral missionaries in government from the 1970s onwards, of which she was but one. From the Jewish beliefs informing the 'cycle of deprivation' thesis advanced by her mentor and acolyte, Keith Joseph, through variously Christian-inflected concerns about the 'poverty trap' and 'social exclusion' that exercised Labour's Frank Field and Gordon Brown, to the much-publicized Damascene awakening that set future Tory Work and Pensions Secretary Iain Duncan Smith on a mission to tackle 'welfare dependency', for 40 years moralizing discourses have been integral to recalibrating the balance between state and market, society and individual.

This chapter explores successive rhetorical reconfigurations since Thatcher's day in political debates around the role and scope of the Welfare State; the balance between rights and responsibilities; and the persistence of discourses discriminating between a deserving and undeserving poor. It does so by examining recurring themes and tropes that have underpinned these shifts and continuities and demonstrating that popular myths about the idle and irresponsible, 'scroungers' and 'shirkers', have rarely been absent.

FROM 'CYCLES' TO 'CULTURES' OF POVERTY: THE 'VOLUNTARY POOR' TODAY

The story of the overarching 'cycles' of poverty theses that gained currency in the 1970s and have repeatedly been reinvented and refocused since is that of tensions (and occasional overlaps) between two intertwined, yet conflicting, conceptions of inter-generational marginalization. One is the enduring conviction (widely held on the political Right) that 'deprivation' is pathological: a condition or lifestyle passed between generations through dysfunctional imitative behaviours, bad genes or a toxic combination of both. The other (generally preferred by the Left) holds that such cultures of poverty as exist result from deep-seated socioeconomic 'disadvantage' caused by structural inequalities beyond the control of individual families or communities.

If the first of these can be traced back to a single origin in the public sphere, this is the 'cycle of deprivation' speech Keith Joseph delivered, as Secretary of State for Social Services in Edward Heath's Conservative government, to a local authority conference on 29 June 1972. Drawing extensively on criminological and psychiatric (as opposed to social work or sociological) literature, it was redrafted 11 times, at one point bearing a title which laid bare the more pathologizing undercurrents of his thinking: 'Cycle of Degradation' (Welshman 2007: 31). True to the interventionist spirit of his day, Joseph's proposals for addressing the problem of 'transmitted deprivation' drew on 'much of the best of concerned progressivism' (Timmins 2001: 289) – from a mass rollout of playgroups and nurseries in urban areas to higher (not lower) benefits for many families. Yet his diagnosis of the *causes* of his 'cycle' was innately conservative. At its heart lay a question both rhetorical and despairing: 'why is it that, in spite of long periods of full employment and relative prosperity and the improvement in community services since the Second World War, deprivation and problems of maladjustment so conspicuously persist?' (Sinfield 1972: 4). Though conceding that the term deprivation embraced 'many disadvantages', which could 'occur singly or in different combinations' (and, significantly, 'throughout society' rather than being confined to the poor), his discussions with 'social workers, teachers and others' had convinced him that the principal 'casualties of society' were the usual abject figures and familiar strangers: 'problem families, vagrants, alcoholics, drug addicts, the disturbed, the delinquent and the criminal' (Welshman 2007: 37).

Joseph began his ensuing policy mission by establishing a 'working party' on 'transmitted deprivation' (its title implicitly assuming intergenerational poverty existed), co-run by the Department of Health and Social Security (DHSS) and the Social Science Research Council. From the outset, its terms of reference were imbued with his personal ideology, including a renewed, neo-Malthusian emphasis on 'family planning', based on his assertions that 'large family size was correlated with delinquency, low intelligence and poor reading skills' (Welshman 2007: 38). Even the term 'deprivation' was semantically loaded: rather than focusing on structural contributors to poverty, such as financial or even educational disadvantage, he chose a noun which might easily have been confused with 'depravation', thereby placing the onus, once again, on the *behaviours* of the poor. This thinking would guide his government's approach to social security until Labour supplanted it in 1974; its introduction of 'area deprivation policies' having the discursive effect of reviving earlier political tendencies to 'mark' or 'other' poor neighbourhoods by symbolically separating them from wider society. And while his decision to increase material support for low-income households contrasts starkly with recent default settings to *withhold* or *withdraw* social assistance in 'problem' cases, his underlying discourse laid the foundations for a reset back to historical ideas about pathological poverty (Welshman 2007: 37). Indeed, it was the long-term legacy of Joseph's speech (largely unpublicized at the time) that proved most significant.

In spirit, if not exact language, it reshaped normative rhetorical approaches to poverty for decades.

Of the many critiques contesting Joseph's thesis along the way, by far the most influential was the superficially similar-sounding (yet qualitatively distinct) 'cycle of disadvantage' concept advanced within four years of his speech by Michael Rutter and Nicola Madge (1976). The discursive shift in their iteration of the 'cycle' concept, towards an emphasis on 'disadvantage' (a term later appropriated, if misrepresented, by Tony Blair) was as significant as it was subtle. While Joseph's thesis rested largely on the problem of unemployment and its consequences for the prosperity and aspirations of those affected, the 'cycles of disadvantage' embraced a far wider range of inequalities, from poverty of access to education, training and democratic participation to lack of cultural, recreational and transport infrastructure. The word 'deprivation' was problematic in that could be construed to cast those in poverty as abject, helpless and all but free of agency. By contrast, 'disadvantage' strained to describe the tangible *inequalities* rendering some people's situations less fortunate than others'. Crucially, while Rutter and Madge conceded that poverty was about more than just lack of money, they had no truck with then popular theories proposing largely non-material solutions. 'A marked overlap', they argued, existed between 'different forms of social disadvantage', and 'for problem families' improved 'social circumstances' might be 'as important as help with personal problems and relationships' (Welshman 2013: 255). Moreover, in a prescient warning to future policy-makers minded to resurrect 'stereotypes of "*the* problem family"', they argued against remedies targeting 'notions of a homogenous group' (Welshman 2013: 255–6).

Before considering in detail how ideas about poverty 'cycles' have continued to inform the rhetoric (and substance) of subsequent welfare policies, it is worth briefly mentioning a related, yet distinct, model of intractable poverty that emerged around the same time as Joseph's. In wrestling with the idea that poverty might be *both* intergenerationally transmitted *and* the consequence of macro-level forces beyond the control of those affected, future Labour Welfare Reform Minister Frank Field (then director of the Child Poverty Action Group) developed a concept that became every bit as influential as the 'cycle' theses: the 'poverty trap' (Field & Piachaud 1971). That this term proved so enduring was because it went beyond offering a neat soundbite to rebrand an already identified problem. Rather, it seemed to encapsulate a sense of intractable impoverishment as recognizable to proponents of Joseph's pathologizing thesis as to adherents of more sociological thinkers, like Peter Townsend (1979), who emphasized the practical (rather than cultural) obstacles faced by people living in poverty. Put simply, the 'poverty trap' argued that some people *were* trapped in lifestyles, even cycles, of poverty – including (though not *defined* by) reliance on benefits. Crucially, this was not because they were wilfully dependent or averse to work: rather, they were 'trapped' by the conundrum that in moving off benefits and into the types of employment available they would lose more money than they gained. Far from being a badge of pathology or corrupt attitudes, then, this vision of a 'culture' of unemployment cast it as a rational response to disempowering forces imposed on claimants from outside.

Like Joseph's thesis, Field's would reverberate down the decades, exercising governments of Left and Right. Its legacy runs through numerous policy ideas (and discourses) to which we will return: from efforts to roll out free childcare to offset the parental costs of entering work to New Labour's introduction of working tax credits and a National Minimum Wage to the concept of Universal Credit: the Coalition's all-in-one benefit designed to 'make work pay' (Osborne & Duncan Smith 2015).

ORIENTALIZING THE EXCLUDED: RETURN OF THE MORAL MISSIONARIES

Defying expert warnings about the flaws in Joseph's thesis, governments of the 1980s and 1990s repeatedly reasserted the existence of cultures of intergenerational dependency. During the 1980s concepts of intractable 'cycles' (whether of 'deprivation' or 'disadvantage') were particularly appealing to Ministers, not least because they offered convenient discursive displacements for all manner of social problems, from the widespread public disorder (labelled 'riots') that rocked inner-city neighbourhoods from Brixton to Toxteth early in the decade to the outbreaks of football violence towards its end. What easier way to deflect attention from politically engineered unemployment caused by large-scale deindustrialization and the long-simmering social (and, at times, racial) tensions these inflamed than by reviving the convenient frame of the unbreakable 'cycle', whose supposed longevity effectively absolved from responsibility the administration of the day? A clear expression of this closed-ranks mindset appeared in the contentious conclusions of Lord Scarman's government-commissioned report into the 'Brixton riots'. While acknowledging that 'flawed and unimaginative policing practices', including racially targeted stop-and-search policies, had contributed to the anger of 'rioters' (McGhee 2005: 22), in condescendingly emphasizing the deep-seated 'racial disadvantage' experienced by African-Caribbean communities Scarman stood accused of 'shifting the object of anti-racist struggle' from 'public institutions' to 'individual' and focusing on 'the problem' of Brixton's community itself (McGhee 2005: 22). In other words, he used 'the wrong things' as a smokescreen, just as ministerial and judicial pronouncements had fuelled a racially tinged 'law-and-order panic' a decade earlier (Hall et al. 1978: vii).

The law-and-order emphasis of such 'crisis' pinch-points repeatedly recurred in state-of-the-nation debates throughout the Thatcher–Major years and into those of Blair, Brown and, ultimately, Cameron. Pathological poverty theses first re-emerged during the late 1980s and early 1990s, principally in the context of two dominant, and intertwined, discursive frames: firstly, the slow-burn media-political problematization of (benefit-dependent) single-parent families; and, secondly, a resurgence of Britain's long-simmering 'juvenile panic' (Morrison 2016a), crystallized by the febrile, underclass-inflected national debate sparked by the murder of toddler James Bulger by two older boys from single-parent households. These twin discourses would both endure, resurfacing repeatedly through everything from later rhetorical (and policy) assaults on 'problem' or 'troubled' families to New Labour's 'amoral panic' about 'antisocial behaviour' (Waiton 2008).

The legacies of these specific iterations of pathological poverty discourse are explored in coming sections. Before we turn to them, though, it is worth briefly revisiting our other linking theme – that of 'moral missionaries' – to consider how the influence of three key individuals contributed to the recycling and reinvention of ideas about cultures of poverty, to establish the *overarching* frameworks for 'welfare reform' through the late 1990s and beyond. In the hands of Blair and Field (his short-lived Minister for Welfare Reform), the term 'cycle of disadvantage' was transformed, like Joseph's 'cycle of deprivation' before it, into a moral mission infused with its adherents' personal beliefs (in this case Church of England Christian). And, within a handful of years, this cycle of *appropriation* would continue, as future Work and Pensions Secretary Iain Duncan Smith (a devout Roman Catholic) emerged from a personal epiphany in Glasgow's deprived Easterhouse suburb to launch the Centre for Social Justice and embark on a quest to 'fix' Britain's 'broken society' (Slater 2014). In truth, both manifestoes for tackling 'social exclusion' – Blair's delivered against the backdrop of London's equally barren Aylesbury estate; Duncan Smith's at a Conservative conference five years after his much-publicized Glaswegian expedition – displayed all the Orientalizing bewilderment of upper-class social explorers emerging into the light from 'darkest England' (Booth 2014). But as sociologist Bev Skeggs argues, citing the social geographer Chris Haylett (2001), while the discourse arising from the Brixton riots othered 'blackness' (specifically black youth) as 'atavistic and backward', Britain's iteration of the US *underclass* concept 'racialized' the poverty characterized by *whites* (Skeggs 2004: 90). In choosing Aylesbury as the backdrop to launch a 'Social Exclusion Unit' tasked with (re)integrating what he called a 'forgotten people', a 'workless class' who had been 'cut off from society's mainstream' (Blair 1997), Blair othered 'a mass of people, in mass housing', who were 'falling out of the Nation' and 'losing the material wherewithal and symbolic dignity traditionally associated with their colour and their class': casting them as 'an ugly contradiction', both 'abject and white' (Skeggs 2004: 90). He was racializing the white working-class poor, dehumanizingly rebranding them as a (savage) 'workless class', in implicit opposition to the (civilized) *working* class: a 'culturally burdensome whiteness' and 'blockage' to 'the development of a modern nation' on the 'global stage' (Skeggs 2004: 90).

How, then, did New Labour's moral missionaries propose to tackle social exclusion? As the linguist Norman Fairclough has shown, Blair's initial approach was crystallized in Frank Field's 1998 Green Paper, subtitled *A New Contract for Welfare*, which was framed around the asserted problem of 'dependency': an objectifying term *defining* swathes of people by their receipt of benefits, rather than identifying this as one *aspect* of their lives. By subverting the previously more popular term 'dependence' (a truism describing low-income households' enforced reliance on benefits) for an implicitly judgemental term casting the act of claiming as a form of deliberate (if abject) agency, Field's wording bore the 'moral' imprint of his Christian-influenced view of social security (Fairclough 2000: 184). Nowhere was this articulated more clearly than in his preachy juxtaposition between two opposing (but paradoxically 'equivalent') states: 'dependency and insecurity' versus 'work and savings'. This stark antinomy was significant in two respects, with far-reaching implications for the discursive (re)construction of social security from this point on. Of immediate note, it rewrote 'the social relations of welfare' as '"helping" relations', framed 'mainly' around a narrow definition of 'getting people off welfare and into work': a message best encapsulated in a single paragraph (5), headed

'The Importance of Work', which showcased a flurry of soon-to-be New Labour buzz-phrases, involving pledges to 'help people move from welfare to work', and ensure 'responsibilities and rights' were 'fairly matched' (Fairclough 2000: 184). More influential, ultimately, was Field's repeated rhetorical distinction between those in 'genuine need' and an implied workless rump not discharging their 'responsibilities' to support themselves. This fused his missionary approach with the more 'contractual' view of welfare Fairclough ascribes to Blair, in a happy alliance reviving the 'moral division between deserving and undeserving poor' (Fairclough 2000: 181).

As coming sections demonstrate, Field's highly personal authorship of New Labour's 'welfare reform' agenda set a rhetorical template for the next 20 years of 'Welfare-to-Work' policy-making, with tensions between 'contractual' and 'ethical' framings of social security (the latter, to Fairclough, redolent of language of the 'New Right') lacing benefit policy even today. Among other things, New Labour consolidated the Major government's symbolic rebranding of 'Unemployment Benefit' as the more active-sounding 'Jobseeker's Allowance' (a payment explicitly conditional on its recipients' continual demonstration that they were 'actively seeking work' – Bochel 2014: 236) by renaming the Department of Social Security (DSS) the Department for Work and Pensions (DWP). Again, the rhetorical onus was placed on claimants (not state) to address the drivers of low income: by working.

Of all moral missionaries, though, it was Duncan Smith, architect of the Coalition's semantically loaded 'Work Programme', whose tenure at the DWP took the thumbscrew-tightening of ever-greater conditionality to a punitive extreme. If Joseph and

Field were throwbacks to an age of conditional charity-giving and gentle moral chastisement, 'IDS' practised a more absolutist philosophy: that almost *any* work (paid or unpaid) was good for the soul, and the unrelenting pursuit of it should underpin entitlement to even the most basic state-funded social protection. His Work Programme imposed this regimen through a suite of schemes and sanctions: from ever-closer monitoring of claimants' efforts to find work, backed by 'three-strikes-and-you're-out' fines for those refusing it (Fuertes & McQuaid 2016: 98), to the self-explanatory 'Mandatory Work Activity', a form of 'Workfare' or 'involuntary volunteering' (Strauss 2008: 100) imported from America.

As with New Labour's prescription (and justification) for tackling long-term unemployment, from the outset IDS was given rhetorical 'ownership of Coalition welfare reform', in a 'political choice' calculated to promote the 'personal narrative' about his 'awakening … to the problem of poverty' and play down the make-up of a cabinet 'dominated by politicians drawn from relatively narrow social strata', with 'high personal wealth' (Wiggan 2012: 386–7). Moreover, the premise for his mission (besides his Damascene conversion) was a series of rhetorical questions and sweeping pronouncements predicated on equally one-dimensional assumptions: namely that 'welfare dependency' was 'an unproblematic and uncontested concept'; claiming benefits contributed to keeping people in poverty; governments 'should seek to reduce social security spending'; and that both poverty and 'dependency' could somehow 'be addressed' by the very act of cutting benefits (Wiggan 2012: 389). A DWP document entitled *21st Century Welfare*, published shortly after his appointment, gave a flavour of what was to come by posing the loaded question: 'what steps should the Government consider to reduce the cost of the welfare system and reduce welfare dependency and poverty?' (quoted in Wiggan 2012: 389). Elsewhere, it casually stated that 'the benefits system' had 'shaped the poorest' and 'trapped generation after generation in a spiral of dependency and poverty', while a follow-up paper later that year would describe 'a life on benefits' as 'a poor substitute for a working life', alleging that the Welfare State was 'maintaining people on benefits rather than helping them to flourish in work' (quoted in Wiggan 2012: 388). As with numerous rhetorical constructs before and since, one of many inconvenient truths ignored by these documents, and the various speeches and announcements leading up to and flowing from them, was the fact that a growing number of *working* people were having to spend 'a life on benefits', whether cast as such or as the in-work 'tax credits' introduced by Brown as Chancellor to incentivize employment by topping up meagre wages.

A nuanced distinction, then, between the New Labour and Coalition Conservatives' emphasis on supposed welfare dependency was Duncan Smith's transformation of a long-running debate about 'the adequacy' of social security for 'raising the living standards of low-income families' into one letting him portray 'the *cause* of poverty and unemployment [author's italics]' as 'originating solely' in a 'culture of out-of-work benefit dependency' (Wiggan 2012: 388). In other words, the Welfare State not only fostered cultures of dependency, but was the reason poverty *itself* existed. Yet if Coalition rhetoric sought to 'renew the validity of behavioural explanations for social problems' while promoting anti-welfarist assertions about 'the supposed failure of "statist" intervention under New Labour', in truth there was more to unite these governments' approaches than divide them. As Wiggan (2012: 385) argues, despite the Coalition's 'greater determination' to *cut* benefits, in other ways it simply hardened and accelerated the 'punitive' measures it inherited.

Flowing from the overarching rhetorical (and policy) preoccupations of recent governments with addressing presumed intergenerational cultures of poverty has been a similar obsession with two related sub-problems. One is the enduring problematization of the human (or sub-human) face of pathological poverty: various personifications of abjection and disgust represented by everyone from 'neighbours from hell' to 'troubled' or 'problem families'. The other has been the cumulative conscription of everyone from people with disabilities to 'NEETS' (young people 'not in education, employment or training') to rough-sleepers, travellers, Romani 'gypsies' and migrants into an economically inactive rump collectively labelled 'workless' (Blair 1997). Weaving in and out of these broad discursive categories has been a further current of concern: one which characterizes these various sub-groups, or the behaviours that supposedly typify them, as 'antisocial', even outright criminal. It is these interwoven sub-discourses we now examine.

PROBLEMATIZING PARENTS: SINGLE MOTHERS, FECKLESS FATHERS AND 'BROKEN' FAMILIES

The origins of today's 'problem family' archetypes can be traced back to policies pursued by Keith Joseph in the early 1970s. Though the term itself (first coined in the 1950s) had fallen into disuse by this time, Heath's government exhumed it, with his Social Services Secretary using an address to playgroup leaders on the first anniversary of his 'cycle' speech to ally the concept to a fledgling DHSS initiative, 'Preparation for Parenthood' (Welshman 2007: 25). Like numerous later (no doubt similarly well-meaning, if patronizing) programmes, this underlying schema, which informed various later 1970s interventions, was nominally universal in scope. In substance, though, it focused on addressing growing concerns about under-aged pregnancy, marital breakdown, domestic violence and – Joseph's personal hobbyhorse – transmitted deprivation by using schools-based education to inculcate children from poorer families specifically (especially girls) with an understanding of the responsibilities attached to parenting.

The discursive DNA of 'Preparation for Parenthood' ran through numerous subsequent policy discourses pathologizing poverty. It insinuated itself into two key reports published under the 1975–9 Labour administration, the Court report on child health (Court 1976) and another from the Select Committee on Violence (1977) (urging Ministers to ensure 'all pupils receive some education in the skills of parenthood') and a string of 1980s university-led projects, including those of Cambridge University Child Care and Development Group and the dedicated Family Policies Study Centre. The then Department for Education and Science also funded three studies into how best to teach parenting to secondary-school children (Hope & Sharland 1997: 9). By the 1990s, meanwhile, Joseph himself was riding back to the rescue, amid a frenzied public debate about the latest crisis of youth: the accumulation of disparate concerns about everything from single mothers to teenage joyriders. In a fresh pamphlet, debated in the House of Lords, he once more crystallized the unfolding panic of the day: a discourse of distrust and disgust that went on to follow a clear trajectory, from the Major government's prolonged preoccupation with unemployed single mothers and 'dangerous masculinities' (Haylett 2001: 358) to the 'problem/troubled' families issue that fixated Blair, Brown and Cameron.

As at earlier junctures in the evolution of scrounger discourse(s), one of the first articulations of creeping concerns about threats to the culturally normative nuclear family ideal came not from a native commentator but an American. In a 1990 dispatch from the netherworld of Britain's 'underclass', Charles Murray blithely identified its core symptom as 'the type of poverty identified by Henry Mayhew in nineteenth-century London': that of 'the "undeserving poor"' (Murray 1990: 3). In Murray's eyes, Britain's underclass was typified by three traits that would guide the central strands of political rhetoric for years to come: out-of-wedlock births (soon personified as jobless single mothers and feckless fathers); violent crime (knife/gun ownership and antisocial behaviour); and unemployment (quoted in Welshman 2013: 162). Attuned to popular narratives of the day, he even linked it to burglaries and vehicle thefts (joy-riding), contriving, in one fell swoop, to pin all contemporary social ills on the maladjusted, morally degenerate rump of the underclass.

This theme of creeping moral degeneracy among the feral lower orders resurfaced repeatedly in 1990s political discourse, fusing the tropes of 1970s 'law-and-order panics' about British youth (Hall et al. 1978) and centuries-long continuums of anxiety about the 'dangerous classes' with which delinquency and hooliganism were invariably aligned (Pearson 1983). Twenty years before 2013's most recent spike in scrounger discourse it reached an earlier peak, when a smouldering seam of anti-welfare sentiment directed at the favoured folk-devil of the day – unemployed single mothers – exploded into a wider panic about familial disorder and dysfunction following the murder of James Bulger. The touch-paper for the already simmering, government-driven maternal panic had been lit several months earlier, in then Social Security Secretary Peter Lilley's near-parodic 1992 Conservative Party Conference speech. Lilley had patented a mantra that would be repeatedly appropriated by later governments: committing himself to 'closing down the something-for-nothing society' (Lilley 1992). In his unfiltered diatribe, woven into a tortuous pastiche of Ko-Ko's aria from *The Mikado*, he extended his discourse of undeservingness to a sweeping panoply of early 1990s abjects, unwaveringly summed up as 'scroungers': from 'bogus asylum-seekers' to 'so-called New Age Travellers', whom he likened (in language reminiscent of Nazi anti-Semitic vitriol) to 'spongers descending like locusts, demanding benefits with menaces'. But if one sound-bite (oft-repeated to this day) came to define the speech it was the lip-curling relish with which Lilley objectified a vicious conspiracy of *familial* scrounger archetypes, from 'young ladies who get pregnant just to jump the housing queue' to 'dads who won't support' their 'kids' (Lilley 1992).

The febrile year of 1993 itself began with a far-reaching appropriation of traditional Conservative moral terrain by the then Shadow Home Secretary: one Tony Blair. In a soon-to-be era-defining *New Statesman* article, he road-tested what became a lasting (if oft-misquoted) political mantra – his determination to be 'tough on crime and tough on the underlying causes of crime' – while implicitly blaming most 'abuse, vandalism and petty disorder' on the deviant poor (Blair 1993). In accusing 'young teenagers' of committing a wave of 'arson or hoaxes' in

Tyne-and-Wear the previous year; conjuring up images of 'our old people' living 'in a state of fear'; and arguing it was 'people who live on inner-city estates' who 'suffer most', he implicitly associated criminality and what he would later reframe as 'anti-social behaviour' with lower-income neighbourhoods and (by extension) those living in them (Blair 1993). Elsewhere there were glimpses of what would be signature tropes of his 1997 Aylesbury address and the preoccupation with 'social exclusion' and 'problem families' it introduced: described here as the blight of 'poor education and housing, inadequate or cruel family backgrounds, low employment prospects and drug abuse', and the risk that letting 'young people' live 'outside mainstream culture' increased their chances of 'going wrong' (Blair 1993).

The timing of Blair's intervention turned out to be darkly prescient. Two weeks to the day after his article appeared, two-year-old James Bulger disappeared. He was later found murdered on a Liverpool railway track, having been abducted and tortured by two ten-year-old boys. The hysterical state-of-the-nation debate that ensued not only strengthened Blair's resolve to address the 'disintegration' of a society 'becoming unworthy of that name' (as cited in Blair 2010: 57). At a more banal level, it was opportunistically exploited in the service of the then-incumbent Tory government's already simmering maternal panic discourse, as crystallized in its renewed drive to revive longstanding Conservative ideals about wholesome nuclear 'family values', by objectifying its supposed equal and opposite: the scrounging, benefit-dependent single mum (and, to a lesser extent, the feckless absent dad). Just as 2013 would be the 'year of the shirker', 1993 was '"the year of the single mother"', with politicians and media seizing on the fact that

Bulger's killers both hailed from 'broken families' to consolidate the already fast-building framing of 'lone mothers' and their 'fatherless, supposedly criminally inclined children' as 'the core of the underclass' and the cause of numerous 'social problems' (Mann & Roseneill 1994: 317). In truth, as cultural theorist Angela McRobbie (1994: 107) has argued, the panic extended more widely than this, embracing 'the breakdown of the family, the growth of crimes committed by children and the powerlessness of the police and judiciary': a toxic cocktail of pre-millennial societal decay which, 'by the time the two boys were charged with murder several months later', had been 'reduced by Ministers and media' to a 'denunciation of "evil"'.

For the Right, this simpleminded positioning of the offenders, their parents and the dysfunctional value systems they were held to represent as antitheses of society's accepted norms had the convenient discursive function of both reactivating long-standing discourses about pathological poverty and justifying a hand-wringing defeatism about the impossibility of civilizing the savages. Yet even if Bulger's killers (and the endemic moral turpitude they symbolized) were irredeemable, for some who had long sought to engineer changes to Britain's post-war social security consensus the cloud of societal decay had a silver lining. And, though Blair (2010: 204) would eventually recant the 'faulty' analysis he applied immediately after Bulger's killing, conceding in his autobiography that he had been wrong to extrapolate from a single extreme case to the 'ultimately flawed conclusion that our society had broken down', his pronouncements at the time set the agenda for a long succession of deeply illiberal interventions. The first was John Major's (ultimately short-lived) 'Back to Basics' campaign, unveiled eight months after Bulger's killing at the 1993 Conservative conference: an eye-catching (if hollow) paean to traditional verities of 'neighbourliness, decency and courtesy', laced with tropes drawn from the background maternal panic discourse, and distinctly Thatcherite emphases on 'self-discipline' and 'family' (Major 1993). It was another year before he unveiled any firm family-friendly initiatives, including an early foray into nursery vouchers to fund pre-school child-care which might have been conceived by Keith Joseph (Major's call for 'self-discipline' and family values blunted, somewhat, by embarrassing revelations about his Ministers' marital infidelities). But if 'Back to Basics' achieved anything meaningful it was to set the scene for the similarly moralistic discourse informing New Labour and the Coalition's approaches to government. Much of Major's 1993 speech aligned his catchphrase with a distinctly post-Thatcher vision of rebalancing state protection with individual self-help. Yet, at other moments, it prefigured thinking that would shape the dual Blairite agendas on social exclusion and antisocial behaviour. In his paean to 'whole communities ... destroyed' when 'terraces' were replaced by 1950s 'tower-blocks', their 'walkways' transformed into 'rat-runs for muggers', and in condemning 'fashionable opinion' which had fed misguided beliefs that it was 'better to rely on the council and social workers' than 'family and friends', Major might have been writing an early draft of the script Blair would use not only at Aylesbury, but in later laments about 'permissive' 1960s attitudes undermining parental discipline (Blair 2002). He was also foreshadowing the paradigm of the 'broken society': a term coined by Blair himself in 1995, but later weaponized by Duncan Smith and Cameron through the all-encompassing montage of problems they ascribed to 'broken Britain': from drug abuse and violent crime to 'teenage delinquency, family breakdown, welfare dependency' and 'loss of traditional values' to 'children who kill' (Thorp & Kennedy 2010).

FROM BROKEN FAMILIES TO BROKEN NEIGHBOURHOODS: CRIMINALIZING COMMUNITIES

Beyond the specific targeting of single-parent families, it would be easy to dismiss the borderline incitement of Peter Lilley's poisonous 1992 speech as a freewheeling rant by an unhinged right-wing ideologue. But his contribution to the Major government's wider reframing of welfare eligibility, and its creeping criminalization of claimants, was profounder than this. Rather, Lilley had begun the process of returning popular narratives around social security to discursive places they had not occupied since at least the 1970s 'scroungerphobia' panic: at times implicitly conflating almost *all* claimants with fraudsters, through his unevidenced assertion that there were 'scores' of 'frauds to tackle' (Lilley 1992). Such discursive leaps paved the way for future governments to bracket together welfare and crime – or, in New Labour's case, antisocial behaviour (ASB).

Hazily defined in law as conduct causing or 'likely' to cause 'harassment, alarm or distress to one or more persons not of the same household' (Great Britain, *Crime and Disorder Act 1998*), the post-1997 concept of ASB built on Blair's insistence years earlier that it was 'people who live on inner-city estates or use public transport' who 'suffer most' from low-level crime and disorder (Blair 1992) and the similarly triangulated elision in his Aylesbury speech between the plight of a 'generation of young men' for whom 'little has come to replace the third of all manufacturing jobs that have been lost' and 'households where three generations have never had a job', occupying 'estates where the biggest employer is the drugs industry' (Blair 1997). For all their differences in tone, there were clear continuities between the vision of 'modern civic society' Blair articulated at Aylesbury and Lilley's baleful diagnosis of the insidious threat of a 'something-for-nothing society'. Blair explicitly alluded to this (albeit more optimistically) by arguing for 'an ethic of mutual responsibility or duty' and 'something for something', based on expectations that everyone would 'play by the rules' and 'only take out' if they 'put in' (Blair 1997). Further, in buying into Conservative myths about 'a generation of young women' for whom 'early pregnancies and the absence of a reliable father almost guarantee a life of poverty' he completed the circuit, by explicitly wedding New Labour to a Tory-led discourse of queue-jumping, under-aged single mums and the inter-generationally 'workless' as influential as his own agenda-setting pronouncements on crime. Hardly surprising that the *Daily Mail* reported his Aylesbury speech under the shouty headline, 'For all our benefit; THE PREMIER CHOOSES ONE OF BRITAIN'S BLEAKEST HOUSING ESTATES TO LAUNCH HIS DRIVE TO MAKE THE SINGLE MOTHERS PAY THEIR WAY', before emphasizing his 'threat' to 'get tough' with 'the workshy young' and 'single parents' (Deans & Hopkins 1997).

This persuasive montage of superficially connected, but disparate (even fanciful), groups later coalesced into an over-arching discursive backdrop onto which years of future social, economic and criminal justice policy would be projected. Despite buying into the ever more ingrained conception of poverty as (at least partly) pathological, New Labour's prescriptions were undoubtedly interventionist, embracing grandly titled 'Third

Way' policies ranging from a 'New Deal for the Unemployed' to Sure Start early intervention centres and credit unions, based on 'a culture of "social capital"' (Welshman 2013: 189). Yet in stressing 'there will be and should be' no 'option for an inactive life on benefit' (Blair 1997), its approach was quintessentially neoliberal: pump-priming a renewed emphasis on condition- ality to prioritize a 'contractual notion of fairness' in which individuals' 'welfare rights' were 'matched with responsibilities' (Haylett 2001: 361). As sociologist Ruth Levitas (1996a: 18) has argued, the very term 'social exclusion' (often interchangeably used with 'underclass') had become integrated into a 'hegemonic discourse' which pointedly contrasted it with 'integration into the labour market' and obscured inequality.

Like other recent governments, the Blair–Brown approach was, then, less to 'provide extra jobs or benefit increases' than to 'facilitate people to make changes within their own lives', revis- iting a continuum of ideas stretching back through Field's 1997 Green Paper to Joseph's 1972 'cycle' thesis. If Blair's words were telling, those of his then Education and Employment Secretary, David Blunkett, were blunter. Introducing the Welfare Reform and Pensions Act 1999, he uncritically accepted the premise of a 'welfare culture' and used the language of sentencing policy to liken the 'help' claimants could expect to 'rehabilitation' (quoted in Haylett 2001: 362). And with the carrot of 'help' came the stick of compulsion: offers of modest benefit top-ups for those without paid jobs who undertook environmental and/or other voluntary work, under the semantically loaded 'Welfare to Work' programme, were paired with 'sanctions' for 'those who fail to put their responsibilities before their rights' (Deans & Hopkins 1997). Moreover, though antisocial acts could theoretically be perpetrated by anyone, in practice ASB policy was transparently targeted at 'inner-city estates' (Blair 1992) and those living on them. Cue a slew of government-commissioned studies and literature reviews linking entrenched poverty, low aspiration and young people predisposed towards criminality or antisocial conduct. As sociologist John J. Rodger (2008: 50–51) notes, 'key criminal justice legislation since 1998 suggests that the main policy for NEETs' had been 'to manage the potential criminality of this group', particularly 'through ASBOs [anti-social behaviour orders]' and various other measures introduced under the '"respect" and antisocial behaviour agendas'. As a result, 'the strong tendency' was to frame 'the issue of NEETs' as a corollary of 'the "underclass" debate' and 'the welfare system' as offering 'perverse incentives to behave badly': the only 'choices' for young people being 'between work' and 'subjection to social surveillance' (Rodger 2008: 51). To this end, a 2000 Department for Education and Skills (DfES) statistical bulletin emphasized how 'living in council housing' and having either unemployed or low-skilled parents increased the risk of young people becoming NEETs (quoted in Rodger 2008: 50). Another DfES document, reviewing empirical literature commissioned from University of Birmingham researchers, emphasized how 'low income, poor housing and large family size' appeared to 'increase the likelihood of developing delinquency', particularly when 'in interplay' (Prior & Paris 2005: 21). While conceding that 'direct links with economic class' were 'weak', it argued that the impact of 'stress caused by low income' and 'reduction in life-chances and resources' were 'more strongly indicated', especially among 'adolescent young men' (Prior & Paris 2005: 21). Two years earlier, the White Paper *Respect and Responsibility* had aligned the ASB 'problem' with lower-income households, insisting a 'small number of families' were 'dysfunctional'. This revived Blair's earlier assertions that (in its words) the 'corrosive effect' of ASB was felt mainly 'in areas of greatest disadvantage' (Home Office 2003: 23). It also sharpened New Labour's focus on *individualized* deviancy, describing how 'two or three families' and their 'network' could 'create havoc' on estates, using tropes familiar from decades of repetition in culture of poverty debates: 'family breakdown' and children's lack of 'a positive role model' (Home Office 2003: 23).

And these strands would continue to dictate the thrust of New Labour ASB policy. By 2008, a supposed 'no-one-works-round-here' culture on council estates was being problematized by Housing Minister Caroline Flint: another moral missionary of sorts, with a *pro*social working-class back-story to legitimize her distaste for the *anti*social antics of the 'workless class' (escape from deprived upbringing by alcoholic single mother to become first in family to reach university – Day 2009). Her controversial solution – condemned by Shelter (2008) as 'a return to the workhouse' – was to force new social housing tenants to sign 'commitment contracts' obliging them to find jobs or face eviction (Flint 2008). Two years later, a Home Affairs Select Committee report stubbornly associated environmental 'risk factors' including 'low income and poor housing', 'disadvantaged' neighbourhoods and 'community disorganisation and neglect' with pathologizing 'family' ones: notably 'poor parental supervision and discipline', 'family history of problem behaviours', 'family conflict' and 'parental involvement in/ attitudes condoning problem behaviour' (Home Affairs Committee 2010). Thus, although one of Blair's stated missions had been to reintegrate a socially excluded 'forgotten people', by consistently criminalizing inner-city areas New Labour's rhetoric had the symbolic effect of further *separating* his 'workless class' from the respectable poor.

Under David Cameron's Coalition, a continuing obsession with 'problem families' (whose intriguing rebranding as 'troubled families' initially raised hopes of a more liberal, less blame-oriented approach to dealing with them) was paired with a decisive switch back to a criminalizing discourse long favoured by Conservatives: their fixation with benefit fraud. For all his early efforts to shake off the Tories' 'nasty party' tag, assisted by the author of that term (then Shadow Work and Pensions Secretary Theresa May) Cameron gave a chilling foretaste of what was to come in the run-up to the 2010 election: vowing to withdraw benefits for three months for claimants convicted of fraud once; six months from second-time offenders; and up to three years for those caught out a third time (Hall 2010). Once in office, his pursuit of this strawman enemy was unrelenting. Under the supposedly compassionate Iain Duncan Smith, May's three-strikes-and-you're-out threat to third-time *fraudsters* mutated into a turbo-charged reinvention of New Labour's sanctions system for claimants failing to engage with 'back-to-work' activities, extending the principle to 'offenders' who repeatedly rejected job offers 'without good reason' or failed to apply for 'suitable posts' (quoted in Porter & Winnett 2010). With one discursive leap, the signatories to new 'claimant contracts' were casually conflated with objectively criminal fraudsters. Meanwhile, Lilley's (in retrospect timid) promise to root out 'bogus claims' was militarized by Cameron's vow to hire private agencies to comb personal bank accounts and household bills of disability benefit claimants in pursuit of undeclared earnings and savings. In framing these agencies as 'bounty-hunters' (Morris 2010), he drew on imagery of pith helmet-clad explorers venturing into a 21st century 'darkest England': a forbidding wilderness inhabited by the feral savages of the 'workless class' (Blair 1997).

As for the loudly heralded 'Troubled Families Programme', of the 'multiple problems' facing the notional 120,000 'disadvantaged families' it set out to address, top priority was given to social ills all too recognizable from previous drives to address pathological poverty: 'parents or children' involved in 'crime or antisocial behaviour', truancy, 'adults out of work' or 'at risk of financial exclusion', young people 'at risk of worklessness' and 'families at risk of domestic violence or abuse' (DCLG 2017). Not only had large swathes of disadvantaged people once more been pathologized; they had also been criminalized. And hand in hand with this criminalization of *poverty*, or the deviant behaviours and culture(s) it was held to promote, came a parallel, interlocking rhetorical shift whose end goal was every bit as invidious: the outlawing of 'worklessness'.

THE RETURN OF VAGABONDS AND STURDY BEGGARS? 'BANNING' UNEMPLOYMENT

An enduring feature of the *fin-de-siècle* iteration of scrounger discourse promoted since the 1990s has been a refusal to countenance almost any kind of 'economic inactivity', however short-term or involuntary (Levitas 1996b). Since Lilley's crackdown on benefit 'cheats', repeated attempts have been made to frame everything from begging by rough-sleepers to claims of incapacity caused by disability as morally and/or criminally suspect. In other words, economic inactivity *itself* has been discursively constructed as fraudulent.

The reasons it has suited successive administrations to follow this script have been, by turns, ideological and pragmatic – though even primarily utilitarian justifications for reducing benefit costs and abuses of the system are ideologically motivated, given their underpinnings by a neoliberal obsession with 'living within our means' (Cameron 2008). There has also been a strong moral missionary strand to this debate, with politicians nominally on Left *and* Right pursuing ideological beliefs of a different kind: for instance, Christian-influenced ideas about promoting self-worth and human potential, and the injustice of allowing anyone to be 'cast on the scrapheap' (Field 1996).

It has long been accepted that the biggest rise in the number of economically inactive people defined (even by Ministers) as incapable of work occurred not on Labour's watch but under that self-styled champion of 'workers' over 'shirkers': Margaret Thatcher. In launching 'invalidity' benefit (discussed in the last chapter) at a time of escalating unemployment caused by mass privatization, market deregulation and de-unionization, much has been made of that administration's *motives* for moving large numbers of newly redundant people onto it, especially in former industrial areas devastated by closures of mines and factories. By classifying these casualties of the post-industrial new order as 'invalid' – obsolete, rather than out of work – this costly move arguably had the perverse consolation of enabling Ministers to massage the true scale of escalating unemployment (Levitas 1996b: 46). A greater long-term injustice, though, has been the repeated subsequent (re)construction of disabled claimants as both a non-contributing, costly burden and morally questionable:

a 'block' to the nation's 'global' onward march (Skeggs 2004: 90) every bit as abject as Blair's 'workless class' (Blair 1997).

This scroungerization of the sick and disabled began in earnest in the 1990s, at the start of an ever-harsher, slow-burn process of redefining eligibility. In the words of social geographer Allan Cochrane (1998: 310), 'the increased rate at which people were claiming invalidity benefit in the early 1990s' fuelled successive 'anti-fraud' drives, combined with efforts to 'define entitlement more narrowly', culminating in Lilley's introduction of 'much tighter medical checks' in 1996, under the subtly rebranded 'incapacity' benefit. The new name suggested it might yet be possible to (re)absorb *some* 'invalids' (back) into serving the economy, while weeding out fit people feigning incapacity. The scene was set for a distrustful reframing of disabled claimants, uncomfortably recalling the language of Medieval scroungers 'whole and mighty of body' but 'given to loytringe' (Golding & Middleton 1982: 9).

Of the ensuing waves of (politically and/or media engineered) 'panic' about the cost of disability benefits, two merit special consideration. The first was the sharp discursive shift latterly adopted by New Labour under Work and Pensions Secretary James Purnell and welfare advisor Lord Freud: architects of the now notorious 'Work Capability Assessments'. The second was the more uncompromising and target-driven rollout of a tougher WCA regime by the Coalition, alongside a slew of compartmentalizing reforms designed to sub-divide claimants into relatively more and less 'able' categories – with the single-minded aim of driving down welfare costs. Assisting both programmes was a significant shift towards 'managerialism' (Newman 2005: 369). Informed by the 'ideological politics of the New Right' (Newman

2005: 369), this cost-sensitive approach (rhetorically justified as a pursuit of 'efficiencies' and 'savings') led to the private-sector outsourcing of core aspects of social security: a trend discursively recasting claimants as 'consumers' and instituting 'a new (marketized and privatized) welfare order' (Newman 2005: 371).

The first of these step-change shifts began in 2008, with the launch of both the WCA regime and another rebranding of disability-related benefits as 'Employment and Support Allowance' (ESA). As with the introduction of 'Incapacity' Benefit and 'Jobseeker's' Allowance 12 years earlier, this loaded term contained a none-too-subtle nudge, recasting claimants previously classified as long-term sick or disabled as *putative* workers: *recovering* or *former* 'invalids' in a metaphorical waiting-room, queuing for 'support' to help them (re)enter the world of 'employment'. Social policy analyst Stuart Connor notes the intertextual ways in which people previously 'written off' (Purnell 2008b) were discursively reconstructed by Ministers as can-do 'jobseekers', regardless of the nature or extent of their conditions. This happened most conspicuously through a high-profile 'Employ Ability' media campaign, which sought to conscript them into a brave new world of 'globalization, flexibility, governance, employability' and (for those locked out or left behind) 'exclusion' (Connor 2010: 42). Implementation of these reforms was accompanied by a series of calibrated ministerial statements designed to reframe all but the most debilitating conditions as only partial and/or temporary obstacles to gainful employment. Thus, in March 2008, Employment Minister Stephen Timms told the Commons the newly published ESA regulations would 'prescribe the conditions of entitlement' for people who 'claim on the basis that their capability for work' is 'limited' (Timms 2008). Precisely seven months later, the Directgov 'newsroom' heralded ESA's launch by proclaiming it both 'tailor-made for disabled people' and those 'with ill-health' and 'part of the Government's radical welfare reforms' to 'get 1 million people off incapacity benefits by 2015': the most explicit admission yet that a key aim was to cut the claimant count (Directgov.uk 2008). For any doubters, it described the new WCA tests as 'designed' to identify what people 'can do', not what 'they can't', helping as many as possible 'get back to work', rather than being 'written off' and 'consigned to a life on benefits' (Directgov.uk 2008). This typically triangulated New Labour rhetoric thus embodied carrot and stick: while implicitly distancing itself from the Thatcherite approach to tagging illness and disability as 'invalidity', it suggested that, by joining a 'work group', all but those with 'the severest disabilities and health conditions' could (re)join the workplace. More sinisterly, underpinning the whole package were an avowed intention to slash the benefits bill and a strong inference that many claimants had long wilfully resisted employment.

As important as Purnell's rhetoric of 'more support for higher expectation' was a subtler discursive shift that signified changes of *substance*, as well as semantics. Woven throughout the press statement were fork-tongued references to both 'claimants' and 'customers': qualitatively different terms that created a symbolic opposition between passive *recipients* of (statist) social protection and active *agents* empowered to (re)engage with an imagined consumer-driven labour market. Just as Tony Blair had set out, a decade earlier, to (re)include the 'socially excluded', a new moral mission (led by an ex-Chancellor facing a post-crash spending crisis) aimed to turn as many claimants as possible into 'hardworking' taxpayers (Brown 1999), by constructing an improbable fusion of the rhetoric of pulpit and market. If one aspect of this latest phase of welfare reform distinguished it from earlier ones, though, this was the appropriation not only of neoliberal *terminology* but its culture, mechanisms and practitioners. In any earlier era Lord Freud's background as an investment banker might have seemed incongruous, even inappropriate, but by this time commercial companies and former captains of industry and high finance had been involved in planning and delivering public services for more than two decades. There was, then, a perfectly logical progression from the creeping privatization begun with the imposition of compulsory competitive tendering on local authorities in the 1980s to the contracting of French IT firm Atos to administer the first fitness-for-work tests.

Fast-forward two years, and the path was already laid for a Tory-led Coalition predicated on debt reduction and swingeing welfare cuts, conditions and crackdowns far more uncompromising, and less ideologically conflicted, than those preceding them. Over the next two (Conservative-led) parliaments, New Labour's relatively modest 12-year target for cutting the number of Incapacity Benefit (IB) claimants was supplanted by compulsory reassessments for all existing claimants; wholesale movement of those 'judged fully capable of work' (whatever their medical histories) onto less generous Jobseeker's Allowance (Cameron & Clegg 2010); and, once the Tories had re-entered government alone, DWP 'performance indicators' incentivizing assessors to reject eight out of ten appeals against refusal of benefits (Sharman 2017). Even the rebranding of the main universal benefit for people with long-term conditions and disabilities, from 'Disability Living Allowance' (DLA) to 'Personal Independence Payment' (PIP), threatened to forcibly *en*able the *dis*abled by strong-arming them into levels of self-reliance for which many were ill prepared. While the term 'personal independence' is laced with the ethos of self-help beloved of conservative-libertarian politicians from Gladstone through Thatcher to Osborne, conspicuous omission of the word 'disability' hints at a further nudge away from the 'sick-note culture' reviled by Duncan Smith, his Tory successors and, before them, New Labour figures like Alan Johnson (BBC News 2008).

For all its viciousness, the relentless rhetorical persecution of claimants who 'can work' but supposedly refuse to – a popular mythology about everyone from picky 'jobseekers' and lead-swinging disability claimants to out-and-out fraudsters that, through the language of media-political discourse, has been transformed into an anti-sociological pseudo-science of 'scroungerology' (Morrison 2013) – only begins to describe the neoliberal parallels to centuries-old 'sturdy beggar' frames. 'Shirkers' of all stripes have repeatedly resurfaced ever since Thatcher coined that pernicious term, from 'so-called New Age Travellers' (Lilley 1992) to 'aggressive beggars' (Waiton 2009) to 'illegal immigrants' (Garland 2008). Much more space would be needed to detail the full discursive effects of these wide-ranging rhetorical constructions of economically inactive 'wasted humans' (Bauman 2004). But if any illustration were needed of how normalized 'class disgust' (Tyler 2013) about 'aggressive beggars' alone had become by 2018 – whether cast as 'scrounging' fraudsters 'in designer jeans', as by Chancellor Kenneth Clarke during the 1990s benefit cheat panic, or the menace to the 'wellbeing' of 'fragmented individuals' conceived by New Labour Ministers obsessed with antisocial behaviour (Waiton 2008: 367–8) – it was the callousness with which, in the depths of a freezing 2017–18 winter, the leader of Windsor and Maidenhead Council wrote to police demanding rough-sleepers guilty of 'preying on residents and tourists' as a 'life choice' be cleared from the streets ahead of the then-upcoming royal wedding of Prince Harry and Meghan Markle (quoted in *Daily Telegraph* 2018). It is, then, hardly surprising that this normalization now extends far further than the old discursive precincts of political debating chambers and the press: into the realms of entertainment.

FROM SOCIAL REALISM TO SOCIAL ABJECTION: THE BIRTH OF 'POVERTY PORN'

One measure of how far a discourse can be said to have seeped into a national psyche is the extent to which it surfaces in contexts beyond those of the news media, politics or even day-to-day social interaction – to take root in popular culture. While an in-depth analysis of the many ways in which UK anti-welfarism and scrounger archetypes have penetrated television, film and the wider arts would require a book in itself, no consideration of the impact of the neoliberal reframing of social security would be complete without a brief review of its most persistent popular manifestations.

The 1980s saw the brutal reality of mass unemployment, deindustrialization and rising social inequality chronicled in a succession of (at times angrily didactic) films, serials and satirical shows – from socially conscious documentary strands like *World in Action* and *First Tuesday* to the work of stalwart social realist dramatists Ken Loach, Tony Garnett, Alan Clarke and Alan Bleasdale, recessionary comedy-dramas like *Auf Wiedersehen,*

Pet and *Prospects* and the Thatcher-bashing tirades of Ben Elton on Channel 4's *Saturday Live*. But by the turn of the millennium the sympathetic, politically charged portrayals of Youth Training Scheme casualties and patriarchal breadwinners struggling to dodge the swelling dole-queues signifying the new era of structural unemployment had mutated into a litany of abject archetypes that (by accident or design) had the discursive effect of bolstering media-political attempts to portray joblessness as pathological.

Though comedic fictions like BBC1's *The Royle Family* and Channel 4's *Shameless* featured affectionate portrayals of working-class (even 'workless class') characters, they lent themselves to being misread and misappropriated as morally dubious (if likeable) wastrels: in essence, scroungers. Meanings change through the process of appropriation, and it is in this context that the abject associations of Jim Royle and, especially, Frank Gallagher are best understood. While Skeggs (2005: 975) observes that *The Royle Family*'s prime concern is to mount 'a sustained attack on middle-class pretensions' from the perspective of working-class Jim's sofa, she rightly recognizes that 'the middle class are likely to misrecognize the nature of the class hatred it contains'. Similarly, Devereux (2007: 200) may be right to argue that, contrary to 'the dominant view of the underclass as being lazy and unresourceful', *Shameless* 'demonstrates how the underclass manages to survive' with the help of 'family and community ties' – fraternal and neighbourly bonds that were in increasingly short supply among almost all classes by the time the drama debuted in 2004. However, as other chapters demonstrate, this has not stopped the term 'shameless' routinely being wheeled out as a shorthand cue-card denoting fraud and fecklessness in media-political portrayals of unemployment and poverty – invariably accompanied by a carefully chosen publicity still depicting an unshaven, straggly-haired Gallagher, pint in hand and fag drooping from his lips. Contrast this studied (if subverted) image of underclass Mancunian abandon with that of Gallagher's closest 1980s counterpart: the PhD-qualified antihero of ITV sitcom *Shelley*, a self-confessed 'professional freelance layabout' who, in everything from his dress sense to bourgeois pseudo-intellectualism, could hardly be further removed from today's popular personifications of shirkers as foul-mouthed, sub-literate and lower class.

It is, then, the relentless association of idleness and unemployment with what might broadly be termed 'the proles' – specifically the denizens of sink estates in post-industrial areas like the imagined Manchesters of *The Royle Family* and *Shameless* – that has tended to set post-millennial TV portrayals of those affected apart from their 1980s antecedents. Combined with this has been the near-total stripping away of any contextualized discursive backdrop to add nuance and meaning in the manner of *Auf Wiedersehen, Pet* or *The Boys from the Blackstuff*'s abandoned building sites. So long gone is the industrial Manchester of brooding factories and textile mills that (occasional anti-Thatcher rant aside) it was almost entirely absent as a background feature, let alone explanatory framework, in the sociological framing of the Royles and Gallaghers. Yet these individualized paragons of post-industrial idleness were as nothing to the glib, pop culture-derived 'scrounger shorthand' offered by the most abject underclass archetype of the late 1990s and early 2000s. Tyler (2008: 28) has shown how the name 'Vicky Pollard' – the inarticulate, council flat-dwelling teenage single mother played by comic Matt Lucas in BBC sketch show *Little Britain* – acquired 'an extraordinary resonance, often replacing the term "chav" as a synonym for' an 'imagined social type' that 'populates negative newspaper and internet forum accounts of white working-class girls and young women'. She demonstrates how Pollard came to be routinely namechecked by everyone from right-wing commentators like James Delingpole, deriding the 'pasty-faced, lard-gutted slappers' she represented as one of 'the great scourges of contemporary Britain', to respected public figures like Deborah Lawson, chair of the Association of Professional Teachers, who told its 2006 conference of her fears about begetting 'a future generation of Vicky Pollards' with poor qualifications and social skills (Tyler 2008: 28).

Abjective and objectifying TV portrayals of this kind ultimately came into their own, however, not through the guises of larger-than-life fictional characters like Pollard or Gallagher but those of the *real-life* caricatures constructed by a popular sub-genre of 'factual' programming that would come to be known as 'poverty porn' (Scott-Paul 2013). Though the earliest example of this strand of stylized, heavily accented 'fly-on-the-wall' documentary (BBC Scotland's *The Scheme*) was broadcast in the formative days of the Coalition, in terms of volume of output it peaked in 2013: the year the frenetic Osborne-instigated welfare reform-cum-cuts programme, and the discursive assault on claimants accompanying it, reached a crescendo. Jensen (2014) gives an encyclopaedic run-down (and characteristically incisive critique) of these shows, observing how they were initially far from confined to the commercial channels (principally 4 and 5) that later became their home. BBC1's 2013 'Cost of Living' season, for instance, included a programme entitled *We Pay Your*

Benefits, which followed four 'taxpayers' as they scrutinized the spending behaviour of four 'welfare claimants': explicitly evoking the Coalition's favoured opposition between the respectable us of hardworking households and the reprehensible them, getting 'something for nothing'. More brazenly, Channel 5's *On Benefits and Proud* slotted into a wider '…and Proud' series which bought into the criminalization of welfare by bracketing claimants alongside unambiguously deviant elements, as illustrated by companion episodes *Shoplifters and Proud* and *Pickpockets and Proud*. A later offshoot, *Gypsies on Benefits and Proud*, symbolized 'a clash of several fantasies in the politics of welfare disgust'. And all this before the BBC opted to accept Ministers' specious insistence that Britain was suffering from a 'runaway problem of benefit fraud', in the form of *Britain on the Fiddle* – a returning series which ran until 2017 (Jensen 2014).

It was not until Channel 4 launched *Benefits Street*, however, that 'poverty porn' hit the big time. If a programme's impact can be judged by its viewing figures, the extent of critical debate (if not always acclaim) it spawns and its seepage into wider cultural consciousness, through the intertextual ways in which its content and characters begin permeating media-political debate, this six-part docusoap, set in inner-city Birmingham, achieved it all. Its first episode, aired on 6 January 2014, attracted 4.3 million viewers and a 17.2 per cent share of the overall TV audience in its timeslot – higher ratings than any other Channel 4 show for more than a year (Plunkett 2014). Episode 2 saw its audience grow by another million, hitting a 20.8 per cent share (Plunkett 2014). And, in the spirit of no publicity being bad publicity, it sparked a swift (but profile-enhancing) counter-discursive backlash, in the form of an online petition demanding it be pulled from the

schedules, which ultimately attracted more than 62,000 signa-
tures (www.change.org 2014). The programme went on to be
nominated for a National Television Award, win the Broadcasting Press Guild's Best Documentary Award and spawn one
enduring celebrity: Deirdre Kelly, aka 'White Dee', who became
a chat show regular, *Celebrity Big Brother* contestant and (most
perversely) public apologist for IDS's short-lived proposal for
'pre-paid cards' to 'prevent claimants spending their money on
"fags and booze"', during her incongruous fringe appearance at
the 2014 Conservative Party Conference (Ridge 2014).

The longer-term legacy of *Benefits Street* has arguably been
more invidious. To messianic (anti-)welfare warrior Iain Duncan
Smith, and his backbench cheerleaders, scenes of claimants
swapping shoplifting tips and nursing industrial-scale cannabis
crops could not have been more serendipitous. Jensen (2014)
notes two occasions when evidence presented by *Benefits Street*
was casually cited as justification for the government's welfare
crackdown: a reply by IDS to a question from MP Philip Davies,
in which he stated that the public '*of course* see it as exempli-
fying the urgent need for welfare reform' and fellow Tory Simon
Hart's unevidenced preamble to a softball question to then Prime
Minister David Cameron, which matter-of-factly asserted that 'a
street like this' existed 'in every constituency in the land'. More
significantly, for anyone who anticipated that 'poverty porn' might
promote, rather than diminish, understanding and sympathy for
the plight of claimants, the findings of early surveys would have
made depressing reading. A poll coinciding with a 2015 conference entitled *Who Benefits? TV and Poverty* – co-organized by the
BBC, Royal Television Society and Joseph Rowntree Foundation
– found that, while there was 'no consistent emotional response'

to such shows, there was a 'slight tendency' for people to say they 'made them feel less sympathetic' towards benefit claimants than they had been previously (Clarke 2015).

Through the prism of TV, then, there has been consistent support (inadvertent and deliberate) for the discursive perpetuation of scroungers as favoured national abjects – and familiar strangers. Though wider popular culture may often have challenged these frames – through the songs of Morrissey, Paul Weller and Billy Bragg, the work of the Tricycle (now Kiln) Theatre, and the novels of authors like Jonathan Coe – the medium of television has repeatedly affirmed and reinforced them, often to huge popular acclaim.

CONTESTING THE CLAIMS: WHITHER THE PATHOLOGICAL 'SCROUNGER'?

But what evidence is there to support the ongoing insistence by problem definers, from Ministers to newspaper columnists to TV producers, on the existence of 'cycles' of intergenerational dependency? How credible is the thesis that worklessness and antisocial (even criminal) behaviour are somehow endemic to low-income communities, let alone handed down from (absent) fathers or (single) mothers to their children?

In sum, empirical evidence for the existence of a distinct 'underclass' or 'workless class' is as unconvincing as that supporting the belief that there is a widespread problem of multiple, successive generations of children being born into environments characterized by long-term dependency. A 1992 collection of Joseph Rowntree Foundation-funded papers, *Understanding the Underclass*, set out an expansive corpus of primary and secondary data indicating that the idea that the economically poorest occupy any kind of homogenous 'class' or sub-class is, at best, far-fetched. Focusing on 'long-term unemployment', sociologist Nick Buck (1992: 19) argued that this was largely explained by structural factors, including the global economic turbulence of the late 1970s and early 1980s and neoliberal market reforms introduced by Thatcher's government. Importantly, it could not be taken as a corollary of a distinctive underclass, primarily because there was no evidence that long periods of joblessness were 'persistent over an entire non-working life' for those affected. Far from being an ingrained norm, long-term unemployment was 'a major interruption' to a long 'working life' for 'the vast majority' of people who experienced it – making them less 'stable members of an underclass' than 'unstable members' of 'the working class' (Buck 1992: 19). In the same volume, fellow sociologist Anthony Heath's (1992: 33) analysis of the 1987 British Election Survey and 1989 British Social Attitudes Survey found minimal evidence for a then widely accepted definition of underclass: 'family units where neither partner … is currently in paid employment' and 'a member has been in receipt of income support'. He concluded that any 'hidden underclass' with 'a culture of dependency' was 'quite a small-scale phenomenon' (Heath 1992: 37). As for the widespread belief that denizens of the underclass opt out of 'political participation', he argued that (to the extent they even existed) they 'simply illustrate tendencies that are widespread in mainstream society as well' (Heath 1992: 37).

In a more recent sociological study, published around the peak of 'shirkerphobia', Robert MacDonald, Tracy Shildrick and Andy Furlong (2014) dismissed the very concept of underclass as a 'zombie category', likening its obsessive pursuit to a 'hunt for the Yeti'. In it they detailed futile efforts to recruit ten families from poor neighbourhoods in Glasgow and Middlesbrough that had experienced three generations in which at least one adult had never worked, by meeting 30-plus community workers, GPs, JobCentre advisors and priests; posting advertisements in local newspapers; leafleting households in low-income streets; and interviewing claimants. Despite the 'close engagement with local communities' of professionals they interviewed, and their 'support' for 'the idea' that intergenerational unemployment existed, they 'were unable' to identify 'any families in which "three generations had never worked"' (MacDonald et al. 2014: 206). When the researchers *did* track down individuals (if not entire families) who had experienced long bouts of unemployment, what they found was hardly a picture of sloth or entitlement: most relayed tales of despondency and dwindling self-esteem caused by their relentless but futile pursuit of work. Fifty-four-year-old Ryan Blenkinsopp from Middlesbrough lamented his 'miserable existence' on the dole (MacDonald et al. 2014: 208), while ex-offender Archie Wilson, 42, from Glasgow, 'got up "early every morning", calling into factories and garages on the off-chance they had jobs going' (MacDonald et al. 2014: 210). The study also debunked lingering myths about lazy single mothers, with women interviewees emerging equally determined to find work as men (MacDonald et al. 2014: 208). Other studies have analysed UK Labour Force Surveys showing that families in which two (let alone three) generations had never worked accounted for 'less than half of one per cent of workless households' (e.g. Gaffney 2010; Macmillan 2011, cited in MacDonald et al. 2014: 206). Moreover, while '*concentrations* of worklessness' were found 'in some neighbourhoods', principally '"Old Industrial Regions"', the 'main problem' for social housing tenants interviewed by labour market researcher Del Fletcher and colleagues was 'not finding work' but 'keeping it', as they became caught in a 'cycle' not of Joseph-style deprivation but 'low-paid, insecure jobs and unemployment' (cited in MacDonald et al. 2014: 201–3). As for those locked in pensioner poverty, a 1980 investigation by the late industrial sociologist Dorothy Wedderburn found this to be a type of socially isolated impoverishment offering 'little opportunity' to develop any kind of 'common culture', let alone one of dependency. Moreover, 'older people who were poor' did not 'necessarily' hail from 'backgrounds of working-class poverty': far from being locked in intergenerational cycles, their younger lives had largely 'not been spent in poverty' (cited in Welshman 2013: 105). This picture of an older generation experiencing unemployment only in later life, following the 'economic dispossession' affecting 'old industrial centres' in 'the last third of the 20th century', was reinforced by MacDonald and colleagues' interviews with this demographic. They recalled 'lives typical of the old working-class', in which 'manual employment predominated': a 'culture of work', not 'worklessness' (MacDonald et al. 2014: 216).

Similarly without foundation are repeated claims of an endemic problem of benefit fraud. According to the latest figures available at time of writing, estimated benefit 'overpayments', due to 'fraud and error', totalled £3.5 billion in 2016–17 (2 per cent of the overall social security budget). While this was more than twice the level of 'underpayments', the latter stood at their 'highest recorded levels': £1.6bn, or 0.9 per cent of the value of all benefits and pensions (National Audit Office 2017: 13).

Contrast this picture with both public perceptions and hysterical media-political claims about the scale of fraud and the true extent of the disconnect between myth and reality becomes apparent. According to the 2016 British Social Attitudes survey, 22 per cent of Britons still believed 'most' unemployed claimants were 'fiddling'. At the height of 'shirkerphobia', meanwhile, popular perceptions were even more misinformed: a 2013 Ipsos Mori poll found that the public believed a quarter of all benefits were fraudulently claimed, putting their estimate 34 times higher than the true level (Work and Pensions Committee 2014). Little wonder, perhaps, that recent Freedom of Information Act requests by, first, *The Observer* and then *The Independent* revealed, respectively, that 85 per cent of allegations of benefit fraud made by members of the public between 2010 and 2015 turned out to be false, while 280,000 tip-offs between 2016 and 2018 alone were dropped by DWP investigators due to lack of evidence (Cowburn 2016, 2018).

Patchy and problematic: this, then, is the shaky empirical basis for the ongoing problematization of 'scroungers'. Let us hold on to this thought as we embark on this book's main purpose: unpacking the myths and misrepresentations popularized through the interplay between newspapers and key claims-makers (including audience members) who collaboratively construct their narratives in today's multi-mediated public sphere.

CHAPTER 3

FRAMING THE POOR

IMAGES OF WELFARE
AND POVERTY IN
TODAY'S PRESS

If 2013 was the peak of Britain's most recent revival of 'scrounger discourse', there is some justification for arguing that it was on the wane by 2016. Returning briefly to Table 0.1, newspapers' use of the term 'scrounger' fell by more than two-thirds between 2013 and 2016 (from 2,103 articles a year to 605) while that of then favoured synonyms, 'shirker' and 'skiver', plummeted by more than half (593 down to 264) and four-fifths (570 to 127) respectively. This was, after all, the year when the architect of Coalition welfare reform, Iain Duncan Smith, publicly condemned George Osborne's pursuit of further cuts in his sudden resignation letter, while his erstwhile Cabinet colleague, Nick Clegg, despaired at the then Chancellor's relentless mining of a 'bottomless pit' of welfare savings (Hattenstone 2016). Ken Loach's award-winning counter-discursive film *I, Daniel Blake* was winning widespread acclaim, while those minded to continue scapegoating marginalized groups for Britain's economic ills had a new focus: immigrants, particularly European Union migrants, rendered newly salient by the impending 'Brexit' referendum.

Yet tempting though it might be to pronounce the end of shirkerphobia, scrounger discourse remained (and remains) very much alive. A closer look at Table 0.1 reveals telling survivals from the prolonged period of claimant-bashing that had slowly built since the 1990s. The number of articles mentioning 'shirkers' and 'skivers' in fact stayed remarkably stable in each year from

2014 to 2016. There was even an upswing in the occurrence of 'workshy'/'work shy', rising by a fifth between 2015 and 2016 (from 466 to 563). And these figures only tell part of the story; as this chapter argues, in-depth analysis of the ways in which the UK press continued to frame poverty and those experiencing it in 2016 give grounds for arguing that the impact of the much-trumpeted counter-discourse is overstated. In fact, far from fading away, discourses problematizing benefit recipients may merely have mutated into new forms, often better disguised than the old. Some mutations can even be glimpsed through close reading of articles that initially appear *counter*-discursive, and the quotes, statistics and truth-claims they use as raw material.

Similarly concerning, in-depth analysis reveals that, by 2016, there was a marked prevalence of 'get both sides' or 'he said/she said' reporting (Mooney 2004), which frequently failed to contest, or even adequately contextualize, highly disputed official claims at a time of mounting empirical evidence of the deleterious impact of 'welfare reform'. Such studiedly neutral articles, whether uncritically reporting Britain's monthly job statistics or Ministers' pledges to pursue full employment, do as much to promote dominant ideologies about welfare claimants as those openly pushing scrounger discourse: by (often mislead-ingly) presenting 'both sides' of an argument as similarly valid, even when one side's claims are much more contentious (Mooney 2004). Such journalism reduces 'objectivity', as Tuchman (1972) once argued, to a 'strategic ritual', whether to preserve illusory norms of impartiality or to deflect ministerial 'flak' (Herman and Chomsky 1988).

This chapter unpacks the multifarious ways in which 'scroungers' – and 'shirkers' – continue to feature, prominently and consistently, in day-to-day press narratives. From conservative tabloids to liberal broadsheets, from honestly labelled opinion pieces to ostensibly balanced news stories, it demonstrates that underlying ideological distinctions between deserving and undeserving poverty remain firmly normalized in media-political discourse. After briefly outlining its textual analysis method and headline quantitative findings, the chapter takes a detailed qualitative look at the ways in which superficially contrasting discursive frames, from openly 'anti-claimant' articles to those adopting broadly counter-discursive positions, largely either explicitly endorse or implicitly accept what remains a dominant consensus on welfare. In so doing, it shows how far there is still to go before countervailing voices can ever be said to have triumphed.

WHAT THE PAPERS SAY: CODING THE FAMES

As this chapter aims to deconstruct the *overarching* ways in which poverty and those experiencing it are discursively framed in today's Britain, it was necessary to go beyond the simple keyword search approach used to track year-on-year trends in pejorative terminology – to analyse the ways in which the UK press positioned poverty *in the round* in the last complete calendar year up to the point when the book was written (2016). This first required gathering a *representative* selection of articles, from across the Left/Right, tabloid/broadsheet, local/national newspaper spectrum, and from all corners of the British Isles. To ensure the sample reflected the *overall* balance of press representations of poverty and related themes, from social security to poor housing and low wages, rather than focusing solely on articles explicitly *problematizing* 'the poor', the search terms also had to be as neutral and denotive as possible. Instead of homing in on pejorative labels like 'scrounger' or 'shirker', therefore, analysis centred on articles featuring the following commonly used terms: 'benefits', 'welfare', 'claimant', 'unemployed', 'jobless', 'workless', 'dole' and 'poverty'.

Taken together, the eight resulting searches produced a total corpus of 3,534 print and online articles, comprising news stories, features, comment pieces, editorials and even reviews of poverty-related TV shows – though some pieces recurred in two or more datasets. The analytical method used was framing analysis: defined as the process of identifying the 'principles of selection, emphasis and presentation' underpinning texts (Gitlin 1980: 6) to present a particular 'aspect of a perceived reality' as 'more salient' than others and '*promote* a particular problem definition, causal interpretation, moral evaluation and/or treatment for the item described' (Entmann 1993: 53). The articles in each dataset were then coded into eight categories identified during initial immersion in the material – ranging from 'hard scrounger' frames promoting unforgivingly critical depictions of benefit recipients to ones that took a defiantly oppositional perspective. The full breakdown of framing categories, and the number of articles coded against each heading across the eight keyword datasets, is shown in Table 3.1, while a more detailed explanation of the overall methodology can be found in Appendix 1.

FANNING THE FRAMES: THE SPECTRUM OF SCROUNGER DISCOURSE

The overall pattern of framing across almost all datasets – especially those generated by the keywords 'benefits' and 'dole'

– showed a startling imbalance between articles presenting claimants sympathetically and those portraying them negatively (or neutrally). Even the 'poverty' dataset, which one might have expected to focus more on overarching issues, contained a small proportion of articles adopting scrounger frames, while seven out of ten adopted 'soft' counter-discursive positions, by highlighting the suffering caused by specific *types* of poverty, but not others.

In terms of unabashed scrounger framing, the 'benefits' dataset is most noteworthy, as it shows how this term was frequently used as a semantic cue in articles focusing on abuses of the system. While more than half of all 'benefits' articles adopted some kind of scrounger frame – whether focusing on straightforward sponging, fraud or so-called welfare tourism – another one in four reported potentially contestable truth-claims neutrally. The latter typically used 'he said/she said' formats to present quotes and/or data from official sources that often contained ideologically hegemonic assertions about, say, the cost of social security or the nature of claimants. Even disregarding the lukewarm counter-claims included in many 'soft' counter-discursive pieces, then, more than three-quarters of all 'benefits' articles implicitly or explicitly accepted the dominant scrounger *framework*, if not *all* of its individual *frames*. Articles using the term 'dole' also tended to problema-tize claimants, with nearly a quarter (97 out of 412) adopting scrounger frames. The remaining three-quarters were almost evenly split between neutral and 'soft', or compromised, count-er-discursive approaches (156 to 155).

Indeed, before examining specific examples in detail, it is worth pausing to consider the overall extent to which counter-discursive frames, whether 'soft' or full-throated, asserted themselves across the eight datasets. Given the understandable recent attention paid to countervailing voices in the welfare debate, one might have expected to see a more assured and uncompromising defence of claimants emerging in newspaper discourse by 2016. In truth, there is little evidence in these figures to suggest that any meaningful counter-discourse has yet achieved serious traction across the print and online press, let alone anything approaching dominance. In all but one dataset ('poverty'), counter-discursive frames were in the minority compared to the combined weight of all other categories, with barely one in five 'benefits' articles contesting a majority scrounger discourse. While nearly two out of five 'dole' pieces were broadly counter-discursive, only four (1 per cent) mounted 'hard' defences of the unemployed, or overtly rejected scrounger discourse. Meanwhile, fewer than 5 per cent of the 611 'jobless' articles (28) were remotely counter-discursive: well under half the number adopting 'scrounger' frames (73). The very high number of neutral articles in this dataset (more than eight out of ten), and the focus of many such pieces on announcements about job statistics, confirms that, when not used pejoratively, the word 'jobless' offers a journalistic shorthand for routine 'bureaucratic' modes of reporting (Fishman 1978). As numerous studies argue (e.g. Tuchman 1972; Fishman 1978; Gans 1979), such normative reporting implicitly reflects the ideological agendas of official/elite sources and can therefore have the effect (if not necessarily the intention) of echoing and reproducing dominant ideologies. Most tellingly, even in the 'poverty' dataset, which contained numerous articles about the nature and scale of social deprivation, most counter-discursive frames were of the 'soft' variety: highlighting 'child

TABLE 3.1 DETAILED BREAKDOWN OF FRAMES FOR EIGHT ARTICLE DATASETS

Discourse-frame	Benefits	Welfare	Unemployed	Jobless	Workless	Dole	Claimant	Poverty	Total
'Hard' scrounger	26 (8.6%)	16 (6.4%)	28 (4.6%)	17 (2.8%)	9 (4.3%)	47 (11.4%)	13 (2.5%)	0	156
'Soft' scrounger	0 (0%)	7 (2.8%)	6 (1%)	0	2 (1%)	11 (2.7%)	7 (1.3%)	9 (1.4%)	42
Cheat-Fraudster	78 (25.7%)	11 (4.4%)	3 (0.5%)	3 (0.5%)		26 (6.3%)	9 (1.7%)	0	130
Incidental scrounger	13 (4.3%)	1 (0.4%)	65 (10.8%)	35 (5.7%)	1 (0.5%)	8 (1.9%)	0	0	123
'Benefit tourist'	47 (15.5%)	2 (0.8%)	0	18 (2.9%)	2 (1%)	5 (1.2%)	3 (0.6%)	0	77
'Hard' counter-discourse	28 (9.2%)	37 (14.9%)	18 (3%)	2 (0.3%)	7 (3.3%)	4 (1%)	3 (0.6%)	18 (2.9%)	117
'Soft' counter-discourse	35 (11.1%)	56 (22.5%)	93 (15.4%)	26 (4.3%)	60 (28.7%)	156 (37.9%)	128 (24.7%)	430 (68.7%)	984
Neutral	77 (25.3%)	119 (47.8%)	391 (64.7%)	510 (83.5%)	128 (61.2%)	155 (37.6%)	356 (68.6%)	169 (27%)	1,905
Total	304	249	604	611	209	412	519	626	

Source: Lexis Library.

poverty', 'pensioner poverty', 'in-work poverty' or debates about 'relative' versus 'absolute' poverty, rather than standing up for those experiencing poverty *across the board.*

WHAT THE PAPERS 'SHOW': TOWARDS INTERPRETING UNDERLYING DISCOURSES

If our headline figures suggest scrounger discourse remains in rude health, how exactly is it manifested in today's press? More importantly, what can the range and nature of these manifestations tell us about the overall state of debate in contemporary Britain around poverty and welfare – and the extent and limits of any counter-discursive shift?

The following sections draw on qualitative illustrations of the ways in which newspaper narratives portrayed poverty and social security in 2016, teasing out revealing trends that help explain how scrounger discourse has survived (and, in some measure, reasserted itself), in defiance of mounting empirical evidence and counter-discursive argument to contest its prejudices and assumptions. In unpacking these frames, let us set aside, for now, the minority of articles classified as 'incidental scrounger' pieces. These are items primarily about subjects *other than* poverty or welfare, but which implicitly promote scrounger discourse by highlighting (often superfluous) details about the socioeconomic statuses and/or lifestyles of their protagonists. As such insidious framing arguably has the potential to exert even stronger normalizing discursive effects than that of explicitly baiting claimants, these articles are examined in in their own right in Chapter 5.

BAITING THE 'BENEFITS CULTURE': CLASSIC SCROUNGER DISCOURSE(S)

Before examining how scrounger frames have begun to take on new and (more varied) guises in press discourse, it is important to acknowledge the continuing prevalence of conventional anti-welfare narratives. Fecund single mothers, feckless fathers and obese couch potatoes were among the rogues' gallery of assorted reprobates reeled out in 2016. In total, they accounted for more than six out of ten scrounger-baiting pieces in each of the 'welfare' and 'claimant' datasets and nearly 80 per cent of 'workless' ones (11 out of 14).

A textbook anti-scrounger 'dole' article was an April *Mail Online* story headlined, '"You get to sit on your bum and lie to kids all day": Obese benefits scrounger boasts about having the best job in the world because he works just FOUR weeks a year as a Santa' (McLelland & Gye 2016). This classic freak-show tale, a trail for then-upcoming Channel 5 docu-soap *On Benefits: Life on the Dole*, mobilized numerous well-worn tropes to portray 'Twenty-six stone Archie' as a grotesque, morally deviant skiver. Not only was he a long-term layabout, claiming '£600-a-month [sic] in state handouts' and having 'not worked full-time for six years', but 'the shameless Father Christmas' described himself as 'a bit of a bully', gloating as he regaled the programme-makers about taunting children before giving them presents. Despite including a quote from an unnamed show 'spokesman', which strained to portray its subjects as 'ordinary people cast adrift by the system' and 'striving just to get by', the story heavily subverted the episode's supposed focus on those with weight-related health conditions that prevented them working by reeling out a list of other featured claimants which read like a procession of circus animals. These included 'Blossom', who 'weighed 25st, wore tattoos all over her face and had multiple health problems', and Gina, who 'weighs 19st' and 'claims' her 'other health problems' stop her losing weight. This unsavoury package was liberally illustrated with photos, their captions loaded with scrounger discourse. Blossom was described as having 'not worked for two decades' and hoodie-wearing Gina and husband Gary as people 'paid more than £10,000 a year in benefits' who 'say they have no money'.

While this mid-market tabloid tale applied the abject freak-show treatment specifically to *overweight* claimants and those with long-term illnesses, a story in the red-top *Daily Star* the previous month had adopted a discourse so sweepingly dismissive it appeared to imply that anyone unemployed was a scrounger. Headlined 'Home rule bid by TV spongers' (Saunders 2016), it opened with the line 'A TOWN's benefits scroungers want to run their own communities', before explaining it was referring to 'jobless Brits' in '"England's poorest town"' (Jaywick in Essex), who wanted to be 'given their benefits' and left to run their local services. As in the *Mail* story, this report (a plug for another Channel 5 show, *Benefits by the Sea*) itemized a list of showpiece scroungers, from 'former burglar Darren, who stole to fund his heroin addict [sic]' and was shown spending 'more than a week's worth of benefits buying an engagement ring and having a meal at a plush restaurant' to 'an alcoholic critically ill in hospital after downing booze he bought with handouts'. By casually conflating claimants with criminality, alcoholism and drug addiction, it portrayed unemployment as a form of *generalized* deviancy, rather than a discrete (socioeconomic) phenomenon. Targeting Jaywick was especially pernicious, given that the town had then recently been named England's most deprived council ward by the then Department for Communities and Local Government (DCLG 2015).

Most articles focusing on claimant deviancy adopted more individualized frames. A January page-seven lead in the *Daily Star Sunday*, headlined, 'Mum-of-12 splurges benefits on boob job', was phrased in a way calculated to enrage hardworking taxpayers. It relayed how 'BENEFITS queen Cheryl Prudham' had 'booked in for a boob job' – and 'you'll be paying for it!' (Dickenson 2016). Illustrated by a photo of pregnant Prudham sitting beside her 11-strong 'brood', the story reminded readers she had previously been 'branded Britain's most shameless' (another reference, perhaps, to the eponymous Channel 4 comedy-drama), as she and husband Robert (a part-time lorry-driver) received £45,000 a year. Pointedly, it added that the couple managed to avoid the 'benefits cap' because of Robert's job: insinuating that, while it was impossible in this case to accuse them of being *jobless* scroungers, they were still playing the system. Similarly framed were 'benefits mother-of-five' Rachael Dower and mechanic partner Keith Birchmore, whose objectification as a devious welfare-dependent couple using their children to leapfrog housing waiting lists on *Mail Online* surfaced in both 'benefits' and 'unemployed' datasets (Moore 2016). Mockingly headlined 'Mother-of-five on benefits demands a bigger home because it's "unfair" that her 11-year-old daughter has to share a box room with her four little brothers', this sprawling article, running for over 1,000 words, spared no effort in framing 'benefit-reliant' Dower as a knowing chancer for demanding 'her housing provider must upgrade her', as 'she keeps having kids'. Despite including Dower's lengthy justification for requesting a bigger home, the story followed it by quoting a 'scathing attack' on the 'benefits scrounger' from Camborne town councillor and ex-mayor Jeff Collins and Facebook posts by 'furious' locals. One angrily entreated Dower to 'stop breeding like a rabbit' if she did not want to 'live in a hutch'. In formulaic freak-show style, the piece was accompanied by several photos of the family, glaring sullenly at the camera from their cramped home.

Though especially prevalent in right-leaning tabloids, 'hard' scrounger discourse was also evident in other areas of the market. A January *Daily Telegraph* story, headlined 'EU report finds Eastern European migrants find work faster', was one of a small number of national broadsheet pieces to adopt this unforgiving frame. It drew an implied opposition between 'hard-working foreigners' and 'lazy natives' (an intriguing inversion of the us-and-them approach frequently used to other invading foreigners in opposition to under-siege Brits), by emphasizing the '"pronounced" difference' between EU economic migrants and the British unemployed – the former being both 'younger and better educated' and more 'motivated to find work' (Holehouse 2016).

Much more marked was the encroachment of scrounger discourse into the provincial press: a significant fact, in that it demonstrates the appeal such narratives are seen to hold not just for 'moral majority' national tabloid audiences (Greer & Jewkes 2005: 21), but readers of more traditionally community-focused local titles (Heider et al. 2005). This point is crucial because, if scrounger discourse has penetrated to all *levels* of the press (as it appears to have done), we are clearly looking at a normalized phenomenon. A good illustration of the widespread appeal of poverty porn-style stories was a *Plymouth Herald* June page-six lead headlined 'Benefits scrounger wants to be next PM', which began by describing its subject (19-year-old Travis Simkins, who had 'starred in' Channel 5's *Benefits Britain*) as a 'self-confessed "benefits scrounger"', despite the fact he was not quoted anywhere making this confession (Waddington 2016). Written in a gently mocking tone, it framed Simkins as a fantasist, describing his 'dreams' to become both Prime Minister and 'a Hollywood star'; quoting his ambition 'to legalise weed', because it would 'bring down crime'; and relating how he wanted to stop 'signing on', as he was 'not actually looking for work'. This was one of many articles that infantilized scroungers: casting them as both feckless and childlike.

More uncompromising in its scrounger-bashing was an outspoken September opinion piece in the *Yorkshire Post*, headlined 'A fair benefits system does not justify social housing for scroungers' (Taylor, G. 2016). In it, children's author (and ex-vicar) G.P. Taylor gave a masterclass in mythologizing claim-ants; drawing on his own experience of 'growing up in a council house on a large estate in Scarborough' to condemn those 'sponsored by the State to stay at home and breed'. Stating that he 'now despise[s] people who are benefit scroungers', Taylor pitted them against an imagined 'us' of deserving job-seekers reminiscent of one-time Conservative Minister Norman Tebbit's infamous (if oft-misquoted) recollection of his father's efforts to get 'on his bike' to find a job (Tebbit 1981). 'When my dad was made redundant', Taylor recalled, 'he went to work as a road-sweeper rather than go on the dole'. For good measure, he included several phrases that might have been lifted wholesale from ministerial speeches, casually referring to 'hardworking people' who were 'paying taxes to keep others in booze and fags', before taking aim at benefit tourists by trotting out the dubious claim (beloved of Eurosceptics) that Britain had 'become the benefits soft touch of Europe'.

These, then, are examples of how classic scrounger discourse continued to surface in press narratives throughout 2016: a year when counter-discursive forces were on the march more volubly than for some time. What, though, of its more disguised and tangential manifestations? The following sections explore these more chameleonic frames.

FROM 'FRAUDSTERS' TO 'FOREIGNERS': MUTATING SCROUNGERS

In at least three datasets, the number of pieces about straight-forward scrounging was eclipsed by a ragbag of frames drawing on assorted variants of the archetype. In the 'benefits' category, simple scrounger-baiting articles were outnumbered nearly five to one (136 to 28) by the combined force of those focusing on criminal fraud; benefit 'tourism' (immigration/migration to exploit Britain's welfare system); and 'incidental' scrounging by those whose claimant status was foregrounded in stories ostensibly about something else. Though less marked, straightforward scrounger narratives in the 'unemployed' dataset were outstripped, two to one, by those focusing on 'incidental scroungers' (with a single 'fraudster' story): suggesting the term 'unemployed' is favoured over 'jobless' or 'workless' when articles about crime or other issues (besides unemployment itself) feature protagonists who happen not to be in work. 'Jobless' articles were similarly mixed, with articles featuring 'incidental scroungers' outperforming those framed around scrounging *generally* two to one, and 'benefit tourists' appearing slightly more frequently (18 times, compared to 17). Let us, then, look at the details of some of these variations, and what they tell us about the way scrounger discourse is evolving in the 'post-shirkerphobia' period.

Familiar frames refreshed: welfare 'cheats', single mums – and hybrids of both
A feature of three datasets was the relatively high percentage of articles focusing on fraud. This applied to nearly half of all scrounger-bashing 'benefits' pieces (78 out of 164) and more than a quarter of those in the 'dole' and 'welfare' datasets (26 out of 97 and 11 out of 37 respectively). 'Fraudster' stories generally fell into one of two sub-categories: tales about cheats pretending to be unemployed or living in households with no wage-earners when they were either working themselves or cohabiting with someone who was; or those about medically fit people pretending to be sick or disabled to avoid work.

To begin with the latter, a prominent pattern to emerge from both 'hard' scrounger and 'fraudster' datasets was the frequency of stories about cheats whose fraudulent behaviour related to either bogus or exaggerated claims of sickness or disability. Given that much of the counter-discourse supposedly so established by 2016 (thanks, partly, to *I, Daniel Blake*) was specifically framed around the callousness of Work Capability Assessments, this is significant. At the very least, it suggests there can be lengthy time-lags between points at which countervailing voices enter the public arena and ingrained, normalized frames favoured by mainstream media are modified, let alone abandoned. More than one in four 'fraudster' articles concerned the cheating conduct of people making false representations about their mental or physical health to qualify for benefits – suggesting this cynical, distrustful frame remained hardwired into press discourse and, by extension, the assumed views of its audiences.

Like the freak-show approach applied to more straightforward stories about lazy scroungers, tales about benefit cheats feigning sickness or disability often had a strong human zoo/ circus dimension that played on readers' voyeurism. Indeed, given that at least some of their subjects had genuine (if exaggerated) disabilities, articles sometimes came close to breaching the Independent Press Standards Organisation's editors' code of practice, by adopting borderline discriminatory language and/or tones (IPSO 2017). Such pieces often implicitly invited readers to poke fun at the outrageously dishonest claims made by grotesque chancers masquerading as invalids. Among those objectified in January 2016 alone were a 'disability benefit cheat' from Lanarkshire 'caught red-handed playing a round of golf', despite claiming 'she could not walk unassisted' (Scott 2016); a

West Midlands woman who said she was 'so disabled she could barely lift a glass', but 'was caught pulling pints while running three pubs' (Metro 2016a); a 62-year-old Southampton man who claimed £18,000 by faking a 'dodgy knee', but was 'caught on camera playing ten-pin bowling' and 'high-fiving his friends' (Logan 2016); and a 'married father-of-five' from Birmingham who 'swindled £67,000 in disability payouts by claiming he could barely walk', but could 'climb 10 flights of stairs' and 'played cricket at the weekend' (Robertson 2016).

As with all 'scrounger' frames, this alternately absurdist and sadistic approach to othering disability fraudsters proved as irresistible to some local papers as it was to national papers. The aforementioned tale of the moonlighting bar manager was first reported on *www.birminghammail.co.uk*, under the objectifying headline: 'Watch benefits cheat who claimed she was crippled pulling pints in a pub' (Day 2016). As its title suggested, the report was accompanied by grainy video footage obtained from 'undercover investigators', showing the tattooed 'cheat' sluggishly serving a customer before leaving the pub clutching a large roll-up cigarette or piece of paper between her teeth and lifting 'heavy items into her car'. The invasive medical details relayed in this account included allegations that, despite being so active, the 59-year-old 'claimed she could barely dress or wash herself' and 'had unbearable arthritis' and 'varicose veins'.

Stories about people falsely claiming to be unemployed were also popular. More audacious examples included those of 'the 72-year-old welfare fraudster' who 'illegally claimed over £34,000 in benefits and Pension Credit' while 'working as a full-time mental health worker' (*Belper News*, 16 May 2016) and the 'dole cheat … job adviser' from Swansea who worked 'full time helping others find employment' while 'raking in £12,500 claiming to be a jobless single mum' (*Daily Star*, 8 June 2016). A story in this category that acted as a singular symbol of the pervasive seepage of scrounger discourse into all arenas of public life (including the normally sober confines of the courtroom) was that of the 65-year-old teaching assistant castigated by a judge for what even the *Telegraph* colloquially dubbed a history of 'scrounging from the taxpayer' (*Daily Telegraph* 2016). In remarks widely quoted in other nationals, Jonathan Foster QC sentenced this serial offender to eight months' imprisonment for her £80,000 fraud, accusing her of stealing from 'community services' paid for 'by every citizen like me' and 'all the other people in court'. By drawing this pointed opposition between himself and his fellow 'citizens' (the respectable 'us') and the 'scrounging' anti-citizen in the dock (a proxy for the deviant 'them'), and uncritically pronouncing 'benefit fraud' a 'prevalent offence' that 'people think they can get away with', Judge Foster both affirmed and reinforced the legitimacy of a fictive folk-devil: the ubiquitous benefit cheat. In so doing, he echoed similarly overblown judicial appeals to British morality (and despair at its decline) quoted in cultural theorist Stuart Hall et al.'s seminal *Policing the Crisis* (1978). Both were legalistic interventions echoing elite-engineered dominant discourses about strawman enemies within: in the 1970s, a law-and-order panic about 'muggers'; in post-millennial, post-crash Britain, 'shirkers'. Judge Foster's us-and-them frame was signified most visually in the *Mail*, which accompanied two widely used, fuzzy photographs of the fraudster (a portly, grey-haired woman flanked by her hoodie-wearing son) with a high-definition portrait of the robed, bewigged QC.

Most reports of fraud based on false claims of unemployment were less colourful, though this was belied by their invariably hyperbolic headlines. A January page-lead in local weekly the *Crawley News* was headlined '£10k fraudster lied about her job to taxman', as if to consciously conflate this tale of low-level abuse with the then high-profile issue of (much larger-scale) tax evasion (Full Fact 2016). As it transpired, the guilty culprit, 46-year-old Sharon Hall, *had* withheld information from the 'taxman', but only briefly (from April to December 2012), after starting a job she correctly deduced would not 'last a long time' (Mackintosh 2016). Moreover, towards the end of the 360-word piece it emerged she had already started repaying the Department for Work and Pensions, and was juggling two jobs to do so. That this article should be glibly angled as the story of a '£10k fraudster' who 'lied' to 'the taxman' marks it out as a particularly invidious example of normalized scrounger discourse. Though we cannot be certain about the whole of Ms Hall's lived reality, from the fragmentary details included it was possible to make reasoned assumptions. Had the story been structured differently, the portrait it painted – of a world of poverty wages; insecure, temporary and/or multiple jobs, and a punitive, bureaucratic state apparatus poised to pounce the moment low- or unwaged claimants fail to declare slight changes of circumstances – would have been starkly different. Indeed, had it focused on such details, it might have conjured up a picture of a 'low-pay, no-pay Britain' (Shildrick et al. 2012) all too recognizable to much of its audience.

One pattern to emerge from stories about bogus unemployment claims was how heavily they drew on a seasoned stereotype from yesteryear: the scrounging single mother. Unlike in the past, though, the subjects of these stories were normally not *genuine* single mothers, but unwaged women *pretending* to live alone, so they could claim benefits (reflecting, perhaps, changes to the system to support lone-parent families, while penalizing two-parent households, since the well-documented 1990s maternal panic detailed in Chapter 2). Reprobates included the 'mum of six' described by *The Sun* (in terms explicitly evoking the imagery of zoo animals) as being 'caged' by an Edinburgh court for a '£100k dole con' involving 'false claims to be a single parent' (Smith 2016) and 'benefit scammer' Anita Brown: 'jailed' in Dundee for claiming to live alone with her adult son so she could draw 'state handouts', despite cohabiting with an 'offshore worker' earning £53,000 a year (Beatson 2016). An intriguing variant of the 'fake single mum' sub-genre, meanwhile, was the handful of similar tales focusing on bogus *bachelors*. These included a December *Yorkshire Post* piece telling how 65-year-old Brian Dockerty hid the existence of his 'common law wife of 20 years' to make 'illegal claims for jobseeker's allowance, housing benefit, council tax benefit and council tax credit' (Gardner 2016). Once again, such narratives proved as attractive to local papers as nationals: with papers from the North West (*Warrington Guardian; Macclesfield Express*) and North East (*Hartlepool Mail*) to Midlands (*Leicester Mercury*) and South West (*Wiltshire Times*) defaulting to variations of the dismissive branding 'cheat' to frame such culprits. In a page-three story published barely 24 hours after the tale shaming Ms Brown, the *Huddersfield Examiner* revealed how 'Deighton woman' Michelle Garnett's fraudulent claim to live alone was betrayed when she let slip her 'long-term relationship' on Facebook (*Huddersfield Daily Examiner* 2016).

Indeed, in a sign of the zeitgeist, stories about fraudsters repeatedly revolved around individuals' nefarious misdeeds being exposed not by anonymous tip-offs from snooping neighbours, but their own social media activities, as they naively posted comments, photos and even videos exposing the falsity of their claims. Perhaps the most atypical story along these lines (but, by extension, one of the most normatively newsworthy and widely covered) was that of 44-year-old hospital doctor and Army reservist Sandra Turnbull, whose fraudulent claim for Disability Living Allowance due to a long-standing hip complaint emerged when, in the *Metro*'s words, she posted on Facebook 'photos of herself being winched onto a helicopter in combat training' (Wilkinson 2016). Turnbull's conviction on three counts of benefit fraud totalling nearly £22,300 over a decade was reported by ten papers, including three locals and two broadsheets (*Times* and *Telegraph*), with the left-leaning *Daily Mirror* delighting as much as right-wing rivals like the *Sun*, *Mail* and *Express* at this atypically middle-class tale of benefit chicanery. Like other papers, it capitalized on the story's commercial appeal by running a gallery of photos of glamorous Dr Turnbull, whose sparkling white teeth, glossy hair and expensive-looking attire (when not in combat fatigues) contrasted strikingly with more typical images of scroungers. Given her privileged background, this could hardly be described as a story demonizing 'poor people', at least in any direct sense. Nonetheless, in that most coverage framed her (linguistically, if not visually) in terms all too familiar from conventional 'fraudster' narratives – as a 'benefit cheat' (*Northern Echo*, *Evening Chronicle*) guilty of a 'disability con' (*Express*), who claimed 'she could barely walk' (*Mirror*) – its widespread coverage meant it still made a strong contribution to reinforcing scrounger discourse.

From 'tourists' to 'terrorists': racializing scroungers

The most striking media mutations of the scrounger paradigm to emerge in 2016 were those that racialized it to construct a hydra symbolizing the supposed growing threat from multifarious scrounging foreigners. Like previous racializations of scrounger discourse, including the marking out of 'culturally burdensome whiteness' (Skeggs 2004: 90) and stigmatization of travellers and Romani 'gypsies', the quintessentially 2016 montage of racialized deviancy drew on a conflated melange of folk-devils: ranging from EU 'benefit tourists' bound for Britain to (*ethnically* othered but home-grown) 'benefit terrorists'.

To understand the salience of this bizarre marriage of frames requires us to consider the politico-economic context of 2016. Following the Conservatives' election into single-party government in June 2015, then Prime Minister David Cameron confirmed plans for a referendum on the UK's continuing membership of the European Union. Besides the longstanding concerns of Tory 'Eurosceptics' about the EU's erosion of British sovereignty, a primary driver behind demands for the vote had been concerns about the scale of economic migration from within the EU, under rules permitting 'free movement of persons' enshrined in the Treaty on European Union 1992 (Marzocchi 2017). Amid official figures demonstrating that, despite Cameron's repeated promises to cut annual net migration to 'tens of thousands', it had reached 333,000 by May 2016 (Office for National Statistics 2017a), he entered the referendum campaign hoping an 'emergency brake' on future free movement recently negotiated with EU leaders would be enough to persuade many sceptical voters to back 'remain'. The brake specifically disqualified EU nationals entering Britain from claiming in-work benefits or social housing until they had lived in the country, paying taxes, for at least four years (quoted in Charter 2016).

The long-term back-story to Cameron's push for this 'emergency brake' had been the slow build-up of a pernicious popular discourse around the supposed strain on public services, the jobs market, social housing and welfare caused by opportunistic 'benefit tourists' lured to 'soft-touch' Britain (Dawar 2012). This discourse had been stoked by Nigel Farage, charismatic then-leader of the agenda-setting United Kingdom Independence Party (UKIP): an anti-EU political movement which, by May 2014, was in the ironic position of being the biggest single UK party in the European Parliament. Fast-forward to 2016 (year of the referendum) and, with most national newspapers explicitly or tacitly backing the 'leave' camp, it is easy to see how the notion of the UK being infiltrated by job-poaching, benefit-grubbing bogeymen came to be viewed as a salient primer by those campaigning for withdrawal and, by extrapolation, an appealing frame for a media keen to capitalize on these fears for commercial gain. But there were other factors conspiring to construct this toxic scrounger/invader hybrid by 2016, besides controversy around free movement. One was creeping popular unease about the downsides of both globalization and multiculturalism, expressed in slow-burn, occasionally eruptive, cultural backlashes against everything from the importation by industrial firms in depressed areas of foreign workers to the perceived self-segregation (and radicalization) of some Muslim communities in cities like Birmingham. Seldom directly addressed by mainstream politicians, this unease, especially visible in (though by no means exclusive to) areas with disproportionately high immigrant populations, was ripe for exploitation by xenophobic groups like the English Defence League (EDL) and (for a time) an electorally successful UKIP. Conflated with the increasingly securitized debates that had come to dominate political and media discourse around the threat of 'Islamist terrorism', this malodorous cocktail of suspicion and distrust could be projected onto foreigners of all creeds and cultures: from third-generation immigrants of Middle Eastern descent to mobile, highly skilled (and, in many cases, *temporary*) migrants from Poland.

The most infamous expression of this conflation of disparate foreign folk-devils was the baleful poster unveiled by Farage barely a week before the referendum, declaring 'Breaking point: the EU has failed us all'. Though it depicted a stream of Syrian refugees crossing the Croatian–German border, and therefore related to the *Mediterranean* migrant crisis rather than intra-EU population movements, it was nonetheless presented as a warning of impending apocalypse should Britain stay in the EU (Morrison 2016d). That this visualization of the imagined 'floods', 'surges' and 'influxes' of migrants casually evoked by politicians and media in their ever-escalating rhetorical arms-race around immigration was launched on the same day that Labour MP Jo Cox (a prominent campaigner for refugees) was murdered by right-wing extremist Thomas Mair, to the cry of 'Britain first: this is for Britain', only added to its toxicity (Rayner et al. 2016).

In the context of welfare, then, by 2016 a perfect storm of cultural and economic factors had coalesced to position marauding, benefit-chasing foreigners as the latest mutation of that long-established enemy within: the scrounger. Hardly surprising, perhaps, that more than a third of the combined total of 'scrounger' articles in the 'benefits' dataset (47 out of 164) and one in four 'jobless' ones (18 out of 73) fell into this category.

One of the year's biggest clusters of UK press coverage of benefit tourism occurred in late January: the point when Cameron was embroiled in frantic negotiations to secure his emergency brake. The sabre-rattling phraseology of a 31 January headline in Rupert Murdoch's longstanding Euro-sceptic mouthpiece, *The Sun*, typified this coverage, dubbing the showdown 'BRAKE POINT; Cam's bid to halt EU migrant cash' (Sabey 2016). The story casually evoked the image of 'EU arrivals receiving benefits', as if this were their sole reason for entering Britain. As in most such articles, nowhere did it qualify the *nature* of the benefits concerned (primarily Working Tax Credits and Child Benefit), let alone contextualize Cameron's negotiating position, by explaining that, by removing migrants' entitlement to tax credits, the government was discriminating between native workers in low-waged jobs who received income top-ups and legal foreign co-workers who would be denied them. Instead, it painted a sweeping picture (by omission rather than inclusion) of generalized scrounging by aliens bound for Britain.

In a sign of how uncritically such claims were absorbed into press discourse, even the *Mirror* reported on benefit tourism in the self-evident, common-sense terms of 'doxa' (Jensen 2014): its headlines and intros incorporating casual references to 'migrant benefits' and 'benefit payments' for 'foreign workers', as if there were no debate about the veracity of such claims (e.g. Blanchard 2016). And, once again, such coverage was not confined to nationals. A January report on the *Belfast Telegraph*'s website began its account of Cameron's negotiations with an intro implicitly accepting the government's assertion of the need to 'ease pressure from migrants on public services'. Not only did it quote him at length, glibly describing the 'problem' of benefit tourism as 'people coming to the UK getting instant access to our welfare system': far from balancing his account with any counter-claims, it added other Eurosceptic voices, including that of Aaron Banks, co-founder of the Leave.EU campaign (www.belfasttelegraph.co.uk 2016b).

While episodically framed freak-show narratives were much scarcer in this category than in those focusing on straightforward scroungers and/or fraudsters (perhaps partly due to the elusiveness of real-world examples illustrative of the stereotype), when they did surface their framing was merciless, even borderline racist. One September *Mail Online* article was headlined 'Two five-bedroom houses turned down as "too small" by a jobless French migrant family of 10 while they rack up a £38,400 hotel bill at the taxpayers' expense' (Glanfield & Gordon 2016). In terms calculated to stoke resentment among 'left-behind' locals in a town which had recently voted to leave the EU, the article described how 'unemployed' migrants Arnold and Jeanne Mballe Sube had rejected two offers from Luton Borough Council of homes 'thought to be worth between £250,000–£270,000', claiming their family needed 'at least six double bedrooms' to 'live comfortably'. Though it made no reference to their ethnicity, significantly an accompanying photo depicted the large black family ranged along a sofa.

Perhaps the most flagrant misrepresentation of the threat posed by EU-generated benefit tourism was an 'exclusive' in the

Sunday Express: almost politically unique, in that (like its daily counterpart) it had backed UKIP in the 2015 election. The story led with a headline as factually misleading as it was hysterical: '12M TURKS SAY THEY'LL COME TO UK: Those planning to move are either unemployed or students according to shock poll' (Wheeler 2016). Not only was Turkey still some way from being granted EU membership, as (to its minor credit) the story's own quote from an ex-Foreign Secretary indicated, but its central claim was based on a survey question so vague as to be unanswerable: namely, 'If Turkey becomes a full member of the EU, and Britain remains in the EU, would you, or any members of your family, consider relocating to the UK?' This the paper itself would grudgingly concede in a 'clarification' published the following month (www.express.co.uk 2016). But given that there was no guarantee those initially exposed to these falsehoods ever saw this belated *mea culpa*, it is worth summarizing the main claims in the original piece, which ran for 1,139 words, as a front-page splash and inside double-page spread. The deceptions began with an intro casually asserting that '12 million Turkish citizens' (extrapolated from a survey sample of just 2,600) 'plan to move to Britain *when* [author's italics]' (not if) Turkey 'joins the EU'. It went on to construct a classic moral panic discourse, with Orientalist trappings, by mobilizing a montage of sinister claims to other the Turkish people as a barbaric enemy *without*: stating that Turkey had a 'murder rate at least four times that of Britain' and quoting sweeping claims from long-term Eurosceptic (and future Brexit Secretary) David Davis that Britain was 'a lucrative target for criminals' and would be besieged by 'young people who want a better life' but could 'overwhelm our public services', have a 'depressing effect on wages' and 'cause real pain' for 'the poorest in Britain' (Wheeler 2016). The fact that any gun-toting Turkish scroungers crossing Britain's border would be instantly subject to its strict firearms laws was one of numerous qualifications omitted in the best sensationalist tradition.

The Turkish example was especially pertinent in that, in othering dark-skinned people from a majority-Muslim country, it implicitly edged towards the most macabre (if inevitable) iteration of the 'benefit tourist' folk-devil infusing a handful of articles concerned with what might be better termed 'benefit *terrorism*'. To a post-Islamic State (IS) press eager to engage and enrage readers for maximum commercial gain, what more malevolent manifestation of moral deviancy could there be than a hybrid of scrounger and suicide-bomber? A good example of an article falling into the 'benefit terrorist' category was a January page-lead in the *Daily Star*, headlined 'JIHADI SID MILKED UK BENEFIT SYSTEM' (Lawton 2016), a play on the media-ascribed alias of then high-profile Kuwaiti-born Briton 'Jihadi John', who had fled to Syria to become an IS executioner (Casciani 2015). The *Star* began by alleging 'the new Jihadi John suspect', Siddartha 'Sid' Dhar, 'funded his trip to join Islamic State with taxpayers' benefit cash', including 'income support, £247-a-month child benefit for four children and tax credits'. With tasteless abandon, it told how the 'former bouncy castle salesman' used 'state handouts' to travel to Syria and become 'the masked killer in a new Isis video' of five prisoners being shot dead.

An even more notorious terror suspect was scroungerized in a convoluted *Scottish Daily Mail* tale that November. Headlined '£3k UK benefits "funded Brussels terror suspect"', it alleged that one of the main Paris and Brussels bombing suspects, Mohamed Abrini, had been handed 'a bag of money' derived from 'benefits payments made to a missing jihadi' who had fled Britain the previous year 'to fight for Islamic State' (Camber 2016). Two months earlier, *The Sun* had run a similar tale of Brussels-bound 'benefit terrorists', entitled 'Bombers' £42k dole'. Most noteworthy about this report – which opened with the attention-grabbing intro, 'TERRORISTS who carried out the Paris and Brussels attacks were paid £42,000 in benefits' (*The Sun* 2016b) – was that this time round the exploited 'handouts' had not been claimed in the UK, but from the 'generous' *Belgian* welfare state (conveniently, *not* a social security system ever mentioned in the same paper's numerous reports focusing on the supposed unique generosity of Britain's). And though 'benefit terrorist' narratives accounted for only a few articles, as with other sub-categories there was evidence of their appeal to locals as well as nationals. In a curious variation of this frame based on a historical mystery, in September the *Derry Journal* reported enduring questions around whether, during the 1980s, Irish Republican terrorist group the IRA had been 'doing the double': 'shaving 10 per cent' off members' 'dole' income to 'pay for guns and explosives' (Mullan 2016).

One other notable sub-genre of the 'foreign scrounger' paradigm emerged from the growing attention paid, from February onwards, to a lively Australian debate about 'dole bludgers'. As noted in Chapter 1, this colloquialism had origin-ally been imported from 19th century Britain (where it referred to pimps), before being transformed into a distinctly Antipodean synonym for 'scrounger' or 'idle or lazy person' (Oxford Dictionaries 2017a, 2017b). The unfolding Austra-lian narrative which insinuated itself into British papers at this time related to a crackdown on the unemployed by Australia's then centre-right government, initially heralded by a rhetorical 'softening-up campaign' (Taylor, L. 2016) prior to the unveiling of its spring 2016 Budget. Like George Osborne before them, Australia's finance ministers sought to drastically cut the country's social security bill, amid figures (cited in a *Mail Online* article headlined 'Are we becoming a nation of bludgers?') supposedly revealing that more than one in five Australian adults was 'claiming welfare' and their numbers had surged from 4.4 to 5.2 million between 2005 and 2015 (Davis 2016). Cue what Cassandra Goldie, chief executive of the Australian Council of Social Service, decried in the *Guardian* as 'story after story', promoted by 'government' and 'parts of the media', that 'unfairly' distorted data to construct 'the unemployed as undeserving dole bludgers' (Taylor, L. 2016). Indeed, since earlier in the year Australian ministers' pronouncements had translated into a gleeful parade of distinctly Antipodean 'scrounger' caricatures in Britain's press: *The Sun* setting the tone in February, with a single-line story headlined 'DOLE IN ONE', about a clampdown on 'unemployed people turning down jobs' because they 'interfere with their golf plans'. On the same day, the *Irish News* had run a story headlined 'Australian government to tighten benefit rules for wannabe actors and sports stars', which reeled out a litany of 'bludgers' exposed by the country's Department of Employment, spanning the spectrum from banal to outrageous. These ranged from a 58-year-old man who refused to work 'for three hours on Sundays' because 'that was when he played golf' to a 19-year-old who 'turned down a job "to follow his dream of becoming an actor"' (Irish News 2016). Even the *Dorset Echo* found space for a short item in its weekly 'ODD NEWS' round-up, under the borderline racist headline 'Idle Aussies'

(Dorset Echo 2016). As so often, though, it was the *Mail Online* which consistently ramped up the 'bludger' discourse, running stories throughout the year. These included a September report supposedly based on frank confessions from culprits themselves, entitled '"I don't want to work my whole life and just die": Hundreds of thousands of young Australians don't work or study – and some vow to NEVER get a job' (Tolj 2016). Revelations in this piece (reminiscent of freak-show coverage of British claimants) came in second-hand quotes lifted from Australia's *Daily Telegraph* purporting to be from 'two women from west Sydney' who admitted 'refusing to get a job, choosing to spend their time "chilling at maccas [McDonald's]" and going off-roading while the government pays their rent'. Significantly, though, not all UK coverage was so honest about the fact these stories referred to Australia, not Britain. One misleadingly worded report in the *Metro*'s Scottish edition was headlined, 'Get a job? Not while I work on my swing'. Its intro read simply 'JOBSEEKERS have turned down work because it clashes with their golf plans or dreams of going on stage', and only near the end of the second paragraph did it (indirectly) reveal that these antics were not occurring in Scotland (Metro 2016b).

The sudden (re-)emergence of 'bludger discourse' in Australia is significant to our UK analysis in two respects. Firstly, the immediate politico-economic context in which bludgers resurfaced was, in many ways, closely comparable to Britain's: a right-leaning government was pursuing austerity policies to reduce an estimated '$240 billion in accumulated deficits and a debt of $317bn' (Sloan 2016). The drivers were there, then, for ministers to want to displace blame for the causes of these ills and divert attention from the pain of wider spending cuts by singling out for especially harsh treatment a plausible scapegoat: the unemployed. Of more *direct* relevance to this chapter, however, was the fortuitous timing of the 'bludger panic': it erupted at precisely the point when *Britain*'s latest wave of scroungerphobia was otherwise waning. We can glimpse this fortuity in the vicarious delight UK papers took in reporting 'bludgers'. At a time when counter-discursive forces were finally getting a hearing, it is significant that one of manifold forces conspiring to sustain and/or reassert shirkerphobia was its manifestation in another country with which the UK has deep-rooted cultural and economic ties. One of many striking features of Australia's discourse (as glimpsed through its extensive coverage in the *Guardian*), moreover, was how grimly redolent it was of the 'shirker' frames that, until recently, had dominated public debate about the UK benefits system. An 18 May story headlined 'Welfare groups say job seekers are being demonised in budget lead up' showed how the term 'shirker' had apparently been imported into the Australian lexicon, through quotes lifted from two stories in the country's *Telegraph*. One was explicitly headlined 'A quarter of dole recipients shirking appointments and jobs', while another adopted language even more dehumanizing, by likening the unemployed to vermin, in a headline containing the pernicious wording 'dole grubs shirking work'. The parallels looked even starker when seen through the prism of Australian ministers' rhetoric. A lengthy retort to critics from the social services minister's spokesman began by denying any 'demonising' of 'jobseekers' – arguing that the aim was simply to stop people 'doing the wrong thing' (Taylor, L. 2016). Not only was the word 'jobseekers' straight out of Britain's post-1990s phrasebook, but 'doing the wrong thing' read like a conscious invocation of the Brown-to-Cameron mantra entreating people to do the 'right' thing, like the 'hardworking' strivers antithetical to 'closed blinds' shirkers (Osborne 2012).

POVERTY AS NATURE/NURTURE: THE 'SOFT' SCROUNGER FRAME

As mentioned earlier, a small minority of pro-hegemonic articles in all but two datasets ('benefits' and 'jobless') adopted 'soft', rather than 'hard', scrounger frames. Articles affirming an *underlying* scrounger discourse, while avoiding more vitupera- tive rhetoric, tended to be those absolving claimants of (some) blame for their perceived behavioural or character flaws. Typi- cally, though, such pieces still adopted regressive socio-political perspectives, in that they fell back on (widely discredited, though oft-revived) ideas about pathological poverty: the condescending suggestion that inherited genetic and/or behavioural flaws meant some people could not help being poor.

Perhaps the clearest example was a *Times* opinion piece by Jenni Russell (a long-time adherent of the 'dependency culture' school – e.g. Russell 2008), which championed Dr Adam Perkins, lecturer in the neurobiology of personality at King's College London, following the cancellation of his scheduled speech at the London School of Economics to publicize his controversial book *The Welfare Trait: How State Benefits Affect Personality*. The book argues that 'welfare-induced personality mis-development is a significant part of the problem' and 'each generation' in receipt of benefits 'has lower work motivation than the previous one' (Palgrave Macmillan 2016). Russell summarized this as an argument that unemployed people 'tend' to be 'more aggressive, antisocial and rule-breaking' than the 'general population', due to 'a mixture of genetics and upbringing', adding that 'the antisocial ones' produce 'children whose personalities are likely to be damaged by growing up with chaotic, irresponsible parents' (Russell 2016). In one sense, then, this (infantilizing) neurobiological take on the pathological poverty thesis did little more than dress up well-trodden conservative ideas casting deprivation as a fault of the welfare system *itself*, rather than structural factors. In another sense, though, Russell's defence of Perkins' readiness to 'think the unthinkable' on welfare (a phrase directly echoing a famous 1997 instruction from Tony Blair to Frank Field) revived the lazy imaginary of the scrounger; with talk of 'workless households' and 'inadequate, self-centred parents'. It did so, though, while trying to perform a discursive back-flip: freeing these people from responsibility by blaming *systemic* failings that gave them 'the opportunity and incentive to produce children ill-equipped for a fulfilling life' (Russell 2016).

'DESERVING' VS. 'UNDESERVING' CLAIMANTS: UNPICKING 'SOFT' COUNTER-DISCOURSE(S)

Although its passion and prominence have been overstated, a growing counter-discourse against long-accepted scrounger myths has undeniably been building. A key argument of this book, though, is that much of this counter-discourse is (as yet) overqualified or 'soft'. Rather than rejecting scrounger discourse outright, it often takes issue with specific *aspects* of it, but not others. Another common approach is to only champion the cause of particular groups. By omitting to stand up for people experiencing poverty *generally*, however, such counter-arguments risk implicitly buying into the discursive *terms* (if not substance) of dominant frames positioning some groups as more deserving than others. These two trends emerged from the frame analysis, especially in 'claimants', 'dole' and 'poverty' datasets. In these cases, articles only *partially* challenging scrounger discourse made up 98, 98 and 96 per cent respectively of all counter-discursive pieces.

The three main forms such qualified counter-discourses took were:

- Articles focusing on the suffering and mistreatment of one or more specific sub-groups of people experiencing poverty (e.g. children or pensioners);
- Articles exposing the failure of welfare changes on grounds of cost, complexity or injustice, while still accepting that 'welfare reform' was necessary;
- Articles implicitly separating 'deserving' from 'undeserving' unemployed people.

From children to pensioners: framing deserving poverty
A form of narrative frame adopted by many articles was that taking up the cause of particular *kinds* of poverty, or group of people experiencing it, rather than advancing a wider-ranging counter-discourse. Though many such pieces were predicated on the impact of benefit cuts on struggling households and communities, only occasionally did they problematize government welfare changes and/or rhetoric outright. Like those affirming dominant discourse(s), counter-discursive opinion-based pieces largely selected themselves, in that they were written (often by high-profile commentators or experts) from openly declared positions. As one might expect, news stories and features required closer initial reading to determine their perspectives, though what tended to distinguish counter-

discursive from neutral ones was their disproportionate emphasis on truth-claims made by *critical* voices in the poverty/welfare debate, sometimes to the exclusion of any direct right of reply from the other side (e.g. Ministers).

One group of claimants generating consistent sympathy in articles highlighting welfare injustice were sick and disabled people claiming Employment and Support Allowance (ESA) and/or Personal Independence Payments (PIPs). Many such articles focused on £30-a-week cuts to first ESA then PIPs proposed by then Chancellor Osborne: measures mobilizing an ever more diverse alliance of opponents, from the House of Lords and Jeremy Corbyn's Labour to Duncan Smith, who (officially) quit the Cabinet over the fact the Treasury had 'repeatedly salami-sliced' the DWP budget (Duncan Smith 2016). A small number (mainly in liberal papers) made effective use of individualized, 'episodic frames' more typically mobilized in scrounger narratives (Iyengar 1991), in this case to *defend* claimants. A May *Independent* story headlined 'DWP overturn ruling which saw man missing half his head declared "fit for work"' reported a successful appeal to maintain ESA entitlement by Kenny Bailey, who had been left with 'severe memory loss' after an operation to remove half his skull following a stroke. Peppering its 277-word account with repeated references to 'unduly harsh' WCA tests, it relayed how he had overturned an initial ruling to cut his benefits on the basis that he could 'walk 200 yards unaided' and 'get up from his chair' (Fenton 2016b). The article subverted episodic framing conventions favoured by freak-show anti-claimant narratives to demonstrate the absurdity of penalizing someone with a manifestly severe disfigurement. However, in focusing on just one type of claimant, and only one individual, rather than the swathes of others suffering similar injustices, it adopted a 'soft', rather than 'hard', counter-frame.

Similarly 'softly' counter-discursive was an article inviting readers to contribute their own experiences to the *Guardian*'s regular 'Hardworking Britain' column that October – the series' premise being to highlight 'stories of individuals affected by government policy, including the austerity agenda' and, specifically, the 'reduction in welfare spending' (Marsh 2016). Though clearly designed to appropriate the idea of what it *meant* to be 'hardworking', by including people struggling to *find* work as well as those subsisting on meagre wages, the effect of labelling the column 'Hardworking Britain' could nonetheless be seen to play into the background rhetoric of 'strivers' versus 'shirkers'. As if acknowledging this, the article's invitation exclusively focused on 'in-work' poverty.

As ever, articles defending specific sub-categories of claimant were as common in provincial papers as in nationals. A February news feature in the *Airdrie and Coatbridge Advertiser* focused exclusively on the potential impact of cuts for people living in 'properties owned by social landlords' or refuges for 'women fleeing domestic abuse' (*Airdrie and Coatbridge Advertiser* 2016). Meanwhile, a lengthy December report on *www.liverpoolecho.co.uk* extensively quoted two organizations responsible for the academic study on which it was based, the Joseph Rowntree Foundation and New Policy Institute, to highlight the devastating effects of shortages of affordable housing for low-income 'in-work' families forced to rent privately (Clay 2016). Not a single quote was included from either Ministers or representatives of those responsible for the escalating costs (e.g. landlords), making the piece undoubtedly counter-discursive. However, in explicitly focusing on the plight of 'private rental tenants in low paid work' and making only passing reference to those receiving 'out-of-work benefits', it adopted a 'softer' stance than if it had been angled around the effects of housing shortages on all claimants.

Moreover, in a telling symbol of the ways even counter-claims-makers often tacitly buy into elite discourses, one of the main government critics quoted, head of analysis at the Joseph Rowntree Foundation (JRF), Helen Barnard, urged Ministers to take 'action' to 'drive up real-term wages, provide more genuinely affordable homes' and 'fill the gap caused by cuts to Universal Credit' for families who were 'just about managing' (Clay 2016). Though she may have intended to subvert ministerial rhetoric, the phrase 'just about managing' (JAM) was a direct lift from the government's then latest discursive construct: recently installed Prime Minister Theresa May's iteration of the 'hardworking families' persistently championed (in implied opposition to scroungers) by all major parties (May 2016). There is nothing especially amiss about countervailing forces appropriating or subverting the rhetorical constructs of government – if nothing else, to expose the *disconnect* between rhetoric and reality. None-theless, the fact that Barnard's critique of government policy/inaction over the inequities of the housing market so deliber-ately mobilized the discursive frame of 'JAMs' demonstrates the power of elite frames to infiltrate, even *dictate*, deliberative terms of debate in the public sphere. In so doing, there is always a danger that those looking to subvert such frames normalize them still further.

To illustrate how pervasive such linguistic terms of reference can become in newspaper (and, by extension, public) discourse, in the 'poverty' dataset the phrase 'just about managing' appeared in 32 individual 'soft' counter-discursive articles between 13 July 2016 (the date May coined it, in her inaugural Downing Street address) and 31 December. This equated to more than 13 per cent of all 430 counter-discursive 'poverty' articles. Moreover, as in the *Liverpool Echo* piece, the phrase frequently surfaced in the words of *counter*-claims-makers, rather than Ministers. In one of many localized stories responding to a 'new child poverty map of the UK' published in November by the End Child Poverty Coalition, the *Bognor Regis Observer* quoted the charity's warning that 'many families' who were 'just about managing today' would not be for much longer if Universal Credit left them 'with fewer pounds in their pocket' (Cartledge 2016).

Another prominent sub-genre of 'soft' counter-discursive local article was that focusing on specific *aspects* of poverty, rather than particular *groups*. Often such pieces appeared propelled by the agenda-led efforts of individual charities, campaign groups or even companies to raise their own profiles. For example, a lengthy November advice column in the *Mid-Devon Gazette*, entitled 'One in seven rural households struggling to pay to heat homes', was penned not by a staff journalist but Neil Colquhoun of the local Citizens' Advice Bureau (Colquhoun 2016). Similarly, a December *Yorkshire Post* story, headlined 'One in ten in Leeds struggling to heat homes', was predicated on 'analysis by price comparison website MoneySuperMarket.com' revealing that 12 per cent of the city's households 'can't afford adequate heating' (Yorkshire Evening Post 2016).

Prioritizing policy failure over injustice
A secondary sub-category of 'soft' counter-discursive articles was that focusing on maladministration, over-complexity and/

or financial inefficiency in welfare policy, rather than injustice. Indeed, many such pieces adopted underlying discursive approaches that were (in the widest sense) *pro-hegemonic*, in that they stressed neoliberal concerns about financial probity, fairness to taxpayers and, in some cases, public-sector wastefulness.

A typical example was a March report in the *Mirror*, headlined 'Outside firms conducting back-to-work tests are costing taxpayer money' (Glaze 2016). Though clearly targeting its criticism less at government agencies *per se* than the latest private-sector companies to which fitness-for-work tests were being outsourced (Maximus and Capita), the article's *overall* thrust was the Commons Public Accounts Committee's charge that disability tests did 'not meet the required standard' or 'provide value for money'. Significantly, despite the fact the committee's criticisms extended to the 'anxiety' suffered by sick and disabled people, the story's overall framing seemed more concerned with injustices to taxpayers than those suffered by claimants. This was symbolized by an opening sentence focusing solely on the charge that the tests were 'behind schedule and costing the taxpayer more money'. As with articles playing back the *language* of government ('just about managing') to expose its emptiness, there are sound arguments for counter-discursive approaches that use the same tactics to expose the flawed thinking behind neoliberal solutions: in this case, market reforms and commercial outsourcing. But without explicitly spelling out such arguments, by incorporating the wider explanatory context needed to transform its account into one that was 'thematically framed' (Iyengar 1991), this article risked projecting an implied *acceptance* of market-based policy approaches – even if it asserted that they had not worked in this instance.

Similarly concerned with failings of policy *process*, rather than *premise* (or outcomes), was a November report in the *Guardian*'s frequently counter-discursive *Society* section, emotively headed 'Spike in food bank usage blamed on delays in benefit claims' (Butler 2016). Unusually, the story (and angry quotes it highlighted from an all-party group on 'hunger' and the Commons Work and Pensions Committee) explicitly included unemployed people, as well as those awaiting disability-related benefits, among the wronged claimants forced to use food banks because of lengthy benefit hold-ups. Yet in opening its intro with a two-word phrase blaming the 'spike' on 'bureaucratic delays' and focusing on the DWP's persistently missed 'targets', it avoided apportioning direct blame for claimants' misery on Ministers behind the system, and even risked masking the contribution made to the uptake of food banks by other issues often highlighted in *Society*, such as the benefits freeze and sanctions. Despite obliquely referring to a 'built-in 42-day delay for processing initial universal credit claims' and 'concerns' that hardship loans and 'cash advances' (though 'technically available') were 'not offered to claimants', the article risked leaving readers with little knowledge of the Byzantine benefits system under the impression that the 'principal reason' for growing food bank use was administrative ineptitude: not the punitive *nature* of welfare reform itself.

'Strivers' and 'saints': the deserving and undeserving jobless
A final 'soft' counter-discursive sub-category worth considering is that containing articles portraying the unemployed and/or other claimants *positively*: but, significantly, only when they could be shown to either be 'doing the right thing' (to paraphrase

politicians), by seeking work, starting their own businesses or demonstrating other virtuous facets, such as community spirit. Like articles focusing on the plight of individual disabled claimants, these pieces tended to adopt episodic frames more commonly seen in anti-claimant stories. This alone meant they could only be classified as softly counter-discursive, in that they were human-interest articles divested of wider (and deeper) contextualization needed to explain/explore the *extent* of difficulties faced by claimants generally. A related feature of these articles was an implicit framing of their subjects as role models for other claimants to follow, by extension patronizing the wider unemployed and distancing the newsworthy (ergo atypically virtuous) people on which they focused from others content to stay on the dole. In other words, these pieces constructed implied oppositions between 'deserving' and 'undeserving' *claimants*: people getting on their bikes to make their own luck and others expecting opportunities to fall into their laps.

A typical 'jobless striver' piece was a November *Hull Daily Mail* story, headlined, 'Hull's young retail stars celebrate their success'. Its intro highlighted 'a group of 16 to 24-year-olds' who had 'struggled to find work' but were now 'graduating from a new pre-employment training programme' designed to 'kick-start a career in retail or hospitality' (*Hull Daily Mail* 2016). What distinguished this from those adopting neutral frames was its strong emphasis on the 'hardworking' *actions* of the claimants (i.e. framing them as *subjects*, not objects, of the story) and their 'success' in either finding jobs, starting businesses or (in this case) completing useful qualifications. A lengthier article focusing on 'hardworking claimants' appeared in October in London's *Evening Standard*. Headlined 'Fighting chance to get back to work', it highlighted the success of 'award-winning' scheme LifeWorks in helping nearly 600 'long-term unemployed veterans' with disabilities and chronic illnesses back into work (Chesworth 2016). Opening with an introduction laced with patronizing clichés about claimants, it implicitly endorsed the 'well-note' approach to disabled people promoted by governments since Blair (BBC News 2008).

A variant on the 'jobless striver' frame was that of 'the jobless saint/hero': stories about claimants focusing on their good deeds, rather than socioeconomic statuses. A textbook example was a January *Mail Online* story about an 'unemployed hero of the floods', who was 'rewarded with a host of job offers' after helping 'save homeowners and their property' (Narain 2016). This concerned the have-a-go exploits of Dan Kenny, who (in words seldom seen in scrounger-bashing tabloids) was 'desperate for a job so he could provide for his new family'. When 'floods devastated his local community', he 'put the job hunt on hold' to work 'round the clock' to 'save homeowners and their property'. Fittingly, this resourceful, responsible 25-year-old father-to-be had since been 'inundated with job offers' by locals impressed by his 'selfless heroism', 'tireless work' and 'good citizenship', and was now working for a property restoration firm. In accompanying photos, the well-groomed young man appeared flanked by new colleagues, leaning on his boss's white van: that timeless symbol of hard graft and the 'moral majority' (Greer & Jewkes 2005). A July story in Teesside's *Evening Gazette* conjured up a similarly positive (if condescending) portrait of jobless saints: a 'team of unemployed young people', who had 'given a colourful makeover' to 'a house provided to homeless people' (Teesside Evening Gazette 2016). By adding both youth and homeless to the mix, this concocted a perfect fusion of three frequently othered (but, here, morally redeemed) groups.

'HARD' COUNTER-DISCOURSE: ITS FEATURES AND LIMITS

What, then, of less compromised counter-discursive articles? What does a 'hard' counter-discursive news frame look like, and how did they manifest themselves in 2016?

Unsurprisingly, many articles adopting positions of outright opposition to dominant representations of claimants were comment-based pieces focusing on the widespread suffering caused by benefit cuts. One such article was a January *www.independent.co.uk* broadside by Siobhan Fenton, headlined 'Osborne isn't even saving money while he penalises the poor: this is about ideology, not economics' (Fenton 2016a). Mounting a scathing attack on the 'rhetoric' of 'austerity' – which she branded a facade for a 'strategic rolling back of the state' and ideological 'removal of support for vulnerable people' – Fenton cited statistics from 'the Government's own spending watchdog' (the National Audit Office) to outline a litany of injustices, ranging from the fact that 'degrading, gruelling' WCA tests were 'costing us more money than they save' to Ministers' 'relentless pursuit of benefit fraud while tax dodging of large corporations and high net worth individuals' was 'ignored'. And (though few in number) anti-scrounger opinion pieces were not confined to broadsheet op-ed pages: TV programme-makers' continued obsession with poverty porn saw weaker copycat shows face a critical backlash, with a February review in the *Mirror* headlined 'Channel 5 is still baiting the unemployed with yet another show about benefits' castigating an '"experiment", which gives three jobless families £26,000 to change their lives' but invites 'ridicule and vitriol' (Postans 2016).

News stories and features adopting 'hard' counter-discursive approaches were rarer. Those that *did* generally applied either broader narrative canvases (e.g. focusing on statistics about the impact of benefit cuts) or widened initially narrow purviews into more general critiques of welfare reform and/or scrounger myths. Though predicated on a contentious UK government decision to redefine *child* poverty, an October *Glasgow Herald* story reported the fury of Scotland's Equalities Secretary, Angela Constance, at the demonization of 'the poor' generally. Its headline stated, 'Constance hits out at depiction of poverty' and its intro quoted her condemning discourses that 'portray poverty as a "lifestyle choice"' (Bews & Paterson 2016).

A BRIEF WORD ABOUT 'NEUTRAL' FRAMES

In that they present the issue of poverty (and those experiencing it) in relatively 'positive' or 'negative' ways, this chapter has unapologetically foregrounded news frames categorized as pro- or counter-discursive. But if there is an 'elephant in the room', it is the fact that, in all but three datasets ('benefits', 'poverty' and, by a small margin, 'dole'), the largest number of articles were best described as 'neutral'. Indeed, in four datasets ('unemployed', 'jobless', 'workless' and 'claimant') these dispassionately framed pieces were in a majority over all other categories combined.

But what do we mean by identifying a 'neutral' frame, rather than one angled to promote 'a particular problem definition, causal interpretation, moral evaluation and/or treatment for the item described' (Entman 1993: 53)? In the context of articles analysed here, a simple test was applied to determine whether they could be defined as neutral. Any article simply *reporting* a poverty-related issue, action or announcement – for example, the latest unemployment figures or loudly hailed anti-poverty policy initiative – was categorized as 'neutral', *in the absence* of accompanying commentary about whether its subject was 'a good or bad thing', other than the purely descriptive (e.g. a bland quote from a press statement). Similarly, articles focusing on more obviously contentious topics that strived to present equally weighted he said/she said comments from claims-makers and counter-claims-makers (e.g. Ministers and anti-poverty campaigners), while avoiding value-laden language in their telling, were coded neutral. Given that comment pieces are (by definition) opinionated, it should come as little surprise that most neutral articles took the form of straightforward news stories and features.

Compared to the various other (agenda-led) categories, though, how much importance should we attach to neutral articles? Surely steering a 'middle way' through issues by applying normative journalistic values of balance and impartiality and avoiding obvious bias can only be a good thing? Well, no: set against the backdrop of the years of shirkerphobia that form the immediate media-political context for this book, the opposite is arguably true. That an article can be classified as discursively neutral does not make it unproblematic. In fact, when concerned with subjects as profoundly important and hotly contested as poverty and social security, news stories and (especially) in-depth features have a duty to properly investigate the matters they report, which sometimes means questioning or even debunking unevidenced truth-claims. As a fall-back position for conventionally trained journalists, adopting detached narrative positions can be an excuse for (at best) lazy, press release-reliant 'churnalism' (Davies 2008) or, worse, a ritualized charade of 'objectivity' (Tuchman 1972). Such approaches implicitly bolster the status quo, by uncritically repeating the platitudes and pronouncements of politicians and policy-makers. Moreover, by neutrally framing stories based on *contentious* (if routine) claims, from the monthly release of official job statistics to ministerial policy announcements, he said/she said reporting can be the antithesis of responsible, public-interest journalism.

FROM 'HARD' TO 'SOFT' COUNTER-DISCOURSES: DO DISTINCTIONS MATTER?

Where, then, do distinctions between various types of counter-discourse leave us? Surely a counter-discourse is a counter-discourse, whether it *wholly* refutes scrounger myths or adopts a more partial perspective: standing up for some claimants, but not others…

Such reasoning would be all well and good were it not for the fact that, by qualifying their position(s) with this caveat or that omission, counter-claims-makers pull their punches: allowing the well-mobilized, uncompromising myth-makers to break through the cracks to reassert their dominance. To quote an incisive 22 December think-piece in *The Independent*, the cumulative effect of poverty campaigners, parliamentary committees and the liberal press focusing only on certain, materially tangible, 'strains of poverty' or the plight of the most obviously 'deserving' groups (children, pensioners, underpaid workers) risks diluting what should be the overriding counter-discursive message: that, in the words of historian Bryce Evans, 'poverty is poverty full-stop' (Hannah 2016). In 'rebranding' poverty to focus on 'terms like "food poverty", "fuel poverty", even "funeral poverty"', argued journalist Felicity Hannah (2016), society could be 'doing those on the breadline more harm than good': enabling 'charities and pressure groups to prioritise their own preferred issues' and 'the state to be seen as tackling an aspect of poverty without having to address the wider issues'. From this book's perspective (poverty *discourses*), the effects of such 'rebranding' might be even more harmful: by presenting certain groups, such as 'fuel-poor' pensioners or 'food/funeral-poor' working families, as intrinsically more deserving than others.

It is with these concerns in mind that we turn to the question of how discourses about poverty in today's multi-mediated news sphere are both responded and contributed to by claims-makers *other* than Ministers, charities and think-tanks: the public itself.

CHAPTER 4

DELIBERATING DESERVINGNESS

THE PUBLIC'S ROLE IN CONSTRUCTING SCROUNGERS

Problematizing news discourses have only limited power if they fail to chime with public perceptions. Only by activating, and magnifying, issues that have recognizable real-world salience for their audiences can even the most persuasively packaged narratives engage and enrage people sufficiently to mobilize them 'for' or 'against' real or imagined threats. During the racially tinged 1970s 'mugging' panic chronicled in *Policing the Crisis*, the measure of how discourse problematizing a supposed surge in street crime resonated with public anxieties manifested itself in the traditional forum of newspaper letters pages (Hall et al. 1978), while the public's buy-in to the later 'scroungerphobia' panic was articulated through correspondence sent to newspaper leader-writers, opinion polls and a survey conducted by academics shortly afterwards (Golding & Middleton 1982: 157). Today, we have an instantaneous, publicly visible measure of lay concerns and opinion: social media.

The balance of influence on popular debate between media producers and audiences was ever a two-way street, as 'market-driven' editors have long been concerned with exploiting the lay concerns of their audiences to sell their output (McManus 1994). So, too, has the media long recognized the commercial value of mining audience members themselves, both for opinions and for story ideas that can be transformed into marketable content: through phone-ins, polls and vox-pops, and more direct appeals for eyewitness accounts and personal experiences relating to newsworthy issues. But the *two-way* street of the pre-digital age has given way to a media environment far more *multidirectional*: social media, comment threads and other user-generated content today places audiences (once largely viewed as consumers) at front and centre of what the media *publishes*. Today people not only discuss and debate news with friends and family over dinner or at the school gates: they respond to stories and argue about them, for all the world to see, by sharing, retweeting and posting lasting records of their views online.

And these developments only begin to explain why web-based social mediation is so significant in the context of scrounger discourse. Where comment threads especially come into their own is not so much in parroting and amplifying (or occasionally disputing) the frames of articles they accompany (though the reinforcing effects of this process are undoubtedly important) as in *consolidating* and *reproducing* their underlying discourses, by bringing *additional* truth-claims to the table that embellish the journalism itself. Though comment posts contributing meaningful additional detail about specific stories may yet be in a minority, those that add asserted personal experience or background knowledge to journalist-led narratives and the source material informing them not only perform an important democratic deliberative function: they can also influence, and even reshape, the terms of public discourse. It is this argument that underpins the focus of this chapter on how the increasingly visible ways in which we all talk about people experiencing poverty are integral to the persistence of ideas about scroungers.

ANALYSING SOCIAL MEDIA:
A BRIEF WORD ABOUT METHODS

For the purpose of this analysis, the term 'social media' is applied in its broadest sense: as 'websites and applications that enable users to create and share content or to participate in social networking' (Oxford Dictionaries 2017d). As the focus is on popular *discourse* about poverty and welfare, rather than the *socializing* function of social media, for analytical purposes the net was narrowed to two discursive arenas: comment threads published beneath online press articles and dialogue about the same stories posted on Twitter.

To control for the strong possibility of posts containing sarcasm or irony or using slang words or colloquialisms (most obviously the terms 'scrounger' and 'shirker'), 'human sentiment analysis' was used (Makarem & Jae 2016). Leaving aside the resource implications of employing computer algorithms, automated analysis might have misconstrued the, at times, figurative or colloquial nuances of social discourse.

Given the hundreds of articles coded for Chapter 3, the final question to address was *which* stories should be selected for analysis. In the end, six 'discursive events' (Wodak 2001: 48) were chosen: equivalent to one for every two months of 2016. Due to the uneven and unpredictable way news cycles unfold, though, some were clustered around specific months, when disproportionate levels of 'chatter' occurred, and all were in the first half of the year: before the UK's domestic agenda became dominated by the run-up to (and fallout from) the June EU referendum. It is also worth noting that March 2016 saw Iain Duncan Smith's successor as Work and Pensions Secretary, Stephen Crabb, rule out further benefit cuts during that parliament, beyond the ones previously announced. This also helps account for the 'quiet' period for welfare-related news in the second half of 2016.

The six events analysed were chosen based on two criteria: they had to relate to stories covered by at least three papers and stimulating discussion on comment threads *and* Twitter; and be representative of the diversity of poverty-related narratives reported during the study period. To this end, they embraced a range of topics, from classic claimant-baiting tales about feckless families to wider issue-based stories about cuts or policy to those that might broadly be described as celebrity-based. The events were:

- A 7 January story about an unemployed couple refused benefits after spending their £50,000 lottery winnings.
- An 11 January story about the jailing of 'Black Dee', a participant in TV docu-soap *Benefits Street*, for dealing cocaine and possessing live ammunition.
- A 25 January story about a Centre for Cities study categorizing almost half of Britain's biggest cities as 'high welfare, low wage' economies.
- A 4 February story about how participants in Channel 5 show *The Great British Benefits Handout* spent a £26,000 windfall setting up an exotic pets party business.
- A 5 April story about Iain Duncan Smith crying in a TV interview while recalling meeting a poor single mother who resembled his daughter.
- A 7 May story about Stephen Crabb's warning to unemployed households that they should find work to avoid an impending cut to the household benefit cap.

TABLE 4.1 BREAKDOWN OF OVERALL READER COMMENT THREAD POSTS BY SENTIMENT

Discourse event	'Hard' scrounger	'Soft' scrounger	Total all scrounger	'Hard' counter-discourse	'Soft' counter-discourse	Total all counter-discursive	Neutral	Other	Total sampled
Lottery winners plea for benefits	153 (49.7%)	76 (24.7%)	229 (74.4%)	3 (1%)	17 (5.5%)	20 (6.5%)	2 (0.6%)	57 (18.5%)	308
Benefits Street star jailed	18 (25%)	28 (38.9%)	46 (63.9%)	0 (0%)	0 (0%)	0 (0%)	0 (0%)	26 (36.1%)	72
'High welfare, low wage' study	53 (14.8%)	19 (5.3%)	72 (20.2%)	23 (6.4%)	69 (19.3%)	92 (25.7%)	0 (0%)	193 (54.1%)	357
Benefits family buy exotic pets	88 (36.1%)	33 (13.5%)	121 (49.6%)	16 (6.5%)	48 (19.7%)	64 (26.2%)	3 (1.2%)	56 (23%)	244
IDS cries for poor mother	36 (9.3%)	52 (13.4%)	88 (22.7%)	135 (34.8%)	87 (22.4%)	222 (57.2%)	3 (0.8%)	75 (19.3%)	388
Warning of benefit cap cut	318 (49%)	47 (7%)	365 (56%)	97 (15%)	55 (8.5%)	152 (23.5%)	2 (0.3%)	131 (20.2%)	650
Total	666	255	921	274	276	550	10	538	2,019

Table 4.1 breaks down the number of posts in each category across all papers publishing threads beneath their online versions of these stories, together with the percentages these represent of total posts about each event. For articles that generated hundreds or thousands of posts, only the first one or two 'pages' of threads were analysed, with comments reordered to ensure the (still large) numbers that *were* coded prioritized the most popular comments among the sites' users. In so doing, the aim was to ensure that coded samples were as representative as possible of overall reader sentiments on each thread. Fuller details of the sampling and coding methodology are given in Appendix 2.

WHAT THE PUNTERS SAID: COMMENT
THREADS AS AUDIENCE DISCOURSE

The overwhelming tone and emphasis of newspaper comment threads relating to the six discursive events was one of disdain towards the unemployed and/or claimants generally. Numerous remarks were tinged with outright prejudice, sometimes bordering on hatred or incitement. 'Scrounging wasters', 'lowlife scrounging bums', 'pond life', 'parasites', 'mindless mouth-breathers' and 'dirty little scummers' were among the insults heaped on the lottery-winning couple who had their benefit claim refused after spending their £50,000 cash prize. More sinisterly, a handful of comments were so aggressive that, had they been aimed at people from specific ethnic or faith groups, they would have broken UK laws banning racial or religious hate speech. Reacting to the news of 'Black Dee's' sentence, a poster on the *Birmingham Mail*'s thread using the alias 'ukmashy' launched into a rant about the 'roundabout' of prison and welfare, describing 'a bullet in the temple' as the only 'sure fire way' of thwarting repeat offenders, while *Metro* poster 'foxy' blasted her as a 'piece of sh##', who should 'rot in jail'. Some went further, using wider-ranging stories about benefits, such as that focusing on the household cap, as an excuse to target other groups they disliked (notably immigrants), in hand-wringing laments about the state of contemporary Britain echoing Duncan Smith's 'broken society' discourse. One such poster on the *Express* site (self-identifying as 'British worker') urged politicians to 'press the "reset" button' on 'the migration magnet' to deter the tide of claimants pouring in from 'cultures that favour huge families, mostly immigrants'.

Significantly, though judgemental and dismissive posts were most common on threads about *individual* cases, they also dominated discussion beneath the policy story focusing on the impending benefit cap change and crept into comments reacting to the think-tank study identifying Britain's 'high-welfare' hotspots. Even readers commenting on the numerous articles sparked by Duncan Smith's teary interview (for satirist Ian Hislop's documentary on Victorian attitudes to poverty, provocatively titled *Workers or Shirkers?*) sometimes skewed their remarks back to the supposed problems of the Welfare State.

In terms of mapping the prevalence of scrounger discourse – posts echoing, affirming and, in some cases, embellishing anti-welfare frames – the figures are most striking in relation to tales about individual claimants. Although a quarter of comments about the couple refused benefits after spending their lottery winnings were sufficiently qualified to be classed as 'soft scrounger', nearly three-quarters adopted some form of anti-welfare stance, with almost half (153 out of 308) strongly condemning them and/or explicitly extending their criticisms to embrace claimants generally. Anti-scrounger posts for this story outnumbered those that were in any way counter-discursive by more than ten to one, with only 6.5 per cent of all comments (20) contesting the overwhelming anti-welfare sentiment. And, though this story was mainly reported in right-wing tabloids, nearly two-thirds of posts published by the supposedly left-leaning *Daily Mirror* (38 out of 60) also bought into scrounger discourse. However, more than half of all posters defending the couple (12 out of 20) also appeared on this thread, with one ('DmX') criticizing the paper for 'demonizing' them.

In the round, anti-claimant sentiment infiltrated almost every thread analysed, across all the discursive events (bar, ironically, some of the 'high-welfare' city ones): outnumbering posts *contesting* this discourse by more than two to one on those revolving around the entrepreneurial unemployed family and the lowering of the benefit cap. And, while more than half of all posts responding to the spectacle of Duncan Smith crying were broadly counter-discursive, equally noteworthy was the fact that, even when responding to a story about the tacit *mea culpa* of a widely reviled former Work and Pensions Secretary, nearly one in four comments (88 out of 388 or 23 per cent) still contrived to steer inter-reader dialogue around to castigating scroungers.

This is not, in any way, to downplay the existence of a counter-discourse. The Duncan Smith story, particularly, generated many angry counter-discursive posts: not only from readers of liberal-left papers but even those of conservative outlets. Indeed, many posters came close to libelling the ex-Minister: branding him a 'liar' or accusing him of presiding over a disability test regime which caused people to become more ill, die prematurely or commit suicide. Well over half the posts this story generated (222 out of 388) criticized both government policy and the discourse(s) it promoted, with six out of ten of these (135) voicing uncompromisingly 'hard' counter-discursive views.

These glimmerings of dissent, were, however, roundly eclipsed by the sheer volume of posts endorsing the overwhelming anti-welfare consensus. Of the 2,019 posts coded, 921 (just over 45 per cent) expressed scrounger-baiting sentiments, compared to the one in four adopting broadly counter-discursive positions. This stark statistic becomes more alarming still when one considers that the longest threads (largely on *Mail Online*) were only coded to the ends of their first pages. In some instances, this left several hundred posts un-sampled: the *Mail*'s lottery story ran to 4,398, of which only the 169 'most rated' (less than 4 per cent of the total) were coded. Given that nearly eight out of ten posts that *were* coded endorsed the scrounger discourse it promoted, had it been feasible to analyse *all Mail* comments the final tally would surely have been far higher.

PRIMING THE ECHO-CHAMBER: CONSTRUCTING EPISODIC SCROUNGERS

Framed throughout as a classic case of feckless scrounging, it was hardly surprising that *Mail Online*'s take on 'jobless' Jamie and Abbie Hort's fruitless bid to persuade the Channel Islands' Social Security department to grant them benefits after blowing a £50,000 Christmas Lottery win earned near-universal condemnation from sampled posters (Tonkin 2016). The report was littered with details portraying the couple as tasteless, immature and irresponsible, with information dredged up about Mr Hort's criminal past (a conviction for spitting in a woman's mouth) to add to the infantilizing impression of a petulant child trapped in a man's body. We learned that, having 'splashed the cash on designer clothes, holidays, new furniture and a giant TV', the pair were evicted when their Income Support and Housing Benefit claims failed. The story was accompanied by several photos, including a selfie of Mr Hort sticking his tongue out and another of the hoodie-wearing couple posing for a press agency photographer on a leopard-skin sofa: the background a riot of stereotypical scrounger paraphernalia, including discarded cigarette packets, a half-drunk bottle of Pepsi and the 50-inch TV set they had bought with their prize money (tuned in, masochistically, to scrounger-baiting daytime programme *The Jeremy Kyle Show*). This near-postmodern touch was emphasized by quotes from Mrs Hort rejecting the charge of Facebook trolls that the couple were 'scroungers' and a screen-grab from a social media post in which she distanced herself from others 'on the social' who 'never work a day in their life's' but still 'get everything payed for [sic]'. This echoed the defensive internal-ization of normative anti-scrounger discourse noted by Golding and Middleton (1982) and ex-MP Sarah Teather (Williams 2013) in their conversations with claimants.

Other papers adopted similar discursive frames. Headlined 'Jobless couple who blew £50k lottery win to beg for benefits claim "we're not scroungers"', the *Express*'s version ventrilo-quized 'outraged taxpayers' who 'blasted' the couple online, only to unleash a 'Facebook rant littered with expletives' from Mrs Hort (Barnett 2016). Again, photos were used as framing devices to portray the couple as abject familiar strangers, sarto-rially inscribed with '"signs of chavness"' (Tyler 2008: 29). These included a close-up of sullen Mrs Hort wearing a duffle coat and vest top, emphasizing her neck tattoo and studded upper lip. *The Mirror* also stressed the couple's 'jobless' status, adding to its photo gallery an unflattering close-up of Mr Hort, foregrounding his straggly beard, facial studs and (presumably) tobacco-stained teeth (Haworth & Bevan 2016). Once more, the scrounger frame also encroached into at least one broadsheet (the *Telegraph*), which ran an agency version of the story opening with the objectifying term 'a couple on benefits' and empha-sizing their 'demand' for more 'state handouts'.

Of all papers reporting the unemployed family's entrepre-neurial party business, the *Mail* adopted the most infantilizing frame: portraying its subjects as, by turns, irresponsible and comically deluded. Its lengthy headline juxtaposed a quote from Scott and Leanne Gavin warning that 'you couldn't give £26,000 in handouts to just anyone' because 'they might blow it' with the revelation they had 'spent £460 on a raccoon and £950 on an inflatable slide after getting all their benefits in one go for Channel 5 show' (Gye 2016). The article opened with a string of bullet-points, emphasizing the couple's 'jobless' status and the fact that they had four children. It also made extensive use of semiotically loaded publicity stills depicting rotund Mr Gavin and his wife surrounded by their children; in close-up wearing hoodies; and toasting their £26,000 windfall with champagne. Another shot featured their eight-year-old son clutching armfuls of banknotes. Though the story conceded Mr Gavin had given up work to care for a son with 'severe behavioural problems', and had now come off benefits to make 'a success' of the new business, these details were undermined by classic freak-show tropes: specifically how, 'within a few days', they had spent £6,000.

The Express took the ridicule further still, its headline relaying how viewers had chosen to 'vent' at the couple's decision to 'splash out £650 on a lizard almost as soon as they were given the case of dosh' (Miller 2016). Intriguingly, it also began by highlighting that they were 'from Liverpool', hinting at an attempt to prompt reader recollections of stereo-typical 'scouse scroungers' familiar from 1980s pop-cultural portrayals, such as BBC1 sitcom *Bread* (Murden 2006: 466). The paper's online presentation of the story also showed how, on websites (just as in print), page furniture and overall layout can be used to reinforce articles' frames, by juxtaposing (and interspersing) them with interdiscursive content. Woven into the text were links to 'related articles', including that of a '"disabled cheat"' who 'took more than £8,500 in benefits' but 'worked at the top of a 446ft hill' and a warning from an 'EU chief' that 'cutting benefits will not stop migrants coming to Britain'; 'related videos' of a 'Benefits Britain teen' who 'wants to go on [reality show] *Big Brother*' and a 'benefits cheat caught working in a pub'; and a voyeuristic 'slideshow' of ten paparazzi shots of a '"Too Fat to Work" benefits couple' caught on camera as they 'binge on KFC'. The Gavins' story, then, was slotted into an invidious multimedia montage of carefully selected freak-shows, so that (taken in totality) the webpage it appeared on presented a persuasive, if wholly unrepresentative, gallery of abject scroungers. Of all papers covering the Gavins' story, only their local paper, *The Liverpool Echo*, was supportive, opting for a rags-to-riches slant, under the playful headline 'It started with a raccoon – now reviewers are raving about new party business' (Margan 2016). Also included were several Facebook posts from satisfied customers, including one praising the couple for 'the best service I've ever had for my party'.

'Black Dee' articles offered an intriguing variation on the scrounger-baiting theme, by introducing Samora Roberts (her real name) as a 'Benefits Street star' (*Mail Online, Birmingham Mail, Daily Star, Daily Telegraph*) but otherwise focusing on her *criminality* (as a drug-dealer), not her wider deviancy (as an unemployed claimant). Nonetheless, tell-tale tropes of scrounger discourse poked through, with most papers drawing attention to '"signs of chavness"' in her attire (Tyler 2008: 29). *Mail Online*, the *Star, Telegraph* and her own local paper, the *Birmingham Mail*, all delighted in the 'full Adidas tracksuit, white trainers, and long black parka jacket' she wore as she 'high-fived her friends and family and cracked jokes before entering the dock' (Kemble 2016). As if readers needed further confirmation of her chavness, every report featured photos, almost all showing her smirking, her hair scraped back into a bun. These included a portrait of her wearing the oft-cited parka and others of her gesturing for a ciga-rette-lighter or scowling into the camera, studded lower lip to the fore. Further signifiers of Roberts' workshy lifestyle included quotes from her lawyer relaying how, since *Benefits Street*, her life had 'come full circle' (a term with connotations of cycles of dependency), as 'adverse publicity' left her living like a 'hermit', on Jobseeker's Allowance, and 'sofa surfing at her sister's house' (www.telegraph.co.uk 2016). Though her drug use had 'stopped entirely', it had been 'habitual' and the 'route [sic] of her evil'.

PARROTING PREJUDICE? QUALITATIVE EXAMPLES OF ANTI-SCROUNGER COMMENTARY

Primed by such episodic frames, scrounger discourse mani-fested itself in a variety of ways on comment threads, with many posts strongly echoing not only the discursive tropes of articles themselves but the gamut of ways in which claimants have been popularly portrayed in media-political discourse for decades. Readers used phraseology evoking everything from Keith Joseph's 'cycle' thesis to lines lifted almost verbatim from speeches by latter-day Conservative Ministers, so aligned were they to their condemnations of 'shirkers' and deifica-tion of 'hardworking' households. The striking recurrence of such tropes, especially on threads published on right-leaning websites, demonstrates how deeply ingrained popular concep-tions of deserving and undeserving poor people have become after decades of (more or less) endless repetition and consolidation. The concept of intergenerational dependency underscored numerous comments on the *Mail* and *Express* sites, with many 'best rated' and 'most liked' posts respectively supporting this diagnosis of social problems symbolized by the spendthrift lottery couple. In a typically demonizing post evocative of age-old underclass rhetoric (and 'liked' by 115 other readers), 'Sophie, Wiltshire' cast the Horts as a breed apart, with the fatalistic lament, 'what chills me to the core' is that these 'bone idle scroungers' have 'bred' and 'their kids will be even worse'.[22] Her view was shared by 'Marg.Oldham' on the *Express* thread, who observed that 'it goes on and on and on'. And rants about intergenerational cultures of idleness were not reserved for the Horts: primed by the *Star*'s mockingly worded freak-show telling of the Gavins' story, 'Veteran44' suggested they should be 'told to use some of the money for compulsory sterilisation', to 'stop them breeding more morons' to reproduce their 'family traditions of sloth and miniscule intelligence'. *Express* poster 'Ray1066' remarked that he felt 'sorry for the animals', living with 'people who have a lower IQ than them'. And so pervasive were perceptions of inherited dependency that they even surfaced on some threads focusing on 'thematically' framed articles (Iyengar 1992), such as the *Mirror*'s sympathetically worded report about the impending benefit cap cut. In its framing, the paper eschewed any obvious scrounger trigger-terms to focus on 'families on benefits' generally (not just those without jobs), while casting the policy as a plan to 'slash' payments that (in a quote from Jeremy Corbyn) was 'devastating for children, devastating for the family and very bad for the community' (Wellman 2016). Yet this failed to deter 'MarcherLord1' from reviving the extreme, atypical case of 'Mick "torch my family for a bigger house" Philpott', and reminding readers how he had claimed '£66k of tax free benefits' for 'breeding another generation of feckless wastrels'.

An even more pernicious strain of us-and-them anti-scrounger comments, at times bordering on incitement, likened claimants (implicitly or explicitly) to animals. To *Mirror* poster 'UltimateJediMaster', the Horts were 'scum', who should be forced 'to live in kennels like the animals they are'. The same paper's thread on the Gavins' party business provoked a stream of invective from 'flnycus', who suggested claimants should 'be left to starve' if, 'after a few weeks' on benefits, they had not done 'something to better themselves'. While insisting s/he was in favour of benefits 'when needed', the same poster added, 'if they are just wasting time being lazy, let them die out', describing this as 'natural selection'. Meanwhile, responding to the *Express*'s benefit cap story, 'Annie1' implicitly likened 'the workshy' to farm animals by saying they 'should be prodded back into work'. Commenting on a *Mirror* 'Best TV' item previewing *The Great British Benefits Handout*, 'ColinLeach' branded its participants 'fat useless pigs'.

More commonplace than examples of undisguised class/ social hatred were those directly parroting then recent ministerial rhetoric. An angry, capitalized post by 'PeterHeal' beneath the *Mirror* TV preview implored the government to 'TELL THEM TO GET A JOB AND NOT LIVE ON THE BACKS OF HARD WORKING TAX PAYERS'. Though especially prevalent in dialogue accompanying stories about the Hort and Gavin families, the 'hardworking taxpayers' refrain surfaced on nearly every thread. In some instances, the plight of taxpayers was used in the same breath as another favourite political imaginary:

Ministers' repeated depiction of benefits as a 'lifestyle choice'. To 'Dogfight, Manchester', the Horts' spending habits were 'just typical behaviour of scroungers on benefits' who 'want hard working tax payers to fund their lives whilst they sit on their bottoms!' In a post rated by 298 others beneath the *Mail*'s benefit cap story, 'tired tax payer, Essex' endorsed Conserva-tive-driven Workfare initiatives, saying s/he was 'not against people claiming benefits' provided they earned them by being forced to 'clean streets, rake leaves or other manual tasks for the good of the community', to teach them 'benefits are not a great lifestyle choice'. And echoing George Osborne's favourite strawman familiar stranger – the 'next-door neighbour sleeping off a life on benefits' while shift-workers leave home 'in the dark hours of the early morning' – 'tsutsugamushi, The shire' won ratings from 432 *Mail* readers for a self-pitying rant about how s/he 'work[s] hard, pay[s] my taxes' and drove a 15-year-old car, while subsidizing a neighbour who was 'on benefits, 5 kids, drives a nice big van and was on majorca [sic] last week'.

A related strain of posts recalled *earlier* governments' rhetor-ical entreaties to get the unemployed on their bikes to find work. An example of how this hardwired discourse continued to permeate press discourse across the gamut, from nationals to local papers in post-industrial areas, appeared on the *South Wales Argus* website, in response to its story about the 'high-welfare' cities report. Recalling his own experience of moving in and out of insecure jobs, 'MrClark' advised the unemployed to develop a 'work ethic' and 'keep plugging away and take whatever you can'. Beyond robustly defending the virtues of work over idleness, he represented a more sophisticated class of poster – going beyond *reacting* to a story, by contributing *evidence* supporting his view, based on asserted first-hand knowledge. Other 'evidence-based' posters included 'dolly dimple, Dollywood, United Kingdom' (rated by 489 readers on the *Mail*'s lottery thread), who self-described as 'one of the people who physically evicts these numbties', and 'purehonesty, the skool of life' (rated by 2,678), who posted this angry autobiographical testimony:

> What a joke you both are, I'm a working single mum and can't afford the rents by greedy private landlords and would embrace a lottery win to secure my future of owning a home, I have to keep moving because the local housing can't offer me anything, I'm now looking again but landlords refuse DSS or not working enough hours and its clowns like you who are irresponsible, expect everyone to look after you, there is work out there, try cleaning toilets like a lot of us HAVE too, lazy gits!

Another poster projecting the deserving/undeserving discourse back onto her own life was 'RuthGower', who responded to the *Mirror*'s report about the Gavins by arguing that 'this lazy pair' of 'spongers' were not prepared to 'get work only if just cleaning', which she 'had to' when she was their age, 'to help with the house keeping'. In eliding such strong associations between these tabloid tales and their own lives, such posters echoed the testimony of many low-waged and unemployed people interviewed by Golding and Middleton (1982: 172), who displayed a similar 'culture of contempt' towards their fellow (low-waged or unwaged) citizens, reflecting the dominance of a hegemonic 'culture' (in the 1980s, as today) that places overwhelming 'stress' on 'the equation of economic success with diligence, endeavour and obedience to the rules of the economic game'.

A related, if subtly distinct, aspect of these autobiographical posts was their irritation (and occasional rage) at articles that appeared to extend definitions of 'welfare' claimants to pensioners, attesting to lay perceptions of a qualitative difference between (deserving) older people and (undeserving) working-age benefit recipients. 'Pensions are not benefits', wailed 'Linda, Milton Keynes' on the *Mail*'s welfare cap thread, evoking the hardworking taxpayer frame to add, 'they are paid for via a lifetime of working and paying NI contributions (for majority)'. Similarly, 'Whoopi do, Tunstall' reacted to the same website's 'high-welfare cities' report by declaring that 'pension is NOT a benefit', and suggesting Ministers' insistence on describing it as such exposed a conspiracy to foment intergenerational resentments by making 'the young people' believe 'oap's are scroungers'. Without directly addressing the question of whether pensions constituted benefits, 'Mike OAP' robustly distanced himself from the unemployed on the *Express*'s welfare cap thread by self-identifying as a pensioner who 'worked from age 16 to 65 and now still pay[s] tax', so that 'the languid work shy can spend their benefits on beer, backy & bingo'. Responding to the 'high-welfare cities' story, equally indignant 'perryorchard, Hartlepool' urged Ministers not to 'refer to the State Pension as a welfare benefit', and rebuked working-age claimants by stating pensions were 'based on the amount of [National Insurance] contributions we have made', making them 'uniquely different' to other payments, which were 'NOT based' on what has 'been contributed'. Importantly, this claim was factually inaccurate, in that the higher rates of both Jobseeker's Allowance and Employment and Support Allowance are both, in fact, contributory.

At times, stigmatization of working-age claimants was extended well beyond the unemployed. Though less commonplace, baiting of sick and disabled people also surfaced, in defiance of any wider '*I, Daniel Blake* effect'. This was particularly the case in relation to thematic narratives, such as the 'high-welfare cities' story, which some readers sweepingly characterized as dead-zones for economically inactive no-hopers. 'How is it', pondered *Mirror* reader 'Darrn300', that the 'pretend disabled' are entitled to 'more than the national living wage'? The *Mail*'s take on this story (run under the misleading headline 'Britain's benefits bonanza' – Denton 2016) spurred 'lindyloux, scotland' to shop 'a neighbour' who was 'faking disability openly' and had 'no intention of ever working'. Despite her 'claims to have arthritis', this scrounger could 'walk back from the shop carrying several litres of cider' and 'bounce on her kids' bouncy castle'. But disabled-bashing sentiments were not confined to threads beneath state-of-the-nation articles: the *Mail*'s party business story prompted 'Martin1977, Preston' to declare, 'scum are scum and will never change', singling out '"men" who use every excuse in the world from depression to bad backs to shy away from work'. Defining himself in opposition to Scott Gavin, he added he would 'rather look in the mirror and know I'm a real man any day'.

Objectification of almost all working-age claimants (often in explicit opposition to pensioners) was also extended to another group frequently othered in media-political discourse: immigrants. 'Import useless, unemployable sponges who have no intention of working, and this is what you get', ranted 'space1999,

Home again, United Kingdom' on the *Mail*'s 'high-welfare cities' thread, while 'Mrs Poldark, Cheltenham' lumped together home-grown and foreign scroungers by invoking a favourite lament of nostalgists despairing of their country having 'gone to the dogs' (Morrison 2016a: 143) – dismissing 'once Great Britain' as 'a dumping ground for lazy workshy benefit seekers born here and abroad', funded by 'a dwindling population of tax payers'. More openly racist was 'outtaEU's' invitation to *Express* readers scanning its benefit cap thread to 'take a walk through wembly and places like that' and 'see them all swanning about in the middle of the day', adding, 'moslems and Africans you pay for all of them'. Meanwhile, 'IMO' used the *Mail*'s household cap story as an excuse to mimic ministerial anti-claimant rhetoric, arguing that benefits were not 'a lifestyle choice' but 'a safety net'; young people should be 'made to look for jobs'; and child benefit should be 'cut to two kids' (a reference to a then-mooted two-child policy for claimants). For good measure, s/he added that 'immigrants who haven't paid anything into the system' should 'get nothing for five years', in full-throated endorsement of Cameron's EU 'emergency brake'. Tougher still was the chippily named 'underpaidEngineer, Cambridgeshire', who declared 'there should not be any benefits', as they were 'one of the lures that bring in millions of free loaders from other countries'.

Perhaps the most significant qualitative difference between the early 1980s survey responses garnered by Golding and Middleton and evidence-based comments in this (late 2010s) sample is that, through comment threads, a minority of *today's* respondents were able to go beyond affirming or contesting received discourses by simply *identifying* with a newspaper scenario or relaying personal anecdotes triggered by it. By contrast, a handful shared additional details or truth-claims *directly pertaining* to specific stories on which they posted, meaning they did not simply *react* to articles, they *enhanced* them. In this sense, they were engaged in a highly active process of co-authorship with journalists: helping to 'complete' narratives otherwise left more 'unfinished' (Morrison 2016b). Such posts were most evident on threads relating to the most commented-upon story: that of the unemployed lottery-winners. In a lengthy *Mail* post providing potentially valuable background on the Channel Islands' benefit system for readers based elsewhere, 'Guerner, Guernsey, Guernsey' described the British protectorate as 'a place where less than 1% of the population are unemployed'. On the *Mirror*'s thread, meanwhile, 'WizzleTeats' asserted s/he had 'family and friends on Guernsey', adding, 'I know a few who have at least a few children to their families and live off around £26,000 a year' and 'manage ok!'

DEFENDING THE DEMONIZED: ASSESSING THE STRENGTH OF COUNTER-DISCOURSE

Despite being in a minority, when counter-discursive posts appeared they were often highly vocal, and disproportionately *evidence-based* compared to those they contested.

An example of an issue provoking a robust counter-offensive was the assertion that pensions were not benefits. Several (brave) counter-claims-makers contested this myth on the *Mail*'s 'benefit cap' thread, notably 'Steven Rochdale', who made the (broadly accurate) point that 'benefits to the over 65s takes up £106 billion of the £167 billion' (Full Fact 2015). This earned him the collective ire of 79 fellow readers, who red-arrowed his comment, with only 18 green ones approving of it. Similarly, 'public X' obliquely referred to the same point on the paper's 'high-welfare cities' thread, stressing 'people on JSA' were only costing '£4.5 billion out of an annual £100+ billion welfare budget', while low-waged workers' pay was topped up by Housing Benefit and tax credits, taking many of their overall household incomes above the £26,000 (let alone £20,000) benefit cap.

In an attempt to correct dismissive assumptions about the laziness of unemployed people living in recession-hit post-industrial areas, 'MrsC, Bucks' reminded readers on the *Mail*'s Duncan Smith thread that 'vast swathes' of Britain had 'never recovered' from having their 'traditional jobs base ... destroyed in the 80s by Maggie T [Thatcher] and her brigade'. Meanwhile, 'Rícky, Sunnyvale Trailer Park, Canada' used this same case to reject the consensus among *Mail* readers on the benefit cap thread, replying to 'peter, wirral's' dismissal of 'layabouts' to accuse him of being 'sucked in by media (and government) propaganda' ignoring the fact that 'the huge majority' are 'genuine' and 'cannot find work' due to 'our crap economy'. Unsurprisingly, such counter-hegemonic talk was much less exceptional on liberal websites, like *The Guardian*'s, in response to whose 'high-welfare' article 'frank-iecrisp, WhetherbyPond' criticized tabloids for promoting their readers' 'bitter and twisted foaming at the mouth' by denying the fact that 'social security includes pensions'. Similar sentiments were expressed by 'EdEdwards', responding to the *Mirror*'s 'Best TV' item. Attacking the exploitation of families on TV shows, he wrote:

Yes there are families out there who would do this type of thing, they are people who have never had any money in one lump sum and have no idea what to do. they were also encouraged by the tv series to make sure they spend as much as they can to drop well below the 16000 POUNDS needed to make a claim in the first place ... its all artificial properganda to turn everyone against each other on the bottom of the scale and to take the attention off the real problems of tax evasions.

Meanwhile, 'DmX' was among several *Mirror* posters who condemned its lottery couple story, specifically the omission of details that did not fit neatly into a scrounger frame. Responding to 'Whacker's' post asking why Mr Hort had not used his winnings 'to re train for other work', he retorted, 'even if he did, the Mirror wouldn't put it in the article', as 'the whole idea' was to anger 'the "middle" class' about '"benefit cheat scum"', diverting attention from those 'really bankrupting us': 'corporations and the super-rich'.

Critical posts blaming *media* (rather than politicians) for colouring public perceptions of claimants was not, however, confined to liberal papers. In a 'soft' counter-discursive post, 'NotInMyName' risked the wrath of *Express* readers by branding the Channel 5 show a 'disgusting program' that 'cherry picked some of the slobbiest wastes of space they could find' to degrade 'anybody on benefits'. Condemning the series' freak-show approach, s/he argued that 'those in a much more privileged position' did not 'see the other side of benefits', and posed the uncomfortable question: 'who the hell wants to watch a programme on somebody budgeting their benefits, not smoking, drinking, feeding a pitbull and not screaming at scruffy kids eating greggs pasties for breakfast?!' This incisive critique, by a poster self-identifying as 'bed ridden (thanks to an NHS botch job)' and having 'to rely on benefits', was notable not only for spiritedly refuting scrounger stereotypes, but also because, *despite* defending claimants, it still implicitly accepted *aspects* of the discourse, by referring to 'slobbiest wastes of space'. In projecting the prejudices voiced by fellow posters onto his/her own status as a (temporary) claimant, and explicitly declaring s/he did not 'want to be associated' with 'these people', the poster once more demonstrated the invidious power of discursive norms: diluting the strength of his/her message with implied *acceptance* of the premise that scroungers exist. Moreover, by insistently separating him/herself from these 'wastes of space', s/he also echoed the prejudices expressed by other self-identifying 'deserving' claimants, such as Golding and Middleton's survey respondents and Sarah Teather's constituents.

SCROUNGER DISCOURSE IN THE TWITTERSPHERE

Analysis of the relative balance between scrounger-bashing, counter-discursive and other Twitter posts was less clear-cut, largely because such chatter as appeared in the Twittersphere around the key discursive events was piecemeal, with few tweets provoking much inter-poster *dialogue*. Unlike the energized Twitter debates analysed in relation to major political events, such as elections and referenda (e.g. Pedersen et al. 2014), even provocative tweeters largely escaped challenge by fellow posters. Moreover, many posts had to be excluded from analysis, either because they simply retweeted links to articles (without *commenting* on them) or were clearly of a marketing or promotional nature (e.g. tweets from those involved in making a TV show or third-party organizations piggy-backing on a story's publicity to promote their own work). It was therefore impossible to code such tweets as 'positive' or 'negative', as they expressed no discernible viewpoints.

The patchy discourse that emerged from Twitter may also partly be the result of the unavoidably imperfect sampling method. Unlike with comment threads, which generated *automatic* datasets (in the form of the posts published beneath articles online), constructing a Twitter sample necessitated experimenting to determine the most appropriate approach for mining as many tweets as possible relating to each news event. The retrospective, rather than contemporaneous, nature of this study also meant it was necessary to use Twitter's own 'advanced search' function, rather than a more analytical commercial tool like Twitonomy. At the time data-gathering was carried out, all the discursive events had occurred more than a year beforehand – making it impossible to use Twitonomy, as the dates were out with its retrospective time limit. Choosing the best search terms also involved trial and error: combinations of terms that initially seemed logical often had to be supplemented by (or substituted with) others to produce more comprehensive datasets.

There was also the question of deciding the appropriate time-frames over which to scrape Twitter in each case. The variable nature of discursive events made it difficult to standardize: for example, a story like that of the lottery-winners unfolded in the news media over the space of a day or two, with all resulting Twitter dialogue around the subject swiftly dissipating as soon as this 'big-bang' coverage was over. By contrast, the buzz around the *Great British Benefits Handout* (and the specific focus on the Gavins' party business) was more prolonged: mobilized initially by PR and media coverage in the week preceding the first episode's broadcast and sustained by ongoing online chatter in the run-up to (and immediately after) episode two, nearly three weeks later. As a result, this story's dataset included considerably more tweets than all the others, running to 125: more than one in five of the total analysed. Moreover, as it was difficult to separate those commenting on the overall nature of the programme (and/or its participants) from ones specifically targeting the Gavins, the decision was taken to code *all* tweets about the show displaying opinions, rather than just those concerning the party business storyline that was the focus of newspaper analysis. Even in the cases of more time-limited events, like the jailing of 'Black Dee', it was generally impossible to limit sampling to the date initial press reports appeared (or even that day and the next) because the way in which newspaper stories are published in today's digital environment is subject to erratic timings, with reports often initially appearing (and provoking reactions) on papers' websites the night before they materialize, and stimulate further debate, in print. For all these methodological hurdles, however, the datasets used here offer as representative a sample of tweets relating to our discursive events as it was possible to assemble, given resource limitations, and are more than adequate for this exploratory level of qualitative analysis. The total break-down of tweet sentiments for each event is laid out in Table 4.2, and Appendix 2 gives fuller details of the methodology used for sampling and analysis.

If, for the purposes of determining the relative balance of Twitter sentiment, we disregard the large number of comments that cannot easily be bracketed 'negative' or 'positive', a sharp and immediate distinction is visible between discursive events relating

TABLE 4.2 BREAKDOWN OF TWEET SENTIMENTS BY DISCOURSE EVENT

Discourse event	'Hard' negative (anti-scrounger)	'Soft' negative	Total all negative	'Hard' positive (counter-discursive)	'Soft' positive	Total all positive	Other	Total tweets sampled
Lottery winners plea for benefits	6 (60%)	3 (30%)	9 (90%)	0	0	0	1 (10%)	10
Benefits Street star jailed	0	1 (50%)	1 (50%)	0	0	0	1 (50%)	2
'Low wage, High welfare' study	0	1 (1%)	1 (1%)	11 (11%)	5 (5%)	16 (16%)	83 (83%)	100
Great British Benefits Handout	26 (20.8%)	12 (9.6%)	38 (30.4%)	3 (2.4%)	8 (6.4%)	11 (8.8%)	76 (60.8%)	125
Ex-minister cries for poor mother	1 (0.3%)	5 (1.5%)	6 (1.8%)	128 (39.6%)	14 (4.3%)	142 (44%)	175 (54.2%)	323
Warning of cut to benefit cap	6 (12.8%)	3 (6.4%)	9 (19.2%)	26 (55.3%)	0 (0%)	26 (55.3%)	12 (25.5%)	47

Source: Twitter Advanced Search.

to *individual cases* versus *issues* around welfare/poverty. Though each event generated many times fewer tweets than newspaper comment posts, it is highly significant that the breakdown of 'positive' and 'negative' sentiments on Twitter was broadly comparable to that visible on threads. As on the news websites, value-laden tweets commenting on *individualized*, episodically framed stories overwhelmingly echoed scrounger discourse(s), with nine out of ten responses to the Lottery couple story condemning their fecklessness, and none openly defending them. Chatter about *The Great British Benefits Handout*, particularly the Gavins' party business, was also dominated by anti-scrounger sentiment, with nearly eight out ten tweets that expressed opinions (38 out of 49) reflecting this standpoint. The one outlier among the episodic events was the 'Black Dee' story, which (despite being retweeted many times) produced only two tweets commenting on it.

Though comparatively mild in tone, 'Elliot Etherington @e_etherington' summed up the consensus on the Lottery story, with a tweet glibly inscribing the Horts as 'a benefit couple' and delivering the damning verdict that they had 'wasted' their 'chance to get out of poverty'. 'Catherine M byrne' dismissed the pair as 'wasters', while 'Ladybirdangel' exclaimed, 'Its ur own frigging fault get a job!' If anything, though, invective aimed at the Gavins was more aggressive, becoming noticeably harsher over time, as the first two episodes of the TV series generated a lively unfolding debate. Tweets focusing on its stars' spending decisions largely echoed classic scrounger frames: 'Scouse' predicted 'these dickheads' would 'fail, spunk the money up the wall and go back on the dole', and 'Bex Chadwick' labelled Scott Gavin 'an electrician with 4 kids claiming = Scrounger!', adding that the programme should be renamed 'The Great British Benefits Cheat'. 'Michael @mickymdc1' asked rhetorically, 'who will support' the families that 'fail', other than 'the tax payer again', while, near the end of the sample period, indignant 'Mike Ashworth @MikeAlphaOne' tweeted, 'Are these fucking disgusting people for real…?'

What, then, of counter-discursive voices? Amid all the vitriol branding the reality show's participants 'peasants' ('@danoliver93'), 'lazy shits' ('Mark Steven Cooper') and 'pathetic loosers [sic]' ('Ferroequinologist @Twoyorkie'), it was easy to miss Kate Miller's kind-hearted remark that the £26,000 windfall represented 'such a good opportunity for them', let alone 'ashley @heartswellss" plea to others to 'stop watching programmes like "the great british benefits handout" (WTF)', as it was 'BILE that scapegoats the poor'.

Significantly, it was the more *issue-based* 'high-welfare' and 'benefit cap' stories, and the episodic story of a different kind focusing on Duncan Smith's teary interview, that spurred counter-discursive voices to assert themselves, at times by lining up to criticize structural social inequality and defend claimants. The 'high-welfare' story moved several posters to cast the Centre for Cities report as evidence of the hollowness of Osborne's repeated pledges to promote economic growth in northern cities. These not only included posts categorized as 'counter-discursive' for *our* purposes (those defending people on benefits and/or criticizing their mistreatment) but numerous 'other' tweets, focusing less on poverty/welfare than the wider macro-economic picture the report painted of a North–South divide. One such tweeter, Carl Durose, declared it was 'no surprise' Birmingham was 'a "low-wage, high-welfare" city' after being 'neglected by central government'. Neil Kennett added sardonically, 'still some work to do on the NORTHERN POWERHOUSE then', while Paul Lewis, presenter of Radio 4's personal finance programme *Money Box*, stretched BBC impartiality rules with the wordplay 'northern workhouse?' More openly countervailing were 'Chris Giles's' remark that 'at least Osborne's housing benefit freeze will help by making people homeless', and 'ASM's' that 'for most citizens up north it's called "Hell-fare"'. As ever, though, the most powerful counter-discursive posts were more evidence-based, with many taking advantage of Twitter's retweet function to add extra information it was impossible to detail within its then 140-character limit. Symbolically self-christened 'nyeanne-bevan' (a reference to post-war Labour Minister Nye Bevan, the founder of the National Health Service) condemned 'rich gits' sitting at a 'Gov table that is probably worth twice' the £6,000 'taken away' from benefit-capped households, after retweeting a capitalized rant from 'Isabeau, #ScotsRef' reminding fellow tweeters that 'STEPHEN CRABB' was a '"COUNCIL HOUSE"

BOY WHO DIDN'T SUFFER "BEDROOM TAX" UNDER A LABOUR GOVT!' Similarly intertextual was the tweet from 'Fiona Kabuki' directing others to Crabb's 2014–15 parliamentary expenses claim for '£14,794 in accommodation costs', and contrasting this with his hypocritical edict that claimants must 'live on £20,000 a year for everything'. Crabb's predecessor suffered even more scabrous critiques, with Noel McGivern tweeting mockingly that 'Iain Duncan Smith weeping over the poor' was 'as convincing as a butcher crying over the poor lambs he is cutting up' and 'I Nobody' comparing 'IDS tearing up for Hislop' with the way 'Hitler cried for [his dog] Blondie'. Other counter-discursive tweets on this subject focused less on the ex-Minister than scrounger discourse itself. These varied from Paul Rogers' mild-mannered observation that 'our attitudes to the unemployed are still both patronising and Victorian' to an authoritative defence of the reputation of Labour Party co-founder Beatrice Webb by the Webb Memorial Trust as someone who, 'though far from perfect', had 'no time for notions of deserving v. undeserving poor', and several tweets wondering (in the words of '(((Keith)))') 'why does nobody talk about deserving or undeserving rich?'

Given the clear disparity between dominant Twitter sentiments sparked by more episodic versus thematic stories, as with the comment threads there are clear grounds for arguing that the way mediatized narratives are *framed* has a strong priming effect on public responses. Despite the oft-asserted bias of social media users towards liberal viewpoints (e.g. Rainie & Smith 2012), and the distinct constituencies generally served by Twitter and newspaper comment threads, it is revealing to note that such a strong *consensus* appears to exist between Twitter-users and (among others) *Mail* readers about the prevalence of scroungers. Turning this argument on its head, readers who post comments on the *Mail* or *Express* websites might be expected to broadly echo the worldviews these outlets espouse, not least because they have chosen to navigate to these specific sites, read their articles and post responses to them. Similarly, given the accessibility and increasing uptake of Twitter, those who choose to tweet on one story but not another are arguably less likely to be representative of tweeters per se than of particular 'ad hoc publics' *within* the Twittersphere (Bruns & Burgess 2011): i.e. the self-selecting minority who have (a) read or heard about a particular story and (b) decided to tweet about it.

In one sense, then, the fact that tweets about the Hort and Gavin families were disproportionately anti-welfare is only to be expected, if we assume that stories about *individualized* fecklessness are likely to appeal to a different constituency to those concerned with more macro-economic issues like that highlighted in the Centre for Cities study. As an indicator, both these stories received more extensive coverage in tabloid papers than other outlets, with the Horts' breaking in the unashamedly claimant-bashing *Express*. That the Duncan Smith story generated so many posts *defending* claimants and attacking his policies (on everywhere from Twitter to the threads of right-wing tabloids) might, at first, seem more surprising. However, it is less so when one considers that even conservative outlets generally slanted their coverage of his teary interview sceptically. Primed by a mix of carefully chosen screen-grabs and/or video clips, coverage of his televised performance invited a string of posts dismissing it as staged: 18 posters used the term 'crocodile tears' in the comment thread sample alone, while

Twitter spawned not only eight tweets vocalizing this term but a dedicated 'crocodiletears' hashtag.

Public responses to the benefit cap story were more intriguing, with a sharp divide discernible between a majority adopting a scrounger discourse on comment threads (365 or 56 per cent of the total) and almost exactly the opposite picture on Twitter, where 55 per cent of tweets were counter-discursive. In part, this reflects differences in the ways papers and social media framed this story. For example, the *Express* opened its report with a misleading portrayal of those facing the cut as idle, describing how Crabb had 'warned benefits claimants to start seeking work', before stating his department had 'published evidence that the Tory drive to cut the welfare bill' was 'working' (Hall 2016). Similarly, the *Mail*'s headline foregrounded Crabb's entreaty to claimants as a stark warning to 'find jobs or your handouts will be cut' (Finan 2016). It supported this line with a string of government quotes reviving misleading comparisons between the financial positions of taxpaying workers and the unemployed: specifically, the manipulatively emotive appeal to voters' ideas of 'fairness' contained in Osborne's statement that it was 'not fair' that 'people out of work' could 'earn more than people in work'.

This familiar alliance between traditional primary and secondary definers (mainstream newspapers and official/ government sources) contrasted starkly with the predominantly counter-discursive forces raising the same story on Twitter. These included *tertiary* definers, such as posters tagging their tweets with explicit (anti-establishment) affiliations, such as an 'I'm with Corbyn' logo and '@kiddycapfury' address, or the official account of Scotland's anti-welfare cuts Black Triangle

Campaign. This is not to say *Express/Mail*-style sentiments were entirely *absent* from Twitter: 'TIM @TheTimble' used the story to rail against '"Benefit Baby Machines" w/multiple kids', while 'Han @WeirdLittleHen' tweeted simply: 'agree with the new benefit cap. 20k untaxed is enough'. Nonetheless, the clear disconnect between the framing of this issue by the press on the one hand and Twitter-users on the other offered the clearest example of a discursive event that drew the attention of wholly distinct constituencies on the two platforms.

FROM SOCIAL MEDIA TO SOCIAL PREJUDICE: NORMALIZING 'SCROUNGER TALK'

The overwhelming picture to emerge from social media analysis, then, is a widespread acceptance of the existence (and persistence) of scroungers. From national and local comment threads to the supposedly more liberal deliberative space of Twitter, nearly four decades after Peter Golding and Sue Middleton anatomized the wave of 'scroungerphobia' mobilized to help cement the hegemonic neoliberal project, a widespread belief in (and aversion to) a sub-class of (anti-)citizens who refuse to 'play by the rules' of that economic system remains deeply ingrained. While there are *some* grounds for optimism about the emergence of counter-discursive voices (as periodically witnessed on Twitter), then, the 'shirkerphobia' of the Coalition years remains remarkably resilient and pervasive.

Chapter 5 begins the process of opening up an even wider exploration of the pervasiveness of scrounger discourse in today's public sphere, by exploring its increasing insinuation into press discourse beyond that directly concerned with 'the poor'.

CHAPTER 5

INCIDENTAL SCROUNGERS

NORMALIZING ANTI-WELFARISM IN WIDER PRESS NARRATIVES

Up to now, this book has concerned itself with examining the dominance of scrounger discourse in media-political narratives explicitly concerned with poverty. The true test of its normalization, however, is the measure of how far it has infiltrated into wider discursive domains beyond policy documents and newspaper articles about unemployment and social security – or the socially mediated forums accompanying and responding to them. This chapter extends our analysis of the agenda-setting output of Britain's national and local press to explore the extent to which news frames problematizing those who experience poverty have come to manifest themselves in articles whose focus, ostensibly, has nothing to do with them, such as stories about children, housing or crime. It demonstrates how often spurious or irrelevant details about the protagonists of such tales – for example, the fact that they are unemployed, claim benefits and/or live in social housing – are included as semiotic cues, primers or markers, to other them or add to existing frames that cast them as deviant.

The chapter further shows that, far from being the preserve of the national press, let alone tabloids, such 'incidental scrounger' narratives are even more commonplace in local newspapers. As a crude indicator, of a 'raw total'[3] of 957 print and online press articles published in 2016 in which the keyword 'antisocial' appeared, 877 (more than nine out of ten) appeared in provincial titles, the caveat being that it would be wrong to suggest *all* such articles concerned people on low incomes and/or benefits. Although the terms 'thug' and 'hooligan' proved relatively more popular in national than local papers (accounting for nearly three-quarters of all occurrences of the former and eight out of ten of the latter), 'yob' and 'vandal' occurred more frequently in the local press. Nearly six out of ten 'yob' articles and 80 per cent of those using the term 'vandals' appeared in locals.

One qualifier might be the fact that there are far more local papers than nationals. Nonetheless, the strong prevalence of articles concerning the issue of antisocial behaviour in the provincial press demonstrates the salience accorded to this subject across the UK, by publications ranging from weekly freesheets serving small market towns and their surrounding villages to major metropolitan evening titles. Moreover, when published in local papers, such tales often featured equally prominently, and were framed in much the same way, as in nationals. By casually, often prominently, incorporating references to unemployment or benefits in stories about drug abuse, alcoholism, violence, truancy and antisocial behaviour (ASB), such tales implicitly associated (even conflated) claimants, council tenants and other low-income archetypes with addicts, delinquents and criminals – conscripting 'welfare dependency' into montages of generalized deviancy.

FROM FECKLESS PARENTS TO FERAL KIDS: THE MANY FACES OF 'INCIDENTAL SCROUNGERS'

The articles forming the basis of this analysis were selected in two ways: from examples of 'incidental scrounger' narratives that emerged from datasets compiled for Chapter 3 and a separate series of Lexis searches using value-laden, pejorative terms relating to news themes that, based on previous research (e.g. Squires 2005; Morrison 2016a, 2016c), could be expected to yield evidence of scrounger discourse. The samples gathered using these search terms were grouped into four thematically linked datasets: 'problem family/ies', 'troubled family/ies' and 'problem parent'; 'single mother', 'single mum' and 'single parent'; 'yob', 'thug', 'hooligan' and 'vandal'; and 'antisocial'.

Once compiled, each dataset was scraped using a simple keyword search to group together all articles referring to one or more other terms commonly used in discourses concerning poverty. These included all the terms used for compiling Chapter 3's datasets – 'benefits', 'welfare', 'unemployed', 'jobless', 'workless', 'dole', 'claimant' and 'poverty' – in addition to others associated with low-income groups, such as 'social housing', 'estate', 'council house' and 'tenant'.[4] Of the Chapter 3 datasets, incidental scrounger narratives were negligible in all but three: 'benefits', 'unemployed' and 'jobless'. The latter two especially (both concerning people without jobs) included significant proportions of articles indirectly othering claimants, by associating their incomes/social statuses with criminality or other deviant behaviours besides dependency. In the case of the 'jobless' dataset, nearly half the 73 articles adopting some form of 'scrounger' frame (35) did so incidentally. This rose to 64 per cent of the 102 'unemployed' articles (65) incorporating scrounger discourse. The terms 'unemployed' and 'jobless', then, appeared to be favoured semantic cues in articles framing unemployment and/or welfare as concepts with *secondary* negative connotations beyond being shorthand for the inherently deviant conduct of claiming benefits itself: e.g. as corollaries for criminality.

While these proportions are striking in many ways, our purpose here is not to *quantify* how many 2016 articles adopted incidental scrounger frames, let alone what precise proportions these comprised of datasets assembled for this chapter using keyword associations outlined above. Rather, it is to analyse some *illustrative examples* of how words and phrases with welfare/unemployment-related connotations have a habit of manifesting themselves in narratives nominally about *other topics entirely* – especially when those topics also relate to behaviours considered morally problematic. A key argument is that the insidious creepage of scrounger discourse into articles ostensibly concerned with non-poverty/welfare issues is problematic precisely *because* of its insidiousness. This is not an issue of overwhelming prominence, let alone ubiquity: a diagnosis that would be grossly over-simplistic, particularly at a time when counter-discursive forces are clearly on the march (even if compromised and outflanked by a still largely hegemonic anti-welfare discourse). Rather, 'incidental scrounger' frames are a concern because they are not always immediately obvious. In fact, some are so well hidden, so *incidental*, that (once again) they might best be described as 'soft', rather than 'hard', in nature. It is the fact that they infiltrate such narratives *at all*, let alone as frequently or forcefully as they sometimes do, that should concern us. The argument is, then, that the more disguised and dishonest the scrounger discourse, the more normalized and malignant it becomes.

As with the various shades of scrounger discourse(s) identified in Chapter 3, clear patterns emerged from qualitative analysis of 'incidental scrounger' articles. With a few exceptions, they fell into the (at times overlapping) sub-categories we now explore.

'BREEDING SCROUNGERS': FECKLESS FAMILIES, PROBLEM PARENTS AND FERAL CHILDREN

A favourite 'problem frame' (Altheide 1997) for many articles incorporating stigmatizing references to benefit claimants (and the underclass) is that of 'troubled' or 'feral' families – as previously observed not only in relation to Britain (e.g. Macnicol 1987; Morrison 2016a, 2016b) but studies focusing on other countries, from Ireland (e.g. Devereux et al. 2011) to New Zealand (Beddoe 2015).

Of all datasets assembled for this chapter, the one containing the most overt incidental scrounger frames was that compiled using the terms 'troubled families', 'problem families', 'troubled parents' and 'problem parents'. This dataset inevitably captured numerous false positives: for example, articles concerned not with particular *types* of parent or household, but 'family troubles', 'parenting problems' or people with 'troubled family upbringings'. However, it also encompassed many pieces associating problematic family set-ups and/or parenting practices squarely with those living in poverty and/or claiming benefits. Given how often terms like 'troubled' or 'problem family' are associated with welfare dependency and feckless lifestyles by politicians, it was perhaps unsurprising to find that, when these terms appeared, they invariably did so in the context of claimants. A textbook example appeared in a prominent page 2 slot in conservative broadsheet *The Sunday Times* in January, under the glib headline, 'Parenting class vouchers to help problem families' (Shipman 2016b). Trailing a speech due to be made by then Prime Minister David Cameron the following day, the story opened with an intro decrying 'the scandal of problem families not knowing how to bring up their children', and wasted no opportunity identifying these 'problem' behaviours specifically with poorer households. Emphasizing 'official figures' indicating that 'families that break up' were 'twice as likely to experience poverty as families that stay together', it relayed how Cameron and wife Samantha hoped to make it '"aspirational"' for them to seek 'parenting classes'. The reporter described the initiative as 'an attempt to reach chaotic families such as those featured in the Channel 4 series *Shameless*, which portrayed life on a sink estate': a framing device underscored by an accompanying portrait of the fictional Gallagher family. This use of *individualizing* welfare discourses explored earlier was further underscored by a lengthy extract from the premier's speech (presumably leaked to this sympathetic paper by his advisors), describing families as 'the best anti-poverty measure ever invented' and 'a welfare, education and counselling system all wrapped up into one'.

A December article in *The Times* offered a similar master-class in the discourse of distancing state (and society generally) from any responsibility for inequality, while othering those who experience it: the idea that poverty was pathological. Headlined 'Depression genes "trap generations in poverty cycle"' (a term echoing Keith Joseph's 'cycle of deprivation' speech), it opened with the gleefully contradictory claim from 'an academic' that poverty was 'biologically entrenched', because 'people with a tendency to depression have children together and then fail to look after them properly' (Moody 2016). The story casually asserted that depressive tendencies were somehow both biologically inscribed *and* socially conditioned. It quoted the study's author, Holger Strulik, chairman of macroeconomics at the University of Gottingen in Germany, describing 'problem parenting' itself as the result of a 'neurobiological poverty-trap' caused by the fact that 'poverty causes stress, and stress causes depression for those individuals susceptible to depression', leading to 'families who are sufficiently poor and genetically susceptible to depression' investing 'less in their children' – thereby bequeathing 'both poverty and depression to the next generation'. Although acknowledging Professor Strulik's study was a 'theoretical paper' that had 'yet to be peer reviewed', and did 'not discuss specific genes or show that they are more common among poor people', the story only included this detail in the second half of its 557-word length – well below the sweeping statement that both 'genes and circumstances' making people 'more vulnerable to depression' were 'found in the most deprived parts of society'. Once more, then, 'problem families' were cast as a breed apart, a different species to the rest of us: denizens of an abject, separate underclass whose antisocial culture(s) were as likely to be genetically determined (and therefore irrevocable) as caused by social disadvantage. Fittingly, the article found space to consolidate the genetic argument by alluding to the similarly paradoxical conclusions of British scholar Adam Perkins, whose *The Welfare Trait* postulated that social security had 'created a social class that was genetically and psychologically "employment-resistant"' (see Chapter 3). As so often, it was also illustrated visually, in this case with a photo of a school-aged girl running away from the camera along an alley between drab back-to-back houses, symbolizing the 'sink estates' of the earlier *Sunday Times* piece.

'Problem family' narratives appeared to hold just as much fascination for local papers as nationals. A case in point was a 290-word, page lead-length October story in the *Fenland Citizen*, headlined, 'Dog poo found smeared over walls and windows after problem family evicted from Sutton Bridge council house'. Implicitly associating this deviant behaviour with social housing tenants, the story made only scant reference to any other (respectable) residents of the estate on which the incident took place – referring to their having 'thanked South Holland District Council's housing team' for evicting the culprits – while placing overwhelming emphasis on the damage done to taxpayer-funded property by vividly describing the errant family's 'doors and walls' being 'removed' and their garden 'littered and overgrown' (Ransome 2016). Significantly, its only quotes came from the local councillor responsible for housing policy, whose comments had the effect (if not intention) of generalizing from these individual acts of vandalism to implicate local tenants generally with antisocial behaviour. In an officious, verbatim quote running to five full paragraphs and 115 words (over a third of the story's length), councillor Christine Lawton pronounced that 'this case should send a strong message out that disruptive behaviour by our tenants will not be tolerated'. An equally stark illustration of hardwired poverty-associated 'problem family' narratives in the local press surfaced in a December comment in the *Yorkshire Post*: one of numerous articles spanning the gamut from news stories to background features prompted by the revelation, in a report by the House of Commons Public Accounts Committee, that a costly 'Troubled Families programme' launched by Ministers four years previously had failed to produce 'long-term sustainable change in families [sic] lives' (Yorkshire Post 2016). While heavily critical of the government's simplistic initiative, which focused on turning around 120,000 so-called 'dysfunctional families', the piece implicitly accepted the premise on which it was based: that 'troubled families' existed and were typically welfare-dependent. In a passage that might have been lifted wholesale from a government policy document or a paper from the Conservative Centre for Social Justice think-tank, it explicitly allied itself to former Work and Pensions Secretary Iain Duncan Smith's belief that it was 'important to wean people off benefits as they made the transition into regular employment', adding that it was 'also key that problem families do not return to their errant ways, such as an addiction with drugs, as soon as the support of local agencies is withdrawn'.

Another trigger-term frequently associated with stigmatizing representations of the unemployed, claimants generally and/or those living in social housing was 'single mothers'. Aside from articles *primarily* about claimants (to which the single mum tag was simply a convenient additional badge of deviancy), stories principally about lone mothers that wove in disparaging references to the fact they claimed benefits were plentiful. As a crude indicator of how widespread this association was, a keyword search of the dataset of 1,496 articles featuring the terms 'single mother', 'single mum' or 'single parent' (which will admittedly have contained duplicates) found 1,061 instances of the term 'benefits'. A classic illustration of the way irrelevant references to single mothers' claimant status were incorporated into stories ostensibly about other subjects entirely was a July *Mail Online* story carrying the lurid headline, 'Drunk single mother trashed an ambulance sent to help her after she was found sitting in the road at 7am after a night out' (Roberts 2016). This regaled readers with the spurious detail that its culprit 'claims employment and support allowance' (a fact which, given the stringency of then fitness-for-work tests used to determine individuals' entitlement to this benefit, ought to have been seen as signifying her status as a *deserving* claimant, rather than a scrounger).

There were also numerous articles, from full-blown features and comment pieces to short TV previews, focusing on the May 2016 ITV1 celebrity-led documentary *Myleene Klass: Single Mums on Benefits*. While some of these were critical of Klass' approach and/or the programme's underlying premise, they were invariably framed around the question of whether such parents 'really' had an 'easy life' or were 'living on the breadline' and mentioned the fact that the show featured 'self-proclaimed "Welfare Queen" Marie Buchanan': an unemployed single mother-of-eight who had 'caused outrage when she publicly declared her £26,000 benefits weren't enough' (*Coventry Evening Telegraph* 2016). In so doing, such pieces bolstered scrounger discourse, even if only by framing the programme as an exploration of the 'issue' of single mothers on benefits.

Similarly commonplace as narratives concerned with benefit-claiming 'single mums', 'problem parents' or 'problem families' were those specifically problematizing *children* from low-income households. Although not every article positioning young people as uncouth or thuggish in the 'yobs' and 'anti-social' datasets included semiotic cues with sufficient poverty or welfare-related connotations to be construed as promoting scrounger discourse, many did. In two of the most explicit conflations of council estates with crime, disorder and ASB, on 10 January both *The Sunday Times* and Northern Irish national *The Belfast Telegraph* reported (in similarly sweeping terms) Cameron's pledge to rid Britain of its 'worst sink estates', by razing to the ground '"brutal high-rise towers" and "bleak" housing' that (in the former's words) were 'often affected by gangs and drug use' (Shipman 2016a). As so often, both stories did as much to expose the wilful association of poverty and crime by *politicians* as to lay bare their own ideological agendas, by relaying how the policy announcement they were trailing (due the following day) would also promise to invest £70 million 'for relationship counselling for troubled families' foregrounded in the previously mentioned story about 'parenting class vouchers', published in the same day's *Sunday Times* (Shipman 2016b). Once more, this ill-defined term was squarely aligned with a specific social group, if not class: projecting a complex, multifaceted problem onto a feckless, antisocial, taxpayer-subsidized 'them' and distancing it from the hardworking, law-abiding, taxpaying 'us'. While the 502-word online *Belfast Telegraph* report at least included Cameron's acknowledgement that some council families could be virtuous – speaking, as he did, of 'warm and welcoming homes' found 'behind front doors' on some 'so-called sink estates' – it also reeled out his all too familiar refrain about 'entrenched' cultures of poverty; 'neglected' estates being the cause of England's 2011 urban 'riots'; and his broader, equally dubious, claim that 'decades of neglect' of tower blocks, with their 'brutal high-rise towers and dark alleyways', were 'a gift to criminals and drug dealers' that 'led to gangs and antisocial behaviour' (www. belfasttelegraph.co.uk 2016a).

Meanwhile, a 530-word October report on Welsh national news site *Wales Online*, under the headline, 'Residents concerned as gang of youths cause "havoc" in neighbouring town after being moved on by police', was one of many to highlight instances of *town centre* (rather than estate-bound) unruly behaviour, specifically in socially deprived post-industrial areas (Mears 2016). Though more measured in tone than some stories (including many local ones) and incorporating quotes from aggrieved locals as well as officials, the article opened with the image of a 'gang of youths' causing 'havoc' in Ton Pentre, and was liberally illustrated with photos, including an apparently staged rear-view shot of a group of shambling, hoodie-wearing teenagers. At the time, 14 per cent of adults living in Rhondda Cynon Taff, the local authority area encompassing Ton Pentre and another nearby town singled out for the 'seriousness' of its 'anti-social behaviour' (Treorchy), were receiving employment-related benefits (StatsWales 2016). A similarly lengthy story, published earlier the same month on the website of Scottish national the *Daily Record*, conjured up an equally baleful picture of a deprived suburb of Wishaw, North Lanarkshire: beginning with images of 'youths as young as 12, many fuelled by alcohol' terrorizing fellow residents of Coltness by 'running riot' and committing a litany of crimes and antisocial acts: 'assaults, underage street drinking, lighting fires in the woods, stealing wheelie bins, throwing stones at buses, shoplifting from Tesco, playing loud music, vandalising private property and entering the nearby building site and breaking machinery' (McKenna 2016). In 2016, Coltness was ranked one of the 10 per cent most deprived neighbourhoods in Scotland (North Lanarkshire Council 2017), and for anyone unaware of its status as an extended residential neighbourhood largely comprised of social housing, the story explicitly alluded to this; relaying how 'parents of the youngsters involved had their council tenancies threatened as a result of their children's behaviour' (an allusion to punitive ASB policies for local authority tenants discussed in Chapter 2).

As with articles explicitly using terms like 'troubled' or 'problem family', feral children archetypes appeared to hold an even keener fascination for local papers than nationals, with articles often running to considerable lengths, accompanied by alarmist headlines and images emphasizing the severity and/or depravity of incidents they relayed. A quintessential example of a local story conjuring up casual images of sink-estate youth disorder appeared in the *Hartlepool Mail* in September, under the headline, 'Vandals slammed after wrecking spree at playpark' (Kirby 2016). Constructing a classic opposition between 'worthy' and 'unworthy' ('good' and 'bad') juveniles (Morrison 2016a), the 457-word report told how 'angry residents' of a 'housing estate' had 'hit out at yobs' (subsequently identified as 'teenage vandals') who 'destroyed' ten 'semi-mature trees, worth about £2,000', and 'dislodged' an aluminium roof panel from 'a bandstand feature within the play area'. It missed no opportunity to dramatize the scale of the 'mindless attack', attributing it to 'a gang of up to 40 or 50 youths' who were 'spotted in the area' around the time it took place, and mobilizing emotive quotes condemning it from those most respectable of community spokespeople: the chairman of the residents' association and the local ward councillor. Of the two, Councillor Paul Beck, vice-chairman of Hartlepool Council's North and Coastal Neighbourhood, provided the choicest juxtaposition between law-abiding, civilized 'worthies' and law-breaking, feral 'unworthies', in relaying the fact that he had received 'lots of complaints' from 'young families living in the area' that their 'enjoyment' of 'an excellent community facility' was 'being spoiled by vandals'. His vow that 'such wanton damage' had to be stopped – a classic example of 'law-and-order' discourse (Hall et al. 1978) – was highlighted in large type beside the main article, and he and his fellow (respectable) community representatives were pictured surveying the damage in two accompanying photographs.

Though it made for undeniably lively news copy, much was journalistically amiss with this article. To begin with, no attribution was given for the sighting of the asserted 'gang' of youths. Nor was there any way of being sure, from scant details included, that the young people spotted in the area constituted a 'gang' in any definable sense or, indeed, 'youths' or 'teenagers', rather than young men (and, potentially, women). Yet, in evoking the image of a marauding mass of violent adolescents, the article provided a textbook illustration of 'juvenile panic' discourse (Morrison 2016a). Moreover, by going on to state that this was 'not the first time the gangs [plural] of vandals have hit', like so many narratives examined in Chapters 3 and 4, it drew on the trope of familiar strangers: shady-looking 'half-known figures we encounter in our daily lives' (Morrison 2016a: 1). The culprits in this case were cast as representatives of a feral underclass: disreputable denizens of the *same* 'estate' as (respectable) 'young families' whose 'enjoyment' of a park they had ruined. The 'gang' (real or imagined) was, then, an *anti*-community to the respectable one symbolized by the pictured dignitaries and 'excellent community facility' it had destroyed.

Comparable images of (feral) 'gangs' of rampaging 'yobs' or 'thugs' blighting (civilized) communities ran like a red thread through other local articles using linguistic cues like 'estate', 'council estate' or 'housing estate' to signify they were set in socially deprived areas. Stories of estates riven by myriad teenage hooligans appeared in papers the length and breadth of the country, from 'yobs' attacking taxi drivers in northern England ('Yob attacks on Bradford cab drivers lead to boycott of Holme Wood estate', *Bradford Telegraph and Argus*; 'Claims that cab drivers being targeted by stone-throwing yobs on Wirral estate',

Liverpool Echo) to 'gangs of youths' bombarding buses and cars in Hampshire with 'eggs, bricks, stones or glass bottles' ('Bus window smashed with rock just days after company threatens to boycott Southampton estate', *Southern Daily Echo*) to 'teenage yobs' who ruined a Christmas family event by shouting 'abuse and obscenities' at Santa ('Teenage yobs hurl abuse and obscenities at Father Christmas during sleigh parade', *Bolton News*) and 'schoolboy yobs', some 'as young as 11', who nearly killed a 'family cat' by repeatedly kicking it in a 'sickening street attack' in Paisley ('Family cat left to die after being kicked "like a football" by schoolboy yobs', *Daily Record*). Almost all these stories ran to several hundred words and were accompanied both by lurid headlines dehumanizing their culprits as 'yobs' or 'thugs' and abundant quotes from and/or pictures of (respectable) community representatives (residents, councillors, business-owners) representing the *human* face(s) of those victimized by these *bestial* forces. In so doing, news frames repeatedly defined these 'yobs', whether they were *of* the same community or invading from outside, in *opposition* to it: as anti-citizens to its citizenry; as invading or revolting savages assailing and affronting its civilized values.

Strikingly, in using these tales of crime and disorder to distinguish between civilization and savagery, some articles went further: placing less emphasis on the existence of this binary opposition *within the bounds* of the estate community than on defining *the estate itself* (and, by implication, its residents) *in opposition to* neighbouring communities and/or its wider surroundings. Locations where such disorderly outbreaks occurred were therefore marked out as *separate* from (and, by inference, antithetical to) the respectable, law-abiding world most people inhabited: the savage 'them' to the civilized 'us'. Skeggs (2004: 89) and others have examined how 'euphemistic transferences' that surface in public policy discourse, such as those juxtaposing 'inner-city schools' with the concept of 'good-enough children', and others 'highlighting, identifying and naming "sink estates" as the "worst housing estates"' can produce 'evidence' of 'an actual physical difference between the respectable and unrespectable, the deserving and undeserving'. In these newspaper narratives this was exactly what happened, with pictorial and linguistic cues used to emphasize the 'spatializing of difference' to draw 'boundaries' around those who 'need policing and containing', so 'the rest of respectable society' can be 'protected from their potentially disruptive, contagious and dangerous impact' (Skeggs 2004: 89). A stark illustration of this was the large photograph published across the top of the *Southern Daily Echo*'s story about the bus company boycotting a Southampton estate after a 'rock' was thrown at one of its vehicles' windows (Kusi-Obodum 2016). Rather than depicting aggrieved or sorrowful members of the community, or even the driver of the bus concerned, it instead showed an aerial shot of the offending estate (Millbrook), picked out from its surrounding area to symbolically define it in opposition to the rest of the city. Moreover, unlike in tales of assaults on festive community events or family cats, the only quotes included were from the bus company and police: local-level primary definers promoting authoritarian 'law-and-order' solutions (Hall et al. 1978) based on segregation and containment. Similarly, the story focusing on threats of a similar estate 'boycott' by Bradford taxi firms contained a string of quotes from angry driver Nadeem Iqbal (and several photos of him beside his cab) but no right of reply from anyone in the community (Mason 2016). With Iqbal branding the teenagers who attacked his car 'hooligans' and 'anti-social and aggressive kids with nothing better to do', while warning their parents to 'get your kids sorted or we won't be coming in', the effect of this framing was, once more, a 'spatializing of difference' that othered an entire neighbourhood (Skeggs 2004: 89). Similarly othering frames directed towards whole communities were discernible in numerous other stories, from a page lead-length *Manchester Evening News* court report that July about the jailing of 'teenage thugs' armed with 'meat cleavers and machetes', who 'robbed four cabbies' in Bury (Rucki 2016) to a September *Daily Record* story about a 'mum stabbed in the back by yobs' as she 'protected her daughter' on a Wirral estate (Fitzsimmons 2016). The latter varied the process of othering by defining the (supposedly) *respectable* locale in which this attack took place in opposition to its less salubrious surroundings, through the words of an unnamed 'neighbour' who described the 'gang of boys' blamed for it as coming from 'an outside area'. While once more calling to mind the familiar strangers paradigm – not least because other nameless residents were quoted as saying they had repeatedly 'noticed groups of youths in the park' – the article's generalized othering of a whole 'area' (and, by implication, its community) also strongly evokes social policy author John Macnicol's description of 'the concept of an inter-generational underclass' existing (socially and physically) 'outwith the boundaries of citizenship, alienated from cultural norms and stubbornly impervious to the normal incentives of the market, social work intervention or state welfare' (Macnicol 1987: 296). Moreover, a January *Lancashire Telegraph* story about 'three teenage yobs' convicted of being 'aggressive and threatening' towards train passengers contrived to other an entire (oft-stigmatized) social group, by labelling them as hailing from 'the travelling community': an irrelevant detail that would have breached clause 12 (ii) of the Independent Press Standards Organization's editors' code of practice had it described their race, colour or religion (IPSO 2017).

To give such articles their due, the recurrence of these feral youth archetypes might, on one hand, be seen to suggest that Britain is genuinely wracked with serious problems of youth disorder; or that, even if reporting of such incidents is overblown and they occur more rarely than journalists' portrayals imply, the phenomenon of teenage 'hooliganism' *exists*, at least as surely as in earlier generations (Pearson 1983). From a *discursive* perspective, though, the persistent associations between such folk-devils and certain kinds of neighbourhood (notably 'council estates', 'estates' and other kinds of urban mass-housing) and the length and prominence given to such stories testifies to a deeper level of signification: one that ascribes added newsworthiness to them when they can be aligned with popular conceptions of a feral underclass. Moreover, the repeated manifestation of unruly youths in news discourse *generally* suggests the social problem delinquency represents is considered a salient one from the point of view of papers' (imagined or actual) audiences. In other words, teenage deviancy is seen as a moral threat *familiar* enough to readers to be used to engage and enrage them for commercial gain.

ANTISOCIAL SCROUNGERS: VANDALS, 'YOBS' AND NIGHTMARE NEIGHBOURS

A related frame frequently used to shoehorn in 'incidental scrounger' discourse to articles ostensibly about other subjects was the broader problematization of antisocial behaviour, especially in relation to the classic 'yob-next-door' archetype of 'neighbours from hell' (Field 2003). Alcoholism, uncollected rubbish, loud music, graffiti and brawling in the streets were among myriad problem behaviours ascribed to low-income households in articles using trigger words like 'yobs', 'vandals' and 'antisocial'. To put it differently, stories nominally about these behaviours were often framed in ways that placed as much emphasis on the lowly social status of culprits as the distress or disorder their conduct caused.

A facet common to several such pieces was that, unlike in straightforward crime or court stories, it was not always simple descriptors like 'unemployed' or 'jobless', or even terms like 'benefits', that betrayed their incidental scrounger frames. Rather, this framing was often subtler (even somewhat disguised), with alternative signifiers of the culprits' poverty and/or claimant status instead used to trigger underclass/welfare associations. Such markers included an array of terms commonly associated with low-income working-class households, such as 'social housing', 'council house', 'council flat', 'council estate' or, simply, 'estate'. As in other cases, an object lesson in this approach appeared on *Mail Online*, in a story entitled 'Trail of filth left behind by "family from hell" as they are finally evicted after a 20-year reign of terror over their neighbours' (Spillett 2016). The story opened with an intro relaying how the 'family of yobs' left their council house 'with £50,000 worth of damage' after being 'evicted for terrorising their neighbours'. Nowhere did it explicitly mention that Tanya Skeldon or partner Shaun Trebilcock were unemployed or on benefits, but, amid all the colourful details about their 'fighting in the street with baseball bats, intimidating nearby residents, drug use, drug dealing and excessive shouting, arguing and swearing', the clear impression was given of an uncouth, dysfunctional family, described by a spokeswoman for their housing provider as having long been 'notorious' and creating 'an absolute nightmare' for fellow tenants. Meanwhile, perhaps the most intriguing article to adopt this association between ASB and council home-dweller was a *www.mirror.co.uk* report focusing not on a real-life case of hooliganism but a simulated incident of mass civil disorder to train members of the emergency services, set on an 'imaginary council estate' (Slater 2016). The story, published on April Fools' Day under the misleading headline 'Footage shows police being pelted with bricks and petrol bombs by "angry mob"', and accompanied by lifelike video clips of hooded rioters, burning vehicles and police officers in riot gear, only fully declared its hand in its third paragraph, with a punchline confessing the 'shocking scene of public disorder' was in fact 'part of a training exercise'. The way the *Mirror*'s website chose to package this story, though, only begins to unpack why this mock riot scenario was potentially pernicious. That the charade played out against the backdrop of a fictional 'council estate', rather than, say, a town centre (the focus of most real-world riots it was meant to be replicating) is significant, as it drew an implicit association between people living in social housing and the 'shocking' images of 'public disorder' it described.

Scrounger signifiers were not always so buried in ASB stories, however. Another *www.mirror.co.uk* piece reeling out the 'neighbour from hell' cliché – this time under the headline 'Yob allowed to keep his home as his victim was moved instead claims he's NOT "neighbour from hell"' – took only until paragraph two to introduce us to 'Jobless Daniel Davies' (Harris

2016). Similarly, a July story on *www.dailyrecord.co.uk* with the headline 'Yob who swallowed drugs to avoid being arrested by cops ends up spewing them up in police car, court hears' again took all of two paragraphs to tell readers that the 'brass-necked yob' of the title was 'Jobless Ian Grady' (Moore 2016). Only marginally more restrained was a December *www.liverpoolecho.co.uk* story, headlined 'Mum who bottled woman damaging her eyesight spared jail – because of her children; Drunk parents launched "disgraceful" unprovoked attacks on bar manager who now must wear glasses for the rest of her life' (Docking 2016). Though, unlike many others, this article could not be accused of frontloading details of the guilty couple's social status, when it finally came to describing their lifestyle it pulled few punches in depicting a dysfunctional family to rival that of Channel 4's *Shameless*, describing how 'jobless' Lyndsey Davies had 'mental health problems' and 'relied on benefits and her husband's income from "sporadic" work, to look after their children, aged two, five and 10'. Couched in different terms, this situation might have conjured up an image of an insecure, zero-hours existence familiar to many of the website's readers. Tucked so low down in a lengthy story heavily framed around the story of two 'drunk parents', though, it only added to an already hardwired portrait of barbaric abandon, particularly when contrasted with the heavy emphasis placed on Davies' lengthy prior criminal record, 'peppered with assaults and drunkenness'.

CRIMINAL SCROUNGERS: INCIDENTAL WELFARE FRAMES IN CRIME AND COURT STORIES

When claimants and social housing tenants were not being vilified for fecklessness, dependency, problem parenting, delinquency, vandalism and their supposedly all-round 'anti-social' lifestyles, they tended to make the news for an even more ignominious reason: outright criminality. Rapists, child-killers, kidnappers and class A drug-dealers were among the deeply unsavoury rogues' gallery of incidental scroungers to emerge from the sample – a trend especially prominent in articles in the 'unemployed' and 'jobless' datasets.

A feature of many such tales in national tabloids was to fore-ground terms like 'unemployed' and 'jobless' as glib, single-word descriptors for criminals (or, in many cases, *alleged* criminals), often at their very start. This suggests that, when it transpired that someone charged and/or convicted of a crime was unem-ployed or otherwise reliant on benefits, a high level of intrinsic newsworthiness was attached to this fact. By extension, the act of labelling an offender 'unemployed' or 'jobless' implicitly doubled-down on the deviancy ascribed to them. In repeatedly associating unemployment or welfare with crime (as some did), papers drew on both the manifest unsavouriness associated with criminals and the 'disgust' (Tyler 2013) separately directed towards feckless claimants. In other words, these two forms of deviancy fed off and consolidated each other: criminals (espe-cially petty ones) became *more* reprehensible, more deviant, because they were jobless; while, conversely, already abject *unemployed* people were rendered *more* abject (and objection-able) by their crimes.

A relatively restrained example of this approach was an April *Mail Online* story under the colourful headline, 'Unem-ployed man jailed for five years after plumbers found his Russian military pistol and silencer on top of his broken boiler' (Duell 2016). This objectifying approach to offenders who happened to be without work was a conspicuously standard approach in titles published by Associated Newspapers (owner of the *Daily Mail*). A grisly *Mail Online* story a month later, entitled, 'Man, 46, is charged with rape after "gentle and kind" widow in her 70s is brutally attacked in her own home', opened with a list of bullet-points, the first reading: 'Unemployed Jason Batchelor accused of raping elderly woman at home' (Matthews 2016). A similarly disturbing July story on the same site, headlined 'Dope-smoking thug who beat his girlfriend's toddler son to death during a drug and alcohol binge is jailed for life – as the mother gets six years for her role in the killing', also opened with the phrase 'an unemployed man' before describing how he 'murdered his girlfriend's 13-month-old toddler son' (Curtis & Baker 2016). And comparable conflations of unemployment with criminality appeared in articles that preferred the term 'jobless'. A *Mail Online* court story headlined 'Jobless mother-of-five denies urinating on town centre war memorial on the anniversary of the Battle of the Somme' lost no opportunity to emphasize her background as an abject claimant, opening with a bullet-point reading 'Jobless Kelly Martin, 42, was charged with outraging public decency' and an intro dismissing her as 'a jobless mother-of-five' (Moore & Joseph 2016).

A near-identical approach was observed in other tabloids. In a baleful tale of betrayed trust in the *Mail*'s mid-market rival, the *Express*, jobless criminals were openly reviled as the dregs of society, through the aegis of aptly named 'unemployed' chancer Daniel Money, whose family branded him the 'scum of the earth' for stealing 'his great-aunt's life savings', having first 'wormed his way into' cancer sufferer Gillian Kirk's 'affections' (Twomey 2016). Indeed, no tabloid, whatever its political stripe, was immune to the appeal of this approach: a July story published online by the supposedly left-leaning *Mirror* was headlined 'Jobless paedophile who pretended to be successful RAPPER to groom underage schoolgirls for sex jailed for 16 years' (Evans 2016). This 609-word report repeated its disquieting association of unemployment with child abuse by reiterating the descriptor 'jobless paedophile' at the start of its intro; including a liberal sprinkling of invectives like 'pervert' and 'predator'; and conjuring up an image of a socially maladjusted homeboy who, despite claiming to be 'a top rapper', was 'still living at home with his mum and dad' while sending '10,000 messages to children on social media, including Facebook and Instagram'. In so doing, the story offered up a perfect cocktail of 'jobless' deviancy, in the person of a sick layabout with infinite time to surf the web in pursuit of outlets for his distorted fantasies about juveniles (deviant ideas that would doubtless be tempered, if not transformed, if he mixed more with other people by entering the socially responsible world of work).

Of all local paper court stories (most concerning low-level offences like theft, affray or possession of class B drugs like cannabis), a handful stood out as particularly noteworthy, both in terms of the prominence they gave to the fact offenders were claimants and the level of imputed deviancy they ascribed to this fact. One such tale was a January report in the *Crawley Observer*, headlined 'Trio charged with GBH and kidnap after man found in stream with broken leg' (*Crawley Observer* 2016). Though it did not open with the word 'unemployed' as a single-word descriptor (unlike many similar national tabloid reports), it went out of its way to emphasize the jobless and/or homeless status of the three accused in a stilted second paragraph, listing them as 'Noel Goode, unemployed', 'Daniel Ellison, 24, unemployed, of no fixed address' and 'Jannai Quacoe, 24, unemployed, of no fixed address', as if this were the limit to their identities.

A more gruesome story placing similar emphasis on the unemployed status of its antagonist was published on *www.birminghammail.co.uk* in June, under the graphic headline 'Drunken killer who beat neighbour to death is jailed for life' (Larner 2016). Its opening paragraph reiterated the word 'drunken' (this time paired with 'thug'), while both the second and third began with the word 'unemployed'. In adopting this repetitive approach, the article drummed in an association between unemployment and not one but two deviant behaviours: extreme violence and drunkenness. Meanwhile, a February crime story in the *London Evening Standard*, headlined 'Jailed: Unemployed fraudster who conned victims out of at least £40,000 to fund jet-set lifestyle', went to even greater lengths to conflate its culprit's claimant status with criminality, implicitly drawing on popular myths associating the very act of drawing benefits with abuse of the system (Bullen 2016). Though the crime concerned was not a bogus *benefit* claim, by dwelling on the incongruous spectacle of this 'unemployed man' living a 'luxury lifestyle' of 'Dom Perignon champagne', 'business-class flights' and 'plush hotel stays in Dubai', this picaresque tale mobilized not just straightforward scrounger discourse but trigger-words (e.g. 'fraudster' and 'swindled') typically used to align the unemployed with cheats.

So where do all these distorted, episodically framed newspaper portrayals leave us? Statistically, there *is* a certain amount of impartial evidence to suggest that 'problem' parenting, ASB and many forms of crime more often occur in low-income neighbourhoods than affluent ones (e.g. Home Affairs Committee 2010). Seen in this light, it is perhaps not *so* surprising (or unjust) that so much attention is paid to stories about delinquency and disorder on council estates and in other poorer neighbourhoods by newspapers – or, indeed, by politicians and the public. But even if it is hard to argue that the overall *amount* of coverage of crime and misdemeanours involving people on benefits or living in social housing is disproportionate, there can be little justification for the *nature and tone* of much of this output: specifically, the disparaging, value-laden language, imagery and other framing devices it uses. How is it justified (let alone necessary) to accompany a story about such serious social issues as truancy, neglect or family breakdown with a photo of the fictional Gallagher family from Channel 4's *Shameless*? What does this do but, at best, trivialize such issues, and, at worst, turn people caught up in difficult and challenging circumstances (admittedly perhaps connected to, if not caused by, their material poverty) into a grotesque freak-show inviting our ridicule and disgust? Similarly, what purpose is served by demonizing young people who upset or intimidate their (respectable) neighbours as 'thugs' or 'yobs', other than to obscure the causes of complex forms of social disorder: casting marginalized citizens, and the 'antisocial' antics a minority of them indulge in, as *causes*, rather than *symptoms*, of often lamentable social disadvantage? What goal can be served by a story about vandalism or disorder on a housing estate only quoting outraged councillors, police officers, bus company owners or other 'official sources' (Fishman 1980), while excluding the voices of the many *blameless* local residents and emphasizing the spatial (and, by inference, moral) separateness of their communities, other than to stigmatize whole neighbourhoods as a 'darkest England' (or Wales or Scotland) inhabited by a wild and deviant 'them' antithetical to the civilized collective 'us'? What relevance do details in court stories telling us that defendants are unemployed, claim benefits or are travellers or 'gypsies' have, other than to consolidate our impression that they are morally deviant, by associating or conflating their class and low-income status or even culture with criminality and a refusal to respect societal norms? In sum, articles associating 'problem families', 'neighbours from hell' or 'feral teenagers' with poverty and/or social security seldom begin to offer an analysis of any underlying conditions that might help explain their 'deviancy' – let alone acknowledge that these may be structural (even global) in origin, rather than the result of personal, pathological failings.

What this short chapter hopes to have achieved, then, is to add another dimension to our understanding of how scrounger discourse has come to be normalized and reproduced in the public sphere, through an intertextual process which involves anti-welfare frames being imported into, and naturalized in, narrative contexts that nominally are not even concerned with poverty or 'the poor'. The encroachment of anti-welfare frames into articles explicitly concerned with poverty and/or benefits is one thing, but when scrounger discourse promoted by ideologically driven politicians and commercially opportunistic newsmakers insinuates itself into stories that have (or *should* have) little or nothing to do with it, the process of normalization reaches a new, more divisive and disturbing, level. What, then, can we do to contest, and ultimately reverse, this normalizing process? It is to this question, above all others, that we turn in our conclusion.

FROM DIVISION TO UNITY

A MANIFESTO FOR REBUILDING TRUST

Stigmatization of Britain's 'undeserving' poor has a long and ugly history. Centuries before the word 'scrounger' became a lightning-rod for repeated reimaginings of a supposed rump of no-hopers content to wallow in shameless dependency, Medieval monarchs, the Church and other early definers were already drawing qualitative distinctions between 'god's poor and the devil's' in their efforts to buy the loyalty of 'good subjects', maintain public order and, in time, martial fit, obedient, productive workforces and military (Golding & Middleton 1982: 9). Fourteenth-century narratives about the 'mobile poor', 'sturdy beggars' and 'vagabonds' were foretastes, then, of a continuum of popular archetypes that would run through the discourses of ensuing generations. They share a common cultural DNA with later mythologies about 'paupers', 'idlers' and the 'shirkers' of today, while also resurfacing in debates about how to cure or *deal with* an imagined wider anti-citizenry – variously defined as the 'residuum', 'social problem group' or 'underclass'.

A thread linking these various iterations of 'scroungers' is an enduring suspicion about the sincerity and motivations of all members of society professing to have little or no viable means of supporting themselves: in today's parlance, those 'taking out' of the system without 'putting in'. Recent moral panics about the supposed undeserving mass who shirk their duties to 'contribute' have singled out as touchstones benefit claimants, especially the unemployed. But, as Chapter 2 illustrates, in late modern Britain the finger of suspicion has extended to all manner of other 'economically inactive' groups, from disabled people to vagrants, travellers and the Roma. Depending on the specific media-political backdrop of the day, multifarious enemies within (or, indeed, *without*) have consistently emerged to assume the dubious 'scrounger' mantle. As Chapter 3's analysis of newspaper frames demonstrates, the run-up to and aftermath of the UK's 2016 referendum on its continued European Union membership saw concerted magnification, in tabloid papers especially, of asserted threats posed to the wellbeing of native citizens and their hard-pressed public services (already ravaged by austerity) by freeloading foreigners popularly constructed as 'benefit tourists'.

A second consistent strand of scrounger discourse, particularly since the late 19th century, has been the repeated reconstruction of poverty as pathological; the fault of 'them', not 'us'. According to this (at times brutally othering) thesis, social 'deprivation', 'disadvantage', 'exclusion' or any of numerous other euphemisms for inequality are ultimately the outcome of deviant inherited characteristics endemic to natives of an alien, socially inferior, 'culture' of poverty. These include inter-generational worklessness, abject antisocial behaviours and dependency on charity and, latterly, state-directed handouts. At the heart of this conception of 'the poor', then, is an us-and-them discourse which problematizes the unemployed, homeless and others receiving alms or benefits as disgusting, inhuman figures who are beyond hope. Moreover, in denying the systemic factors contributing to poverty, by blaming the victim, such discourses not only legitimize our collective failure to address it: they enable elites to repeatedly ration or conditionalize social assistance, while demonizing or even *criminalizing* its recipients.

The ever broader brush-strokes used to tar larger, more diverse swathes of our fellow citizens with the stain of the scrounger has been mirrored in a diversification of the discursive arenas in which these pervasive archetypes are (re)constructed. In today's fluid, participatory online news sphere, as Chapter 4 shows, we are witnessing much more than the mass production and *consumption* of anti-welfare narratives (though that is certainly happening). Rather, the digital news environment has become a bubbling, multidirectional discursive interface in which journalists and their (agenda-led) sources are involved in a process of narrative negotiation and *co-production* with 'audience members'. People who post their own opinions, and testimony, to comment threads or wider social media are not passive observers or consumers of discourse: they are active participants in its construction, validation and reproduction in the public sphere. And the ubiquity of the scrounger has become such that this odious phantom now extends even further afield, creeping into narrative contexts to which he/she/it ostensibly has no relation. As Chapter 5 demonstrates, scroungers rear their heads, incidentally, in articles with no intrinsic relevance to subjects like poverty or welfare: stories about juveniles, crime and antisocial behaviour routinely including claimants among their casts of stock characters and/or focusing on borderline irrelevant details that allow their protagonists to be slotted into the scrounger mould. This is to say nothing of the many ongoing manifestations of scrounger discourse in popular culture, from *The Jeremy Kyle Show* to *Benefits Street*. Moreover, the extreme, atypical caricatures so often put up for public spectacle, and framed as *typifying* a feckless, feral underclass, both reflect and reinforce the paradoxical tension between our *appetite* for abject archetypes as sources of freak-show infotainment and our *disgust* at the deviant values they are held to manifest.

But the insidiousness of today's lingering throwback to 1970s 'scroungerphobia' penetrates deeper even than this. As our critique of more *counter*-discursive newspaper frames and social media posts suggests, even in contexts where scroungers are explicitly *absent* they are often implicitly *present*, thanks to the conspicuous omission of certain (undeserving) groups from the 'deserving' ones that countervailing voices defend. In Chapters 3 and 4, we observed how the much-heralded amplification of counter-claims since the latest highpoint of scrounger discourse (2013) had been overstated. On one hand, our analysis of newspaper frames and social media sentiment *does* support the assertion that sweeping misrepresentations of 'the poor' are increasingly being questioned – and the suffering of low-income groups during a period of ongoing welfare and wider public-spending cuts is finally being publicized. Yet it also found that politicians, charities, pressure groups, journalists and news outlets that had latterly taken up the cause of those forced to choose between food and fuel often confine themselves to championing groups based on their own narrow campaign agendas, or those most easily framed as deserving: from pensioners and children to poverty-paid workers trapped in cycles of insecure zero-hours contracts, usurious pay-day loans and morale-sapping visits to foodbanks. All these groups indisputably merit sympathy, and our anger and agitation at the deregulated, exploitative economic system that has caused their suffering. However, the problem with mounting such selective, *single-issue* counter-discourses is that, by not standing up for *all* those experiencing poverty (in, lest we forget, one of the world's ten largest economies – Gray 2017), they implicitly endorse the divide-and-rule discourses of those who *intentionally* separate out everyone not falling into neat, self-evidently worthy categories, such as the unemployed. One of many ironies about George Osborne's pernicious polarization of the (deserving) early-hours 'shift-worker' and the (undeserving) neighbour 'sleeping off' a 'life on benefits' was his denial of the fact that many shift-workers are as likely to spend 'a life on benefits' as those without work, such is the job insecurity and wage stagnation wrought by the unfettered free markets he championed.

Another undermining aspect of the 'soft' counter-discursive approach is its unhelpful contribution to the muddy *political* framing of various sub-categories of (socially deserving) actors glibly labelled 'vulnerable'. While it has long been judged acceptable to *problematize* those living in financial and material poverty related to unemployment, homelessness and (asserted) sickness and disability, terms like 'the vulnerable' or 'most vulnerable in our society' are routinely used to defend sweeping groups, like pensioners, many of whom are far from socially or economically disadvantaged. An extension of this principle is the tendency for politicians to portray pensioners as *uniformly* deserving recipients of social security, regardless of financial need; whether they have debilitating illnesses or disabilities; or even whether their OAP status *necessarily* means they have all, *ipso facto*, contributed sufficiently to the National Insurance pot during their working lives. In this vein, premier-in-waiting Cameron's 2010 'invitation to old people' to vote Conservative repeatedly equated pensioners with contributing citizens who, *by definition*, had 'worked hard all their lives' (Cameron 2010).

Moreover, when Opposition politicians dare to publicly question the direction of 'welfare reform', they invariably choose highly selective 'vulnerable' groups as the locus for their concerns. Hence, in June 2011 then Labour leader Ed Miliband framed his assault on the Coalition's then latest plans to cut disability-related benefits as a defence, specifically, of recovering cancer patients – a diverse group of people he glibly asserted had 'worked hard all their lives, done the right thing' and 'paid their taxes' (quoted in Wintour 2011). Less than two years later, at the height of shirkerphobia, he and his Shadow Work and Pensions Secretary, Liam Byrne, used a proposed 1 per cent working-age benefits freeze as an opportunity to align themselves with the 'hardworking' households of popular folklore: framing it as a 'strivers' tax' and an assault on hardworking families (Byrne 2013). Though this time Miliband implicitly extended the catchall term 'most vulnerable' to defend seldom-championed groups, including the unemployed, he avoided mentioning them explicitly (Miliband, E. 2013). Pointedly, Byrne used the same soundbite to ally himself with *workers* on benefits; emphasizing that the cap would hit Working Tax Credits, and lamenting Labour's image as the party of 'shirkers not workers' (quoted in Hall 2013).

Such mealy-mouthed defences of 'the vulnerable' are, then, rhetorically inadequate for debunking scrounger myths. By (implicitly) exempting this group or that from defences of 'vulnerable' people – or, worse, explicitly *buying into* aspects of scrounger discourse, by tortuously triangulating their policy prescriptions – they present conflicted cases that crumble under relentless attacks from those with no qualms about promoting anti-welfare narratives. As observed in numerous studies of othering discourses, hegemonic constructions of social reality come about not only through the united determination of elite actors to drown out dissenting voices, but also the compromised or conflicted counter-claims mounted by critics. Thus, at the height of shirkerphobia, Labour diluted its counter-arguments by accepting a Conservative-led reframing of social security as almost solely a reward for (previous) hard work, payment of taxes and National Insurance contributions: in sum, a history of putting in, rather than taking out. Under Byrne's successor, Rachel Reeves, Labour also recast itself as harder on benefit tourism than the Tories, by pledging to refuse new EU migrants working-age benefits for up to four years after their arrival in Britain. Speaking to *The Sun on Sunday* in August 2014, Reeves argued it 'isn't right' that 'somebody who has worked hard all their lives' and 'contributed to the system' is 'entitled to only the same as somebody who has just come to this country' (quoted in Woodhouse 2014).

Such approaches implicitly suggest deserving claimants are only those who are both 'vulnerable' *and* have 'worked hard all their lives', along with the fallacy that this category and its antithesis (those Osborne cast as spending a 'life on benefits') are mutually exclusive. Yet this false dichotomy masks the harsh reality that today's insecure labour markets leave numerous 'hardworking households' experiencing frequent spells of unemployment, as they drift between low-paid, part-time, short-term and/or zero-hours jobs. In other words, it denies the inconvenient truth that it is possible (even usual) for one and the same person to be *both* hardworking *and* unemployed. And this is to say nothing of the many who 'worked hard all their lives' until the seismic market reforms of the 1980s consigned them to unemployment.

It is often argued that, if there is one last acceptable prejudice in contemporary Britain, it is homophobia. Yet with significant advances in LGBT rights at long last having been achieved (including under Cameron's Coalition), there is a strong case for arguing that this dubious mantle would more accurately be applied to *social*, or *class*-based, stigmatization. Othering people based on the way they speak or dress, what they do for a living and (most of all) whether they are unemployed and/or claim benefits has become so disturbingly socially acceptable that it is only now being recognized as an issue. For this reason alone, it remains a long way from being adequately addressed.

INSECURITY, ALIENATION AND SOCIAL DISTRUST: SCROUNGERS AS FAMILIAR STRANGERS

A connecting thread between the successive historical manifestations of 'scroungers' this book explores has been their reappearance and/or magnification in popular discourses at pinch-points when the prevailing order of the day (and dominant value system sustaining and reproducing it) has been threatened. Precise contextual reasons for these outbreaks of elite/societal insecurity have varied hugely: ranging from pressures caused by population growth, economic competition or warfare to environmental catastrophe. As abundant literature testifies (e.g. Hall et al. 1978; Cohen 2002), when such disruptive events or forces are at work, the default positions of struggling elites is to retrench and build barricades: often by constructing (or resurrecting) phantom foes. These phantoms can serve as short-term diversions, to distract from elites' own culpability for a situation (or their impotence to solve it), or as longer-term, hegemonic instruments of social control.

For phantom foes to succeed they must be plausible, and plausibility requires them to be recognizable. This is where familiar strangers come in: abject and untrustworthy archetypes that, in the case of 'scroungers', can easily be projected, via podium, pulpit and popular press, onto any number of unkempt-looking, uncouth-seeming others we pass or glimpse as we go about our lives. But defining plausible familiar strangers is only part of the process of myth-making needed to construct a durable discourse. To mobilize the full weight of public opprobrium against an identified foe also requires the threat it poses to be magnified. Moreover, for battles against phantom foes to offer the hope that security, stability and morality might be *restored*, the foe must be assailable; and what foe could be easier to overcome (and subjugate) than that with the least resources to defend itself?

As Chapter 1 demonstrated, the scrounger-bashers of history used every megaphone at their disposal to demonize and objectify the 'undeserving poor' of their day: from the language and imagery of Christian sermonizing and pagan superstition to the moralizing of the Victorians to the alternately infantilizing and criminalizing discourses that problematized the 'residuum' and 'underclass', to the 'hardworking', 'taxpaying', 'play-by-the-rules' orthodoxies of neoliberalism. The shadow of the Black Death saw the 'mobile poor' demonized to aid the conscription of almost anyone capable of standing into the service of a country on its knees after a near-apocalyptic loss of life and land. The global competitive pressures underpinning Elizabeth I's mercantilist policies saw the revival of earlier panics about the 'sturdy beggar' into finely honed distinctions (weaponized by statute) between those even the Tudors conceded were of little practical use to their expansionary hegemonic project – the orphaned, chronically sick or elderly 'impotent' – and the 'rioters, vagabonds and the idle' lumped together as 'thriftless' (Golding & Middleton 1982: 10). And successive later 'crises' saw politician, preacher and press baron unite to, by turns, castigate, coerce and criminalize 'idlers' and 'shirkers': through the mass-mobilization of workers needed to oil the cogs of the Industrial Revolution to the mass-conscriptions of soldiers to defend Britain's dwindling imperial interests throughout the 19th and early 20th centuries. By the 1970s, decades of social security consensus, underpinned by relatively stable economic conditions, began to fracture, against a backdrop of growing global instability and mounting industrial unrest. It was this socially tensile atmosphere that gave us 'scroungerphobia': a mounting moral panic discourse widely promoted by politicians and the news media, but critiqued in the wider realms of popular culture, through the social-realist films of Ken Loach, Alan Bleasdale's *The Boys from the Blackstuff*, and memorably counter-discursive TV plays like *The Spongers* (1978), *Dog Ends* (1984) and Alan Bennett's *The Insurance Man* (1986).

What, then, in our current epoch, is responsible for resurrecting the scrounger again, this time in the guise of that baleful post-millennial familiar stranger: the 'shirker'? As a starting-point, various seminal studies have argued that the late modern, post-industrial West is best understood as a 'risk society' (Beck 1992), characterized by generalized jitteriness, even panic, that reaches beyond the more limited (but definite) panics of the past (see Cohen 2002). The late sociologist and philosopher Zygmunt Bauman (2000: 116 and 113) developed this thesis to fine-tune the problem of 'liquid modernity': a fluid, more socially atomized way of living and interacting with our fellow citizens (locally and globally), fostered by 'software capitalism' and the accompanying fragmentation of previously solid bonds represented by neighbourhood community networks and other traditional socioeconomic structures, such as trades unions and co-ops. One aspect of this uncertain new age – evident in today's daily communications with people we never physically meet, in the placeless dialogical spaces of email and social media – is that, while we may feel increasingly devoid of tangible real-world community ties, we are more likely than ever to regularly interact with 'strangers' (Bauman 2000: 94–109).

This conceptual framework is key to understanding the revolution in social relations, both vertical (hierarchical) and horizontal (peer-to-peer), that both foster and are fostered *by* neoliberalism. And it is neoliberalism, and the deregulated and depersonalized social framework it engenders, that most contributes to (and depends on) the repeated reconstruction of familiar strangers. Perhaps the most corrosive and damaging symptom of an economic system which fractures previously solid interpersonal relations; disperses individuals who once belonged to situated communities; and ushers in an anarchy of deregulated, globalized 'software capitalism' devoid of the long-term, full-time, nine-to-five certainties of the past is that, in atomizing neighbourhoods and networks, it risks breaking the bonds of social trust. The literature on the slow-burn erosion of trust over the past 40-plus years in neoliberal states is so extensive as to require little introduction. To give a flavour, numerous studies have identified corollaries between high levels of social inequality and economic insecurity found in liberal free-market societies like Britain's and declining trust between individuals, families and communities (e.g. Hall 1999; Harper 2001; OECD 2001; Li et al. 2005; *World Values Survey* 2015; LLAKES 2011). A 2001 report by the Centre for Educational Research and Innovation found the proportion of UK residents professing to 'generally trust others' plunged by half (from 60 to 31 per cent) between 1959 and 1995 (OECD 2001: 101). Moreover, by 2005 levels of 'general trust' towards 'other people' (a broad group embracing almost anyone we encounter outside our immediate circles) had dropped yet another percentage point, compared to its relative consistency in 'social market' countries like France and the Netherlands, and in stark opposition to the high levels of social capital in 'social democratic' Scandinavian societies (LLAKES 2011: 3). Yet more damningly, a processual study by the political scientists Bo Rothstein and Eric M. Uslaner (2005: 45) used statistical tests to demonstrate that 'the causal direction' between socio-economic inequality and declining trust 'starts with inequality'. Individual case studies support these conclusions, while (in some) specifically relating the trust/distrust equation to policies and discourses concerned with 'the poor'. A recent study by another political scientist, Cecilia Guemes (2017: 18), focusing on 'neoliberal welfare reforms and trust' in Argentina, argued that 'welfare policy framings, discourses and tools can negatively impact social trust'. Guemes builds persuasively on the idea that dwindling trust in neoliberal states *facilitates* the demonization of 'welfare' recipients, to suggest that the sequence at work is more a circuit than a straight line: distrust becomes both a *product* of anti-welfare discourse and its cause.

The discourse of 'scroungers' and 'shirkers' is, then, the product of a *nexus of neoliberalism*. As Guemes and others demonstrate, the language and imagery used to demonize, other, mark and inscribe claimants are themselves neoliberal constructs. More significantly, though, the societal *causes* and conditions that enable these discourses to take root and flourish are also neoliberal: individualism, ever-widening economic inequalities, market liberalization, rising financial and personal insecurity and the resulting slow-burn collapse of interpersonal trust. Onto this backdrop those keen to obscure the underlying structural imbalances and injustices that have engendered these processes – and/or to deflect blame from those responsible (including themselves) – can project montages of hazily defined, yet plausibly *familiar*, strangers. Beyond the ongoing socio-political context of post-crash austerity, the concepts of 'abject figures' (Tyler 2013) and familiar strangers offer useful paradigms for conceptualizing the ever more 'liquid' (Bauman 2000) and malleable forms into which today's folk-devils are moulded. It is the task of those hoping to restore social cohesion and break free from the tyranny of 'government *for* the market, rather than of the market' (to paraphrase Foucault et al. 2008) to expose these straw-men enemies as the empty vessels they are.

However, before we move on to more optimistic terrain, by considering how the durability of scrounger myths might be overcome, it is worth pausing to consider how truly *ideological* shirkerphobia discourse can be said to be. A common refrain when George Osborne was Chancellor was that he was ideologically wedded to cutting the size and scope of the Welfare State as a tool for engineering a 'hegemonic' project that would cement the political supremacy of 'The New Normal' the Conservatives sought to establish in power (Spours 2015: 12). It was the emerging 'New Normal' Labour's David Miliband confronted as he fought through howls of laughter from the Tory benches to denounce the 'rancid' cuts in the 2013 Benefits Uprating Bill and condemn the 'dividing-line politics' Osborne had used to '"frame" the debate' through a process of 'invent your own enemy' and 'spin your campaign to a friendly newspaper editor', in his 'intolerable' attempt 'to blame the unemployed for their poverty and our deficit' (Miliband, D. 2013). Similarly, a *Guardian* Editorial sparked by that year's Budget despaired that Ministers were 'succeeding on an unprecedented scale' in an 'ideological crusade to reduce the role of the welfare state' (*www.theguardian.com* 2013). And such prognoses were not confined to Opposition benches or liberal papers. Towards the end of his spell in coalition, Liberal Democrat Deputy Prime Minister Nick Clegg leapt on Osborne's statement that a planned further £12 billion cut to the benefits budget would leave Britain's welfare system 'permanently smaller' to accuse him of being 'driven' by 'two very clear ideological impulses': to 'remorselessly pare back the state' and ensure 'the only section of society which will bear the burden of further fiscal consolidation are the working-age poor – those dependent on welfare' (quoted in Dominiczak 2014). By contrast, an insightful paper published the following year by Labour think-tank Compass warned that the reality of Osborne's strategy for conquest (and the challenges it presented to the Left) was more 'complex' than his popular caricature as a 'neo-liberal ideologue [sic]' implied (Spours 2015: 12). It argued that (whatever his underlying motives) Osborne was engaged in a process of neo-Blairite triangulation involving a combination of 'consensus and coercion': in essence, 'manufacturing consent'

(Herman & Chomsky 1988). By appropriating Labour policies (and language) with proposals for a 'National Living Wage' and 'Northern Powerhouse' to address the economic imbalance between North and South, while also plotting 'the next stage of market-centred social and economic liberalisation' (Herman & Chomsky 1988), he was busily constructing a 'new centre of British politics' (quoted in Wintour 2015).

Whatever the true mix of hard-line political beliefs and hard-nosed pragmatism informing Osborne's quest for 'supremacy' (Spours 2015), it was undoubtedly assisted by neoliberal ideology in several important respects. In his relentless drive to cut Britain's deficit, he (like many European counterparts) became wedded to what Nobel Prize-winning economist Paul Krugman branded 'the austerian ideology': a determination to balance the books regardless of the casualties created in the process, backed by a misguided 'doctrine of expansionary austerity' which counterintuitively argued that swingeing spending cuts boosted consumer and investor confidence, promoting economic growth (Krugman 2015). In making deliberate political choices to cut this departmental budget rather than that, Krugman argued, the Tories were acting in an *implicitly* ideological way: exploiting the opportunity offered by a new continental consensus on austerity to pursue long-held instincts. By fuelling and mobilizing a 'hard right turn in elite opinion, away from concerns about unemployment', Ministers used 'the alleged dangers of debt and deficits' as 'clubs' to 'beat the welfare state and justify cuts in benefits' (Krugman 2015).

Ideology also entered the equation in another respect. As this book's newspaper analysis demonstrates, anti-welfare discourse continues to dominate popular portrayals of claimants, and the agenda-setting effects of both this and the political rhetoric that stokes and echoes it can also be seen in sentiments expressed about news stories and related issues by their 'audience members' online. Ideology relies on language (lexical *and* visual) to gain expression, but it is the *act* of expressing it that manifests it. This is why, in a nutshell, discourse *matters*: it is through the discursive *process* that social relations of power and identity, including ones explicitly or implicitly problematizing particular groups, are negotiated, affirmed and reproduced. As Fairclough (1992) has consistently argued – including in the context of the discourse of (New Labour) 'welfare reform' policy – by asserting, accepting and repeating discursive practices, social actors (including the public) normalize the truths they are held to enshrine. And when discourse promoted by politicians and the news media becomes increasingly enmeshed with normative truth-claims and imaginaries reflected in wider popular culture (for instance 'poverty porn' TV shows) this intertextual process helps solidify ever more dominant constructions of social reality, as the different discursive sites become reciprocally reinforcing. In this respect alone, whatever the individual or collective *motivations* of newspaper editors and their sources for promoting scrounger discourse, in doing so they are articulating, and legitimizing, an ideology. More prosaically, even if their principal motive for dramatizing tales about benefit-scroungers and invading welfare tourists is simply to sell papers and drive online traffic, they are *still* acting ideologically, in that they are prioritizing an implicitly neoliberal goal of profit over balance, truth and public interest. And let us not forget that dominant, endlessly repeated, discourses can have serious real-world consequences. As criminologist Jon Burnett argues, in a chilling 2017 critique of Britain's post-crash 'discourse of hate', 'when resentment to welfare and free movement is legitimised, hate becomes normalised'. In real-world terms, this has led to 'certain forms of violence' being 'intensified under the rubric of austerity', as testified by 'campaign groups, support centres and self-organised networks' and 'one in six' disabled people who reported 'being verbally or physically assaulted' in terms parroting 'scrounger rhetoric' in a 2015 Disability Hate Crime Survey (cited in Burnett 2017). If any statistic should embolden us to take on 'the discourse of hate', exposing its lies and distortions, it is surely this.

TOWARDS RESTORING TRUST

In arguing for the persistence of scrounger discourse, this book risks appearing pessimistic. It is not. There is no doubt that, compared to five years ago, we are in a better place. The very *existence* of a fast-building (if broad) 'anti-cuts' sentiment, and the focus of many counter-claims-makers on exposing the suffering of those experiencing poverty (however selectively defined), smacks of progress. Similarly encouraging is the apparent softening of public opinion towards the unemployed displayed in recent British Social Attitudes surveys, perhaps fuelled by the fact that, while the headline 'unemployment rate' is at its 'lowest since 1975' (ONS 2017c), more people are experiencing *bouts* of joblessness than ever in today's 'gig economy'. In Jeremy Corbyn's Labour Party we also glimpse a reframing of the social security policy debate by an Opposition at last unafraid to speak its name: one whose leader openly condemns 'disgraceful, divisive terms like "scrounger"' (Corbyn 2016). An equally welcome illustration of the emerging toxification of such terminology (at least when openly voiced by politicians) came with the immediate calls to resign new Conservative Party Vice-Chair Ben Bradley faced in January 2018, following the emergence of a six-year-old blog-post in which he had suggested benefit-claiming 'chavs' be given free vasectomies to stop Britain 'drowning in a vast sea of unemployed wasters' (quoted in Gregory & Bartlett 2018). Meanwhile, despite the overall UK-wide appeal of scrounger narratives that emerged from Chapter 3's newspaper analysis, there were heartening signs of this discourse being *relatively* less popular in some parts of Britain, with papers in Scotland (other than the *Scottish Sun*, *Mail* and *Express*) generally adopting 'softer' frames and publishing more counter-discursive articles than elsewhere, in keeping with the country's more social democratic political climate.

But turning points (if one *is* nearing) do not come from nowhere. Even in the dark, divisive years of the Coalition – and the shirker-bashing rhetorical arms-race it fostered – seeds of resistance were brewing, not just among grassroots activists and service-user networks but in the notable (if under-publicized) efforts of writers and artists. In May 2013, with the tide of shirkerphobia peaking, the Black Triangle Campaign mounted a noble fight, backed by 40 leading charities and medical professionals, to persuade Ministers to exempt disabled claimants at risk of suicide from fitness-for-work tests. Meanwhile, Calum's List had begun the heartrending task of memorializing the tens of thousands of people thought to have died or taken their own lives as a result (at least partly) of the tyranny of WCAs and/ or hardship caused by loss of benefits. Much earlier, a steady drumbeat of dissent had been building among a coalition of writers, in two volumes of poetry and creative writing: the first, *Emergency Verse*, published impressively close to Osborne's hyperbolically framed 2010 'emergency' Budget, and the second, *The Robin Hood Book*, two years later (Morrison 2010; Morrison & Topping 2012). Each collection featured poems by a mix of more and less established writers, from former beat poet Michael Horovitz to author Jeremy Reed, and forewords by, respectively, then Green Party leader Caroline Lucas and Mark Serwotka, general secretary of the Public and Commercial Services Union (PCS). More recently, the cause of debunking anti-welfare myths and restoring public trust in social security principles has been taken up by everyone from Ken Loach to ex-Smiths guitarist Johnny Marr and his actor collaborator Maxine Peake.

For a meaningful and resilient counter-discourse to flourish, though, there needs to be a wider popular rediscovery of the mutual interests that bind us and a rejection of the prejudices that would divide us. Beyond this, to restore and reinvigorate the bonds underpinning Britain's post-war social security settlement – trust, community and co-dependency – the only solution, in the end, is to organize. This means harnessing social networks to promote progressive messages over discourses of distrust. But it requires us to go beyond using the connecting tools of the new (virtual) public sphere to simply link up *online*: to pursue meaningful dialogue, collaboration and, ultimately, change in the *real* world. During the dark years of distrust and division, we have seen the beginnings of this: in the physical camps the Occupy movement built in financial centres to protest against global elites' failure to reform the banking system whose misdeeds condemned millions to austerity; and in the flash-mob sit-ins staged by UK Uncut as it mounted its short, sharp, successful campaign to expose the scale of tax evasion and avoidance endemic among owners of leading British companies. Also piercing the febrile fog of shirkerphobia were countless online petitions launched via digitally savvy, post-crash campaign platforms, including 38 Degrees, change.org and Avaaz. However, to have any hope of a game-changing impact, of resoundingly defeating the hegemonic neoliberal paradigm that has long prevailed, we must organize on a much larger, more tangible and permanent scale. This means recreating the 'solid' bonds of the earlier modern era (Bauman 2000) – through local neighbourhood networks, mutuals, cooperatives and other common endeavours – while utilizing the 'liquid' tools of late modernity to establish national, even global, networks of common purpose: ones putting people and the ideal of shared community (as opposed to the interests of disparate, potentially conflicting, 'communities') above everything else. In so doing, we must band together to restore the mechanisms of the market to our service, rather than letting it remain our master. And to mobilize support means taking control of discourse, which, in the absence of long-overdue press reform or Ministers' willingness to do more than fire occasional rhetorical barbs at vested interests, involves finding ways of shouting louder (and messaging wider) than politicians or papers.

There are encouraging signs of this starting to happen, including through the ongoing Joseph Rowntree Foundation-funded *Talking about Poverty* project, which seeks to address the 'gaps and overlaps' between 'public and expert understandings of UK poverty' (Volmert et al. 2016). But what would an inclusive, democratic, powerfully progressive *movement* look like? Though still in its infancy, one potential model is offered by influential grassroots Labour membership group Momentum. In harnessing social media and other emerging technologies to recruit and mobilize supporters on the doorstep, on the stump and at the ballot-box, this stands as an example of how an alliance of one-time clicktivists and apathetic non-voters can be transformed into an active, dynamic campaign. And the campaign ahead of us could not be more urgent. 'The moral test of government', observed former US Vice-President Hubert Humphrey, is how it 'treats' people 'in the dawn' and 'twilight' of their lives, as well as those 'in the shadows of life': 'the sick, the needy and the handicapped' (quoted in Alker 2011). It is to the task of restoring this principle that we must now move, and in haste.

APPENDIX 1

FRAMING ANALYSIS METHODOLOGY

The Lexis Library database of UK newspapers was used to collect a series of relevant datasets spanning all national and regional titles from 1 January to 31 December 2016 inclusive. Search terms used were: 'benefits', 'welfare', 'claimant', 'unemployed', 'jobless', 'workless', 'dole' and 'poverty'. A search was also initially carried out for the all-embracing term 'the poor', but the resulting dataset was abandoned, as it contained a high number of 'false positives' (Soothill & Grover 1997): e.g. 'the poor child'.

Searches were conducted using the Lexis 'moderate similarity' filter to, first, group together identical pieces published multiple times (on the same date, by a single paper) and manually sift out duplicates. The 'overall' corpus of 3,534 articles represented the raw sum of all those collected across the eight datasets, but for coding purposes it was necessary to individually analyse each dataset. Treating the total as a 'master dataset' would have led to extensive double-counting, as numerous articles recurred across two or more datasets (e.g. the terms 'benefits' and 'welfare' often appeared in the same piece).

In coding articles' frames, a two-stage approach was applied, beginning with immersion in the datasets (in this case, an initial read-through): a process known as 'inductive category development' (Mayring 2000: 3). This necessitated refining, and increasing, the number of categories during the exploratory read-through, as unanticipated variations emerged: e.g. the early appearance of ostensibly counter-discursive articles which, on closer inspection, adopted more conflicted positions led to the identification of 'soft counter-discourses'. Eight categories of discursive frame were finally identified: 'hard scrounger', 'soft scrounger', 'cheat/fraudster', 'benefit tourist', 'incidental scrounger', 'neutral', 'hard counter-discourse' and 'soft counter-discourse'.

To ensure initial coding was reliable enough to be replicated, one-tenth of the total sample was recoded eight months after initial analysis, producing a 97.2 per cent match. The small minority of articles coded differently the second time (10 out of 353, or 2.8 per cent) were mainly 'soft' counter-discursive pieces previously coded neutral (or vice versa). This highlights the compromised, insubstantial nature of many broadly countervailing frames and the relative clarity, forcefulness and certainty (and resulting dominance) of scrounger discourse.

APPENDIX 2

SENTIMENT ANALYSIS
METHODOLOGY

As with the framing analysis, initial immersion in the comment dataset(s) again identified a wider spectrum of posts than ones that were straightforwardly 'negative' (affirming scrounger frames), 'positive' (counter-discursive) and 'neutral'. These ranged from 'hard' positives or negatives to *qualified* (or 'soft') variants of these broad categories, to *tangential* comments that either veered off-topic or were sentimentally ambiguous (coded, broadly, as 'other'). Posts were therefore grouped into six categories.

As certain newspaper websites, notably *Mail Online*, ran many hundreds, if not thousands, of reader posts beneath some stories, it was impossible to code every post within time and resource limitations. To ensure the comments analysed constituted a representative sample, in such cases posts were reordered using the websites' 'most rated', 'most liked' or 'recommendation' tabs, and the first full page of these, along with their top 'replies', were coded. For sites, like the *Guardian*'s, which ran fewer than 100 comments per page, the first two pages were sampled, to ensure large enough snapshots were captured. In all cases, samples were significant, often amounting to 200-plus posts.

Twitter search terms used for the six events were as follows: Lottery story – 'couple and benefits and lottery' and 'couple lottery' (two searches) between 6 January 2016 and 8 January 2016; 'Black Dee' story – 'Black Dee Benefits Street' (one search) between 10 January 2016 and 12 January 2016; 'high-welfare' story – 'high welfare' and 'Centre for Cities' (two searches) between 24 January 2016 and 26 January 2016; Great British Benefits Handout story – 'Great British Benefits Handout or British or benefit or benefits or handout' (one search) between 1 February 2016 and 22 February 2016; IDS story – 'Hislop or Duncan Smith or Workers or Shirkers' (one search) between 6 April 2016 and 8 April 2016; benefit cap story – 'Stephen Crabb' and 'benefit cap' (two searches) between 6 May 2016 and 9 May 2016. False positives were generated by some searches, necessitating some tweets being manually removed from the sample. For example, the name 'Stephen Crabb' produced several tweets commenting on the Minister generally, rather than in the context of the benefit cap story.

Coding tweets was more problematic than categorizing comments, with five classes of sentiments identified: 'hard' and 'soft' negative (anti-scrounger); 'hard' and 'soft' positive (counter-discursive); and an extensive, highly variable 'other' category. This embraced the many tweets that diverged into debating wider questions about society and economy, rather than explicitly taking pro- or counter-hegemonic positions on the scrounger question. No 'neutral' category emerged because tweets that might otherwise have been coded this way generally did little more than describe topics as, say, 'interesting', rather than adopting any clear *position* on them.

NOTES

1   The consistent popularity in Google searches for the term 'scrounger' in 2012 and 2013 was not matched by similarly persistent patterns for either 'skiver' and 'shirker' (Google Trends 2018b, 2018c) – suggesting that *media* discourse may have tapped into and/ or reflected public attitudes and interests more closely than that favoured by politicians. Nonetheless, searches for 'shirker' did reach a then all-time peak of 60 in November 2012, around the time of George Osborne's notorious speech castigating the unemployed for 'sleeping off a life on benefits'. Another, lower, spike (of 31) followed in April 2013, the month of Philpott's conviction. 'Skiver' reached its Coalition-era peak earlier than 'scrounger', hitting 51 in January 2011, at the start of the year in which ministers announced details of their ambitious signature welfare reform policy: Universal Credit.

2   Note: where possible, comments and tweets have been quoted exactly as written, with typos, punctuation/spelling errors and capital letters intact, to preserve the authenticity of original posts.

3   The term 'raw total' refers to the initial figure for the number of results generated by a Lexis Library database search, using the 'moderate similarity' filter to group together very or moderately similar articles. A total of 957 articles were initially generated, but this total was recalibrated by Lexis to 751 when the dataset was downloaded. The breakdown between national and local articles is based on the 'raw' figures, as it was only at this level that an itemized list of news sources was available.

4   The full list of terms used to scrape these datasets was as follows: 'benefits', 'welfare', 'unemployed', 'unemployment', 'jobless', 'workless', 'dole', 'claimant', 'poverty', 'estate', 'council estate', 'council house', 'council flat', 'social housing', 'housing association', 'tenant', 'rented', 'homeless', 'beggar', 'begging', 'hostel', 'deprivation', 'traveller', 'gypsy/ies'.

REFERENCES

Airdrie and Coatbridge Advertiser (2016) 'Benefit cap plan puts refuge places at risk; Impact could be devastating, says Women's Aid manager', *Airdrie and Coatbridge Advertiser*, 24 February, p.7.

Alker, J. (2011) 'Children in the dawn and shadows of life should be a top priority in budget talks', ccf.georgetown.edu, 14 July, https:// ccf.georgetown.edu/2011/07/14/children_in_the_dawn_and_ shadows_of_life_should_be_a_top_priority_in_budget_talks/, accessed 8 January 2018.

Allen, K. (2013) 'Wage cuts for British workers deepest since records began, IFS shows', *The Guardian*, 12 June, https://www.the guardian.com/money/2013/jun/12/workers-deepest-cuts-real-wages-ifs, accessed 23 January 2018.

Altheide, D.L. (1997) 'The news media, the problem frame, and the production of fear', *The Sociological Quarterly*, 38(4): 647–668.

Artz, F.B. (1953) *The Mind of the Middle Ages*, New York: Alfred A. Knopf.

Atkinson, J. (2013) 'Our welfare state is just rewarding feckless behaviour', *Daily Express*, 8 March, https://www.express.co.uk/comment/ expresscomment/382644/Our-welfare-state-is-just-rewarding-feckless-behaviour, accessed 15 January 2018.

Barnett, H. (2016) 'Jobless couple who blew £50k lottery win to beg for benefits claim "we're not scroungers"', *www.express.co.uk*, 8 January, https://www.express.co.uk/news/uk/632827/Jobless-couple-blew-lottery-win-benefits-claim-not-scroungers, accessed 9 January 2018.

Bauman, Z. (2000) *Liquid Modernity*, Cambridge: Polity Press.

Bauman, Z. (2004) *Wasted Lives: Modernity and its Outcasts*, Cambridge: Blackwell.

Baumberg Geiger, B., Reeves, A., and de Vries, R. (2017) 'Tax avoidance and benefit manipulation: views on its morality and prevalence', in R. Harding (ed.) *British Social Attitudes: 34th Report*, http:// www.bsa.natcen.ac.uk/media/39144/bsa34_benefit_tax_final.pdf, accessed 20 December 2017.

BBC News (1997) 'Blair's speech: single mothers won't be forced to take work', 2 June, http://www.bbc.co.uk/news/special/politics97/news/06/0602/blair.shtml, accessed 21 December 2017.

BBC News (2008) 'Bid to tackle "sick-note culture"', 20 February, http://news.bbc.co.uk/1/hi/health/7253577.stm, accessed 21 December 2017.

Beatson, J. (2016) 'Jail for benefit fraudster', *Scottish Express*, 6 January, p.22.

Beck, U. (1992) *Risk Society: Towards a New Modernity*, trans. M. Ritter, London: Sage.

Beddoe, L. (2015) 'Making a moral panic: "feral families", family violence and welfare reforms in New Zealand. Doing the work of the state?', in V.E. Cree (ed.), *Gender and Family*, Bristol: Policy Press, pp.31–42.

Beveridge, W. (1942) *Social Insurance and Allied Services*, London: Her Majesty's Stationery Office.

Bews, L. and Paterson, L. (2016) 'Constance hits out at depiction of poverty', *Glasgow* Herald, 26 October, p.6.

Blair, T. (1993) 'From the archive: Tony Blair is tough on crime, tough on the causes of crime', *New Statesman*, 28 December 2015, https://www.newstatesman.com/2015/12/archive-tony-blair-tough-crime-tough-causes-crime, accessed 21 December 2017.

Blair, T. (2002) 'My vision for Britain: by Tony Blair', *The Observer*, 10 November, http://www.theguardian.com/politics/2002/nov/10/queensspeech2002.tonyblair, accessed 21 December 2017.

Blair, T. (2010) *A Journey: My Political Life*, London: Vintage.

Blanchard, J. (2016) 'David Cameron rejects European offer for an "emergency brake" on migrant benefits', *Daily Mirror*, 29 January, http://www.mirror.co.uk/news/uk-news/david-cameron-rejects-europe-an-offer-7272658, accessed 22 December 2017.

Bochel, H. (2014) *Social Policy*, Abingdon: Routledge.

Booth, C. (1888) 'Condition and occupations of the people of East London and Hackney, 1887', *Journal of the Royal Statistical Society*, 51(2): 276–339.

Booth, W. (2014) *In Darkest England and the Way Out*, Cambridge: Cambridge University Press.

Borromeo, L. (2015) 'These anti-homeless spikes are brutal. We need to get rid of them', *The Guardian*, 23 July, https://www.theguardian.com/commentisfree/2015/jul/23/anti-homeless-spikes-inhumane-defensive-architecture, accessed 21 December 2017.

Brown, G. (1999) Speech to Labour Party Conference, 27 September, https://www.theguardian.com/politics/1999/sep/27/labour conference.labour7, accessed 20 December 2017.

Brown, G. (2007) Speech to Labour Party Conference, 24 September, http://news.bbc.co.uk/1/hi/uk_politics/7010664.stm, accessed 20 December 2017.

Brown, G. (2008) Speech to Labour Party Conference, 23 September, http://www.britishpoliticalspeech.org/speech-archive.htm?-speech=180, accessed 20 December 2017.

Brown, G. (2017) 'Theresa May is creating an epidemic of poverty. Don't give her a free hand', 12 May, https://www.theguardian.com/commentisfree/2017/may/12/theresa-may-poverty-tories-children-labour-gordon-brown, accessed 20 December 2017.

Bruns, A. and Burgess, J. (2011) 'The use of Twitter hashtags in the formation of ad hoc publics', *Proceedings of the 6th European Consortium for Political Research (ECPR) General Conference*, 25-27 August, University of Iceland, Reykjavik.

Bruns, A., Highfield, T. and Burgess, J. (2013) 'The Arab Spring and social media audiences: English and Arabic Twitter users and their networks', *American Behavioral Scientist*, 57(7): 871–898.

Buck, N. (1992) 'Labour market inactivity and polarisation: a household perspective on the idea of an underclass', in D.J. Smith (ed.) *Understanding the Underclass*, London: Policy Studies Institute, pp.9-31.

Bullen, J. (2016) *London Evening Standard*, 24 February, 'Jailed: Unemployed fraudster who conned victims out of at least £40,000 to fund jet-set lifestyle', https://www.standard.co.uk/news/crime/jailed-unemployed-fraudster-conned-victims-out-of-at-least-40000-to-fund-jetset-lifestyle-a3188446.html, accessed 21 January 2018.

Burnett, J. (2017) 'Austerity and the production of hate', https://www.plutobooks.com/blog/austerity-and-the-production-of-hate/, accessed 23 January 2013.

Butler, P. (2016) 'Spike in food bank usage blamed on delays in benefit claims', *The Guardian*, 14 November, https://www.theguardian.com/society/2016/nov/14/spike-food-bank-usage-blamed-delays-benefit-claims-frank-field, accessed 22 December 2017.

Byrne, L. (2012) 'Britain's new bargain: social security for One Nation Britain', 1 December, http://liambyrne.co.uk/research_archive/britains-new-bargain-social-security-for-one-nation-britain-my-speech-to-the-fabian-society-on-the-70th-anniversary-of-the-beveridge-report-1st-december-2012-toynbee-hall/, accessed 20 December 2017.

Byrne, L. (2013) 'IDS is in trouble over his strivers' tax – and he knows it', *New Statesman*, 2 January.

Camber, R. (2016) '£3k UK benefits "funded Brussels terror suspect"; "Man in the Hat" given dole money that was being paid to IS fighter, court told', *Scottish Daily Mail*, p.27.

Cameron, D. (2006) 'Modern Conservatism speech', 30 January, https://www.theguardian.com/politics/2006/jan/30/conservatives.davidcameron, accessed 30 May 2018.

Cameron, D. (2008) 'Living within our means speech', 19 May, http://www.ukpol.co.uk/david-cameron-2008-living-within-our-means-speech/, accessed 16 January 2018.

Cameron, D. (2010) 'An invitation to older people', 18 April, http://conservative-speeches.sayit.mysociety.org/speech/601488, accessed 23 January 2018.

Cameron, D. (2011) Immigration speech, 14 April, http://www.bbc.co.uk/news/uk-politics-13083781, accessed 20 December 2017.

Cameron, D. (2013) Speech to Conservative Party Conference, 2 October, http://www.telegraph.co.uk/news/politics/david-cameron/10349831/David-Camerons-speech-in-full.html, accessed 20 December 2017.

Cameron, D. and Clegg, N. (2010) *The Coalition: Our Programme for Government*, London: Cabinet Office.

Canter, L. (2013) 'The misconception of online comment threads: Content and control on local newspaper websites', *Journalism Practice* 7(5): 604–619.

Cartledge, L. (2016) 'Child poverty in Bognor and Littlehampton at 24 per cent', *Bognor Regis Observer*, 8 November, https://www.bognor.

co.uk/news/child-poverty-in-bognor-and-littlehampton-at-24-per-cent-1-7666186, accessed 22 December 2017.

Casciani, D. (2015) 'Islamic State: Profile of Mohammed Emwazi aka "Jihadi John"', BBC News, 13 November, http://www.bbc.co.uk/news/uk-31641569, accessed 22 December 2017.

Chambliss, W.J. (1964) 'A sociological analysis of the law of vagrancy', *Social Problems*, 12(1): 67–77.

Charter, D. (2016) *Europe: In or Out – Everything You Need to Know*, London: Biteback Publishing.

Chesworth, N. (2016) 'Fighting chance to get back to work', *London Evening Standard*, 31 October, p.57.

Clarke, S. (2015) 'Who benefits? TV and poverty', *Royal Television Society*, 1 December, https://www.rts.org.uk/article/who-benefits-tv-and-poverty, accessed 22 May 2018.

Clay, O. (2016) 'Fears in-work poverty caused by high rents could be affecting Halton families', *Liverpool Echo*, 9 December, http://www.liverpoolecho.co.uk/news/fears-work-poverty-caused-high-12297748, accessed 22 December 2017.

Clegg, N. (2010) Speech on 'Fairness Premium', 15 October, https://www.libdems.org.uk/nick_clegg_announces_7bn_fairness_premium, accessed 20 December 2017.

Clegg, N. (2011) 'We'll help the Alarm Clock heroes keep Britain ticking' , *The Sun*, 11 January, https://www.thesun.co.uk/archives/news/299662/well-help-the-alarm-clock-heroes-keep-britain-ticking/, accessed 20 December 2017.

Coates, K. and Silburn, R. (1970) *Poverty: The Forgotten Englishman*, London: Penguin.

Çoats, A.W. (1976) 'The relief of poverty, attitudes to labour, and economic change in England, 1660–1782', *International Review of Social History*, 21(1): 98–115.

Cochrane, A. (1998) 'What sort of safety-net? Social security, income maintenance and the benefit system', in G. Hughes and G. Lewis (eds.) *Unsettling Welfare: The Reconstruction of Social Policy*, London and New York: Routledge, pp.291–333.

Cohen, S. (1972) *Folk Devils and Moral Panics*, St Albans: Palladin.

Cohen, S. (2002) 'Moral panics as cultural politics: introduction to the third edition', in *Folk Devils and Moral Panics*, 3rd edn, London: Routledge, pp. vvi–xliv.

Colquhoun, N. (2016) 'One in seven rural households struggling to pay to heat homes', Mid Devon Gazette, 7 November, p.22.

Connor, S. (2010) 'Promoting "employ ability": The changing subject of welfare reform in the UK', *Critical Discourse Studies*, 7(1): 41–54.

Corbyn, J. (2016) Labour leadership campaign speech, 21 July, https://www.newstatesman.com/politics/staggers/2016/07/jeremy-corbyns-campaign-speech-full-i-came-politics-stand-against, accessed 20 December 2017.

Court, S.D.M. (1976) *Fit for the Future: Report of the Committee on Child Health Services*, London: Her Majesty's Stationery Office.

Coventry Evening Telegraph (2016) 'Best of the Box', *Coventry Evening Telegraph*, 31 May, p.21.

Cowburn, A. (2016) 'More than 85% of public tips on benefit "fraud" are false', *The Observer*, 27 February, https://www.theguardian.com/society/2016/feb/27/false-benefit-fraud-allegations, accessed 1 February 2018.

Cowburn, A. (2018) 'Benefit fraud "witch-hunt": 280,000 public tip-offs led to no action taken due to lack of evidence', *The Independent*, 15 January, http://www.independent.co.uk/news/uk/politics/benefit-fraud-public-tip-offs-legal-action-police-no-evidence-dwp-work-pensions-department-a8144096.html, accessed 1 February 2018.

Crabb, S. (2016) Maiden speech as Work and Pensions Secretary, http://www.bbc.co.uk/news/uk-politics-35863776, accessed 20 December 2017.

Crawley Observer (2016) 'Trio charged with GBH and kidnap after man found in stream with broken leg', *Crawley Observer*, 8 January, https://www.crawleyobserver.co.uk/news/crime/trio-charged-with-gbh-and-kidnap-after-man-found-in-stream-with-broken-leg-1-7151485, accessed 21 January 2018.

Cunningham, H. (1991) *The Children of the Poor*, Oxford: Blackwell.

Curtis, J. and Baker, K. (2016) 'Dope-smoking thug who beat his girlfriend's toddler son to death during a drug and alcohol binge is jailed for life – as the mother gets six years for her role in the killing', *Mail Online*, 29 July, http://www.dailymail.co.uk/news/article-3714255/

Dope-smoking-killer-toddler-Noah-Serra-Morrison-jailed-life. html, accessed 21 January 2018.

Daily Telegraph (2016) 'Judge tells benefit fraudster she is taking money "from people like me"', *Daily Telegraph*, 23 December, http://www. telegraph.co.uk/news/2016/12/23/judge-tells-benefit-fraudster-is-taking-money-people-like/, accessed 22 December 2017.

Daily Telegraph (2018), 'Clear beggars from streets of Windsor ahead of royal wedding, says local council leader', *Daily Telegraph*, 4 January, http://www.telegraph.co.uk/politics/2018/01/04/beggars-should-cleared-streets-windsor-ahead-royal-wedding-says/, accessed 17 January 2018.

Davies, N. (2008) *Flat Earth News: an Award-winning Reporter Exposes Falsehood, Distortion and Propaganda in the Global Media*, London: Chatto and Windus.

Davis, A. (2016) 'Are we becoming a nation of bludgers? Australians on the dole jumps by 70 per cent in just 10 years', *Mail Online*, 10 October, http://www.dailymail.co.uk/news/article-3829907/ Are-nation-bludgers-Australians-dole-jumps-70-cent-just-10-years.html, accessed 22 December 2017.

Dawar, A. (2012) 'Go to Britain for benefits says EU', *Daily Express*, 14 May, https://www.express.co.uk/news/uk/319981/Go-to-Britain-for-benefits-says-EU, accessed 18 January 2018.

Day, E. (2009) 'Whoever said British politicians are dowdy?', *The Guardian*, 10 May, https://www.theguardian.com/lifeandstyle/ 2009/may/10/caroline-flint-uk-politics, accessed 24 January 2018.

Day, H. (2016) 'Watch benefits cheat who claimed she was crippled pulling pints in a pub', *Birmingham Mail*, 12 January, http://www. birminghammail.co.uk/news/midlands-news/watch-benefits-cheat-who-claimed-10722647, accessed 22 December 2017.

DCLG (Department for Communities and Local Government) (2015) *The English Indices of Deprivation 2015*, https://www.gov.uk/govern-ment/uploads/system/uploads/attachment_data/file/465791/ English_Indices_of_Deprivation_2015_-_Statistical_Release.pdf, accessed 17 January 2018.

DCLG (Department for Communities and Local Government) (2017) *Supporting Disadvantaged Families - Troubled Families Programme*

2015 to 2020: Progress so Far, https://www.gov.uk/government/
uploads/system/uploads/attachment_data/file/611991/Supporting_
disadvantaged_families.pdf, accessed 21 December 2017.

Deacon, A. (1978) 'The scrounging controversy: public attitudes
towards the unemployed in contemporary Britain', *Social Policy &
Administration*, 12(2): 120–135.

Dean, H. (1991) *Social Security and Social Control*, Abingdon: Taylor &
Francis.

Dean, H. (2012) 'The ethical deficit of the United Kingdom's proposed
universal credit: pimping the precariat?', *The Political Quarterly*,
83(2): 353–359.

Dean, T. and Taylor-Gooby, P. (1992) *Dependency Culture: The Explosion of a Myth*, London: Harvester Wheatsheaf.

Deans, J. and Hopkins, N. (1997) 'For all our benefit; The premier
chooses one of Britain's bleakest housing estates to launch his drive
to make the single mothers pay their way', *Daily Mail*, 3 June, pp.
12–13.

Debord, G. (1967) *The Society of the Spectacle*, trans. Donald Nichol-
son-Smith, Paris: Buchet-Chastel.

Denton, J. (2016) 'Britain's benefits bonanza: 29 UK cities have "low
wage, high welfare" economies – and one has seen its benefits
bill jump 45%', *www.thisismoney.co.uk*, 25 January, http://www.
thisismoney.co.uk/money/news/article-3415396/Britain-s-
benefits-bonanza-29-UK-cities-low-wage-high-welfare-economies-
one-seen-benefits-bill-jump-45.html, accessed 9 January 2018.

Department for Work and Pensions (2012) *Fraud and Error in the Benefit
System: 2011/12 Statistical Release*, https://www.gov.uk/govern-
ment/uploads/system/uploads/attachment_data/file/265788/nsfr-
final-291112.pdf, accessed 20 December 2017.

Devereux, E. (2007) *Understanding the Media*, 2nd edn. London: Sage.

Devereux, E., Haynes, A. and Power, M.J. (2011) 'At the edge: media
constructions of a stigmatised Irish housing estate', *Journal of
Housing and the Built Environment*, 26(2): 123–142.

Dickenson, I. (2016) 'Mum-of-12 splurges benefits on boob job', *Daily
Star Sunday*, 17 January, https://www.dailystar.co.uk/news/latest-
news/488072/Benefits-mum-boob-job, accessed 22 December 2017.

Directgov (2008) 'Incapacity Benefit replaced by Employment Support', 27 October, http://webarchive.nationalarchives.gov. uk/20100408181946tf_/http://www.direct.gov.uk/en/Nl1/ Newsroom/DG_172466, accessed 21 December 2017.

Disability News Service (2017) 'Disability hate crime', http://www. disabilitynewsservice.com/tag/disability-hate-crime/, accessed 21 December 2017.

Docking, N. (2016) 'Mum who bottled woman damaging her eyesight spared jail – because of her children', *Liverpool Echo*, 23 December, http://www.liverpoolecho.co.uk/news/liverpool-news/mum-who-bot-tled-woman-damaging-12366296, accessed 21 January 2018.

Dolan, A. and Bentley, P. (2013) 'Vile product of Welfare UK', *Daily Mail*, 3 April, p.1.

Dominiczak, P. (2014) 'Osborne's welfare cuts spark fury from Clegg', *Daily Telegraph*, 6 January, http://www.telegraph.co.uk/news/ politics/nick-clegg/10554721/Osbornes-welfare-cuts-spark-fury-from-Clegg.html, accessed 8 January 2018.

Dorset Echo (2016) 'Odd news: a round-up of the bizarre stories making the news this week – Idle Aussies', *Dorset Echo*, 23 February, http:// www.dorsetecho.co.uk/news/14296146.ODD_NEWS__A_ round_up_of_the_bizarre_stories_making_the_headlines_this_ week/, accessed 12 July 2018.

Douieb, T. (2012) 'Workers and shirkers', *Huffington Post*, 11 July, http:// www.huffingtonpost.co.uk/tiernan-douieb/workers-and-shirk-ers_b_1664564.html, accessed 21 December 2017.

Dowell, B. (2007) 'Kyle show "human bear baiting"', *The Guardian*, 24 September, https://www.theguardian.com/media/2007/sep/24/ television, accessed 22 May 2018.

Duell, M. (2016) 'Unemployed man jailed for five years after plumbers found his Russian military pistol and silencer on top of his broken boiler', *Mail Online*, 18 April, http://www.dailymail.co.uk/news/ article-3546068/Man-jailed-five-years-plumbers-Russian-military-pistol-silencer-broken-boiler.html, accessed 21 January 2018.

Duncan Smith, I. (2015) Speech on work, health and disability, http:// www.reform.uk/publication/rt-hon-iain-duncan-smith-mp-speech-on-work-health-and-disability/, accessed 21 December 2017.

Duncan Smith, I. (2016) Full text of resignation letter, BBC News, 18 March, http://www.bbc.co.uk/news/uk-politics-35848891, accessed 22 December 2017.

Easton, M. (2010) 'Welfare: can the Tories save billions in benefits?', 9 April, http://news.bbc.co.uk/1/hi/uk_politics/election_2010/parties_and_issues/8611173.stm, accessed 21 December 2017.

Entman, R.M. (1993) 'Framing: toward clarification of a fractured paradigm', *Journal of Communication*, 43: 51–58.

Evans, S. (2016) 'Jobless paedophile who pretended to be successful RAPPER to groom underage schoolgirls for sex jailed for 16 years', *www.mirror.co.uk*, 29 July, https://www.mirror.co.uk/news/uk-news/jobless-paedophile-who-pretended-successful-8525097, accessed 21 January 2018.

Fairclough, N. (1992) 'Discourse and text: linguistic and intertextual analysis within discourse analysis', *Discourse & Society*, 3(2): 193–217.

Fairclough, N. (2000) *New Labour, New Language?*, London: Routledge.

Fenton, S. (2016a) 'Osborne isn't even saving money while he penalises the poor - this is about ideology, not economics', 12 January, *The Independent*, http://www.independent.co.uk/voices/osborne-isn-t-even-saving-money-while-he-penalises-the-poor-this-is-about-ideology-not-economics-a6807741.html, accessed 22 December 2017.

Fenton, S. (2016b) 'DWP overturn ruling which saw man missing half his head declared "fit for work"' *The Independent*, 24 May, http://www.independent.co.uk/news/uk/home-news/dwp-overturn-ruling-which-saw-man-missing-half-his-head-declared-fit-for-work-a7046671.html, accessed 22 December 2017.

Field, F. (1996) Contribution to 'right to work' debate, https://www.theyworkforyou.com/debates/?id=1996-06-26a.263.4, accessed 16 January 2018.

Field, F. (2003) *Neighbours from Hell: The Politics of Behaviour*, London: Politicos.

Field, F. and Piachaud, D. (1971) 'The poverty trap', *New Statesman* 3: 772–773.

Finan, V. (2016) 'Benefits cap to be slashed from £26,000 to £20,000 per family: claimants told "find jobs or your handouts will be cut"',

Mail Online, 7 May, http://www.dailymail.co.uk/news/article-3578279/Benefits-cap-slashed-26-000-20-000-family-Claimants-told-jobs-handouts-cut.html, accessed 9 January 2018.

Fishman, M. (1980) *Manufacturing the News*, Austin: University of Texas Press.

Fitzsimmons, F. (2016) 'Mum stabbed in the back by yobs "as she protected her daughter" in park', *Daily Record*, 6 September, https://www.dailyrecord.co.uk/news/uk-world-news/mum-stabbed-back-yobs-as-8776669, accessed 21 January 2018.

Fletcher, D.R. (2015) 'Workfare – a blast from the past? Contemporary work conditionality for the unemployed in historical perspective', *Social Policy and Society*, 14(3): 329-39.

Flint, C. (2008) Housing speech, 5 February, https://www.theguardian.com/politics/video/2008/feb/05/housing.council.flint, accessed 21 December 2017.

Foucault, M., Davidson, A.I. and Burchell, G. (2008) *The Birth of Biopolitics: Lectures at the Collège de France, 1978–1979*, New York: Springer.

Fuertes, V. and McQuaid, R. (2016) 'Personalised activation policies for the long-term unemployed: the role of local governance in the UK', in M. Heidenreich and D. Rice, *Integrating Social and Employment Policies in Europe: Active Inclusion and Challenges for Local Welfare Governance*. Cheltenham: Edward Elgar Publishing.

Full Fact (2015) *The Welfare Budget*, 10 July, https://fullfact.org/economy/welfare-budget/, accessed 9 January 2018.

Full Fact (2016) *Tax: Evasion and Avoidance in the UK*, 7 October, https://fullfact.org/economy/tax-avoidance-evasion-uk/, accessed 21 December 2017.

Gans, H.J. (1962) *Urban Villagers*, New York: Simon and Schuster.

Gans, H.J. (1979) *Deciding What's News: a Study of CBS Evening News, NBC Nightly News, Newsweek and Time*. Constable: London.

Gardner, T. (2016) 'Leeds pensioner made £26,000 of false benefit claims', *Yorkshire Evening Post*, 29 December.

Garland, D. (2008) 'On the concept of moral panic', *Crime, Media, Culture*, 4(1): 9–30.

Garthwaite, K. (2011) '"The language of shirkers and scroungers?" Talking about illness, disability and coalition welfare reform', *Disability & Society,* 26(3): 369–72.

Garthwaite, K. (2012) 'The "scrounger" myth is causing real suffering to many in society', http://blogs.lse.ac.uk/politicsandpolicy/ the-scrounger-myth-is-causing-real-suffering-to-many-in-society/ #author, accessed 20 December 2017.

Garthwaite, K. (2014) 'Fear of the brown envelope: exploring welfare reform with long term sickness benefits recipients', *Social Policy & Administration,* 48(7): 782–98.

Garthwaite, K. (2016) *Hunger Pains: Life inside Foodbank Britain,* Bristol: Policy Press.

Gitlin, T. (1980) *The Whole World is Watching,* Berkeley: University of California Press.

Glanfield, E. and Gordon, A. (2016) 'Two five-bedroom houses turned down as "too small" by a jobless French migrant family of 10 while they rack up a £38,400 hotel bill at the taxpayers' expense', *Mail Online,* 7 September, http://www.dailymail.co.uk/news/article-3777922/Couple-eight-children-say-neglected-council-offered-new-five-bed-home-didn-t-dining-room.html, accessed 11 July 2017.

Glaze, B. (2016) 'Outside firms conducting back-to-work tests are costing taxpayer money', *Daily Mirror,* 31 March.

Golding, P. and Middleton. S. (1982) *Images of Welfare,* Oxford: Mark Robertson.

Goldson, B. and Jamieson, J. (2002) 'Youth crime, the "parenting deficit" and state intervention: a contextual critique', *Youth Justice,* 2(2): 82–99.

Goode, E. and Ben-Yehuda, N. (1994) *Moral Panics: the Social Construction of Deviance,* Oxford: Blackwell.

Google Trends (2018a) 'scrounger' search term, https://trends.google. co.uk/trends/explore?date=all&geo=GB&q=scrounger, accessed 19 July 2018.

Google Trends2018b) 'shirker' search term, https://trends.google. co.uk/trends/explore?date=all&geo=GB&q=shirker, accessed 19 July 2018.

Google Trends (2018c) 'skiver' search term, https://trends.google.co.uk/trends/explore?date=all&geo=GB&q=skiver, accessed 19 July 2018.

Gray, A. (2017) 'The world's 10 biggest economies in 2017', *www.weforum.org*, 9 March, https://www.weforum.org/agenda/2017/03/worlds-biggest-economies-in-2017/, accessed 8 January 2018.

Great Britain (1998) *Crime and Disorder Act 1998: Elizabeth II. Chapter 1*, London: The Stationery Office.

Greer, C. and Jewkes, Y. (2005) 'Extremes of otherness: media images of social exclusion', *Social Justice*, 32.1(99): 20–31.

Gregory, A. and Bartlett, N. (2018) '"Vasectomies are free": Tories' new vice chair urged jobless to stop having kids or UK would "drown in wasters"', *Daily Mirror*, 17 January, https://www.mirror.co.uk/news/politics/tory-mp-promoted-theresa-role-11862840, accessed 23 January 2018.

Güemes, C. (2017) 'Neoliberal welfare policy reforms and trust: connecting the dots', *Journal of Iberian and Latin American Research*, 23(1): 18–33.

Gye, H. (2016) 'You couldn't give £26,000 in handouts to just anyone ... they might blow it, say couple who spent £460 on a raccoon and £950 on an inflatable slide after getting all their benefits in one go for Channel 5 show', *Mail Online*, 4 February, http://www.dailymail.co.uk/news/article-3431729/The-Big-Benefits-Handout-Jobless-couple-Channel-5-reveal-cash-transformed-lives.html, accessed 9 January 2018.

Habermas, J. (1996) *Between Facts and Norms: Contributions to a Discourse Theory of Law and Democracy*, trans. W. Rehg, Cambridge: Polity Press.

Hall, M. (2010) 'David Cameron: benefit cheats ... three strikes and you're out', *Daily Express*, 10 April, https://www.express.co.uk/news/uk/168357/David-Cameron-Benefit-cheats-3-strikes-and-you-re-out, accessed 20 December 2017.

Hall, M. (2013) 'Party is over for benefit skivers', *Daily Express*, 9 January, https://www.express.co.uk/news/uk/369554/Party-is-over-for-benefit-skivers, accessed 21 December 2017.

Hall, M. (2016) 'Exclusive: New drive to slash benefits as the family limit will be cut to £20,000 a year', *www.express.co.uk*, 7 May, https://

www.express.co.uk/news/uk/667935/benefits-family-limit-cut-stephen-crabb-welfare , accessed 9 January 2018.

Hall, P. (1999) 'Social capital in Britain', *British Journal of Political Science*, 29: 417–461.

Hall, S., Critcher, C., Jefferson, T., Clarke, J., and Roberts, B. (1978) *Policing the Crisis: Mugging, the State and Law and Order*, London: Macmillan.

Hannah, F. (2016) 'New definitions of poverty are re-defining financial hardship', *The Independent*, 13 April, http://www.independent.co.uk/money/spend-save/food-poverty-fuel-poverty-funeral-poverty-are-re-defining-financial-hardship-a6982431.html, accessed 22 December 2016.

Harper, R. (2001) *Social Capital: a Review of the Literature*, UK: Office for National Statistics, Social Analysis and Reporting Division.

Harris, J. (2016) 'Yob allowed to keep his home as his victim was moved instead claims he's not "neighbour from hell"', *www.mirror.co.uk*, 31 May, https://www.mirror.co.uk/news/uk-news/yob-allowed-keep-home-victim-8005618, accessed 21 January 2018.

Hattenstone, S. (2016) 'Nick Clegg: "I did not cater for the Tories' brazen ruthlessness"', *The Guardian*, 3 September, www.theguardian.com/politics/2016/sep/03/nick-clegg-did-not-cater-tories-brazen-ruthlessness, accessed 12 July 2018.

Haworth, J. and Bevan, T. (2016) 'Couple blow their £50k lottery winnings in just one year – and are now battling to apply for benefits', *www.mirror.co.uk*, 7 January, http://www.mirror.co.uk/news/uk-news/benefits-couple-blow-50k-lottery-7133000, accessed 9 January 2018.

Haylett, C. (2001) 'Illegitimate subjects? Abject whites, neoliberal modernisation, and middle-class multiculturalism', *Environment and Planning D: Society and Space*, 19(3): 351–370.

Heath, A. (1992) 'The attitudes of the underclass', in D.J. Smith (ed.), *Understanding the Underclass*, London: Policy Studies Institute, pp. 37–47.

Heider, D., McCombs, M. and Poindexter, P.M. (2005) 'What the public expects of local news: Views on public and traditional journalism', *Journalism & Mass Communication Quarterly* 82(4): 952–967.

Helm, T. (2013) 'The week the welfare war broke out', *The Observer*, 6 April, https://www.theguardian.com/politics/2013/apr/06/welfare-debate-osborne-mick-philpott, accessed 21 December 2017.

Helm, T. (2014) 'Ed Miliband: we will introduce tougher rules on benefits for new migrants', *The Guardian*, 11 October, https://www.theguardian.com/politics/2014/oct/11/ed-miliband-toughen-benefit-rules-for-migrants, accessed 20 December 2017.

Herman, E.S. and Chomsky, N. (1988) *Manufacturing Consent: the Political Economy of the Mass Media*, New York: Pantheon.

Holehouse, M. 'EU report finds Eastern European migrants find work faster', *Daily Telegraph*, 21 January, http://www.telegraph.co.uk/news/worldnews/europe/eu/12114022/EU-report-finds-eastern-European-migrants-find-work-faster.html, accessed 21 December 2017.

Home Affairs Committee (2010) 'The Government's approach to crime prevention', in *Home Affairs Committee: Tenth Report*, 16 March, https://publications.parliament.uk/pa/cm200910/cmselect/cmhaff/242/24202.htm, accessed 21 December 2017.

Home Office (2003) *Respect and Responsibility: Taking a Stand against Anti-social Behaviour*, London: The Stationery Office.

Hope, P. and Sharland, P. (1997) *Tomorrow's Parents: Developing Parenthood Education in Schools*, Lisbon: Calouste Gulbenkian Foundation.

Huddersfield Daily Examiner (2016) 'Woman's false claim of £34k in benefits', *Huddersfield Daily Examiner*, 7 January, p.3.

Hull Daily Mail (2016) 'Hull's young retail stars celebrate their success', *Hull Daily Mail*, 8 November, http://humberbusiness.com/news/hulls-young-retail-stars-celebrate-their/story-3494-detail/story, accessed 22 December 2017.

IPSO (Independent Press Standards Organization) (2017) *Editors' Code of Practice*, https://www.ipso.co.uk/editors-code-of-practice/, accessed 21 January 2018.

The Irish News (2016) 'Australia to tighten benefit rules due to growing number of wannabe actors and sports stars', *The Irish News*, 24 February, http://www.irishnews.com/news/2016/02/24/news/australia-to-tighten-benefit-rules-due-to-growing-number-of-wannabe-actors-and-sports-stars-428288/, accessed 12 July 2018.

Iyengar, S. (1991) *Is Anyone Responsible? How Television Frames Political Issues*, Chicago and London: University of Chicago Press.

Jensen, T. (2013) 'A summer of television poverty porn', *Sociological Imagination*, 9 September, http://sociologicalimagination.org/archives/14013, accessed 20 December 2017.

Jensen, T. (2014) 'Welfare commonsense, poverty porn and doxosophy', *Sociological Research Online*, 19(3): 3.

Johnson, J. (2008) *The Use of the Internet by America's Largest Newspapers (2008 Edition)*, 18 December, *bivingsreport.com*, accessed 20 December 2017.

Jones, O. (2011) *Chavs: The Demonization of the Working Class*, London: Verso.

Jones, W.R. (1980) 'Pious endowments in medieval Christianity and Islam', *Diogenes*, 28(109): 23–36.

Kaufmann, M. (1907) *The Housing of the Working Classes and of the Poor (Vol. 2)*, https://archive.org/stream/housingworkingc01kaufgoog/housingworkingc01kaufgoog_djvu.txt, accessed 21 December 2017.

Kelsey, D. (2015) 'Defining the "sick society": discourses of class and morality in British right-wing newspapers during the 2011 England riots', *Capital & Class*, 39(2): 243–364.

Kemble, H. (2016) 'Benefits Street's "Black Dee" jailed for seven years for keeping drugs and live ammo', *www.dailystar.co.uk*, 11 January, https://www.dailystar.co.uk/news/latest-news/486805/Benefits-Street-Black-Dee-jailed-keeping-drugs-live-ammo, accessed 9 January 2018.

Kennedy, S. (2011) *Uprating of Social Security Benefits*, House of Commons Library Research Briefing, http://researchbriefings.files.parliament.uk/documents/SN06141/SN06141.pdf, accessed 20 December 2017.

Kennedy, S., Wilson, W., Apostolova, A., Keen, R. (2016) *The Benefit Cap*, House of Commons Library Research Briefing, http://researchbriefings.files.parliament.uk/documents/SN06294/SN06294.pdf, accessed 20 December 2017.

Kirby, S. 'Vandals slammed after wrecking spree at play park', *Hartlepool Mail*, 22 September, https://www.hartlepoolmail.co.uk/news/

vandals-slammed-after-wrecking-spree-at-play-park-1-8139843, accessed 21 January 2018.

Krugman, P. (2015) 'The case for austerity was a lie. Why does Britain still believe it? The austerity delusion', *The Guardian*, 29 April, https://www.theguardian.com/business/ng-interactive/2015/apr/29/the-austerity-delusion, accessed 8 January 2018.

Kusi-Obodum, M. (2016) 'Rock thrown through bus window just days after company threatens to boycott Southampton estate', *Southern Daily Echo*, 28 September, http://www.dailyecho.co.uk/NEWS/14767518.Bus_window_smashed_with_rock_just_days_after_company_threatens_to_boycott_Southampton_estate/, accessed 21 January 2018.

Lansley, S. and Mack, J. (2015) *Breadline Britain: The Rise of Mass Poverty*, London: Oneworld Publications.

Larner, T. (2016) 'Drunken killer who beat neighbour to death is jailed for life', *www.birminghammail.co.uk*, 7 June, https://www.birminghammail.co.uk/news/midlands-news/drunken-killer-who-beat-neighbour-11438470, accessed 21 January 2018.

Lawton, J. (2016) 'Jihadi Sid milked UK benefit system', *Daily Star*, 7 January, p.9.

Lazerri, A. (2013) 'After the Philpotts' shameless crocodile tears, here are other monsters caught crying their lies out', *The Sun*, 4 April, https://www.thesun.co.uk/archives/news/642136/after-the-philpotts-shameless-crocodile-tears-here-are-other-monsters-caught-crying-their-lies-out/, accessed 21 December 2017.

Levitas, R. (1996a) 'The concept of social exclusion and the new Durkheimian hegemony', *Critical Social Policy*, 46: 5–20.

Levitas, R. (1996b) 'Fiddling while Britain burns? The measurement of unemployment', in R. Levitas and W. Guy (eds) *Interpreting official statistics*, London: Routledge.

Li, Y., Pickles, A., & Savage, M. (2005) 'Social capital and social trust in Britain', *European Sociological Review*, 21(2): 109–123.

Lilley, P. (1992) Speech to Conservative Party Conference, https://www.youtube.com/watch?v=FOx8q3eGq3g, accessed 21 December 2017.

Lister, R. (2004a) *Poverty*. Cambridge: Polity Press.

Lister, R. (2004b) A politics of recognition and respect: involving people with experience of poverty in decision-making that affects their lives' in J. Anderson & B. Siim (eds), *The Politics of Inclusion and Empowerment*, London: Palgrave Macmillan, pp.116–138.

LLAKES (Centre for Research on Learning and Life Chances in Knowledge Economies and Societies) (2011) *Education, Opportunity and Social Cohesion*, London: Institute of Education, University of London.

Logan, R. (2016) 'Benefits cheat who claimed £18,000 by pretending he had "dodgy knee" caught ten pin bowling', *Daily Mirror*, 16 January, http://www.mirror.co.uk/news/uk-news/benefits-cheat-who-claimed-18000-7190822, accessed 23 December 2017.

McCann, K. (2016) 'Iain Duncan Smith resignation: EU claims are a "deliberate attempt to discredit me" IDS claims after emotional Andrew Marr interview', *Daily Telegraph*, 20 March, http://www.telegraph.co.uk/news/politics/conservative/12199301/iain-duncan-smith-resignation-reaction-live.html, accessed 20 December 2017.

MacDonald, R., Shildrick, T. and Furlong, A. (2014) 'In search of "intergenerational cultures of worklessness": Hunting the Yeti and shooting zombies', *Critical Social Policy*, 34(2): 199–220.

Mackintosh, T. '£10k fraudster lied about her job to taxman', *Crawley News*, 20 January, p.11.

McLelland, E. and Gye, H. (2016) '"You get to sit on your bum and lie to kids all day": obese benefits scrounger boasts about having the best job in the world because he works just FOUR weeks a year as Santa', *Mail Online*, 21 April,

http://www.dailymail.co.uk/news/article-3550211/Obese-benefits-Meet-26-stone-man-loves-four-weeks-year-job-Santa-sit-bum-lie-kids-day.html, accessed 22 December 2017.

McGhee, D. (2005) *Intolerant Britain? Hate Citizenship and Difference: Hate, Citizenship and Difference*, New York: McGraw-Hill Education.

McIntosh, M.K. (2011) *Poor Relief in England: 1350–1600*, Cambridge: Cambridge University Press.

McKenna, L. (2016) 'Teen gangs run riot in Coltness as five youths are charged by police', *Daily Record*, 5 October, https://www.dailyrecord.co.uk/news/local-news/teen-gangs-run-riot-coltness-8981543, accessed 21 January 2018.

McManus, J.H. (1994) *Market-driven Journalism: Let the Citizen Beware?*, London: Sage Publications.

Macnicol, J. (1987) 'In pursuit of the underclass', *Journal of Social Policy*, 16(3): 293–318.

Macnicol, J. (1999) 'From "problem family" to "underclass", 1945–95', in R. Lowe and H. Fawcett (eds) *Welfare Policy in Britain: The Road from 1945*, London: Palgrave Macmillan, pp.69–93.

McRobbie, A. (1994) 'Folk devils fight back', *New Left Review*, 203: 107.

Major, J. (1993) 'Back to Basics' speech, 8 October, http://www.johnmajor.co.uk/page1096.html, accessed 16 January 2018.

Makarem, S.C. and Jae, H. (2016) 'Consumer boycott behavior: an exploratory analysis of twitter feeds', *Journal of Consumer Affairs* 50(1): 193–223.

Mann, K. (1994) 'Watching the defectives: observers of the underclass in the USA, Britain and Austialia', *Critical Social Policy*, 14(41): 79–99.

Mann, K. and Roseneil, S. (1994) 'Some Mothers Do 'Ave 'Em': backlash and the gender politics of the underclass debate', *Journal of Gender Studies*, 3(3): 317–331.

Margan, M. (2016) 'It started with a raccoon – now reviewers are raving about new party business', *www.liverpoolecho.co.uk*, 5 February, http://www.liverpoolecho.co.uk/news/liverpool-news/started-raccoon-now-reviewers-raving-10849826, accessed 9 January 2018.

Marsh, S. (2016) 'In-work poverty: do you struggle to get by on your wages?', *The Guardian*, 12 October, https://www.theguardian.com/commentisfree/2016/oct/12/in-work-poverty-wages, accessed 22 December 2017.

Marx, K. and Engels, F. (1977) *The Communist Manifesto*, 12th edn, London: Penguin Books.

Marzocchi, O. (2017) 'Free movement of persons', http://www.europarl.europa.eu/atyourservice/en/displayFtu.html?ftu-Id=FTU_4.1.3.html, accessed 18 January 2018.

Mason, V. (2016) 'Yob attacks on Bradford cab drivers lead to boycott of Holme Wood estate', *Bradford Telegraph and Argus*, 22 September, http://www.thetelegraphandargus.co.uk/news/14756617.Yob_attacks_on_cab_drivers_lead_to_estate_boycott/, accessed 21 January 2018.

Matthews, A. (2016) 'Man, 46, is charged with rape after "gentle and kind" widow in her 70s is brutally attacked in her own home', *Mail Online*, 16 May, http://www.dailymail.co.uk/news/article-3591229/Man-46-arrested-gentle-kind-widow-70s-brutally-raped-home.html, accessed 21 January 2018.

May, T. (2016) 'Just about managing' speech, https://www.gov.uk/government/speeches/statement-from-the-new-prime-minister-theresa-may, accessed 21 December 2017.

Mayring, P. (2000) 'Qualitative content analysis', *Forum: Qualitative Social Research*, 1(2), https://ci.nii.ac.jp/naid/10026506554/, accessed 22 December 2017.

Mears, T. (2016) 'Residents concerned as gang of youths cause "havoc" in neighbouring town after being moved on by police', *Wales Online*, 31 October, http://www.walesonline.co.uk/news/local-news/residents-concerned-gang-youths-cause-12103101, accessed 21 January 2018.

Metro (2016a) '£26,000 benefits cheat caught pulling pints', *The Metro*, 13 January, p.17.

Metro (2016b) 'Get a job? Not while I work on my swing', *The Metro*, 24 February, p.9.

Middleton, A. (1997) 'Acts of vagrancy: the C version "autobiography" and the statute of 1388', in S. Justice and K. Kirby-Fulton (eds), *Written Work: Langland, Labor, and Authorship*, Pennsylvania: University of Pennsylvania Press, pp.208–317.

Miliband, D. (2013) Speech on Benefits Up-rating Bill, 8 January, https://hansard.parliament.uk/Commons/2013-01-08/debates/08a50f90-b656-4c51-871a-cf44abe9cd3a/CommonsChamber, accessed 21 January 2017.

Miliband, E. (2013) Speech on welfare, *The Guardian*, 6 June, https://www.theguardian.com/politics/blog/2013/jun/06/ed-miliband-welfare-live-blog, accessed 21 December 2017.

Miller, A. (2016) 'Great British Benefits Handout viewers vent as family spends £1,000 on a lizard and racoon', *www.express.co.uk*, 17 February, https://www.express.co.uk/showbiz/tv-radio/644750/Great-British-Benefits-Handout-lizard-racoon-home-zoo-Scott-Leanne-Twiter, accessed 9 January 2018.

Moody, O. (2016) 'Depression genes "trap generations in poverty cycle"', *The Times*, 3 December, https://www.thetimes.co.uk/article/depression-genes-trap-generations-in-poverty-cycle-qg09zhtpk, accessed 22 December 2017.

Mooney, C. (2004) 'Blinded by science', *Columbia Journalism Review*, 6.

Moore, C. (2016) 'Mother-of-five on benefits demands a bigger home because it's "unfair" that her 11-year-old daughter has to share a box room with her four little brothers', *Mail Online*, 19 July, http://www.dailymail.co.uk/news/article-3697629/Mother-five-benefits-demands-bigger-home-s-unfair-11-year-old-daughter-share-box-room-four-little-brothers.html, accessed 22 December 2017.

Moore, C. and Joseph, A. (2016) 'Jobless mother-of-five denies urinating on town centre war memorial on the anniversary of the Battle of the Somme', *Mail Online*, 3 July, http://www.dailymail.co.uk/news/article-3672219/Arrest-woman-photographed-urinating-town-centre-war-memorial-100th-anniversary-Battle-Somme.html, accessed 21 January 2018.

Moore, R. (2016) 'Yob who swallowed drugs to avoid being arrested by cops ends up spewing them up in police car, court hears', *www.dailyrecord.co.uk*, 8 July, https://www.dailyrecord.co.uk/news/local-news/yob-who-swallowed-drugs-avoid-8377102, accessed 21 January 2018.

Morris, N. (2010) 'Cameron calls in "bounty hunters" to catch benefit fraudsters', *The Independent*, 10 August, http://www.independent.co.uk/news/uk/politics/cameron-calls-in-bounty-hunters-to-catch-benefit-fraudsters-2049096.html, accessed 17 January 2018.

Morrison, A. (ed.) (2010) *Emergency Verse: Poetry in the Defence of the Welfare State*, Brighton: Caparison.

Morrison, A. (2013) 'Scroungerology; O Beveridge, where art thou?', *www.therecusant.org.uk*, April, http://www.therecusant.org.uk/april-is-the-cruellest-month/4575298213, accessed 21 January 2018.

Morrison, A. and Topping, A. (eds.) (2012) *The Robin Hood Book: Verse versus Austerity*, Caparison.

Morrison, J. (2016a) 'Finishing the "unfinished" story: online newspaper discussion threads as journalistic texts', *Digital Journalism*, 2: 213–232.

Morrison, J. (2016b) *Familiar Strangers, Juvenile Panic and the British Press: The Decline of Social Trust*, London: Palgrave Macmillan.

Morrison, J. (2016c) 'Framing families: "deserving" vs "undeserving" households and neighbourhoods as glimpsed through juvenile panic stories in the online press', *Proceedings of the 66th International Conference of Political Studies Association Annual Conference: Politics and the Good Life*, 21–23 March 2016, Brighton, UK.

Morrison, J. (2016d) 'Break-point for Brexit? How UKIP's image of "hate" set race discourse reeling back decades', in D. Jackson, E. Thorsen, and D. Wring (eds) *EU Referendum Analysis 2016: Media, Voters and the Campaign*, Bournemouth: The Centre for the Study of Journalism, Culture and Community, p.66.

Morrison, J. (2018) 'Online news audiences as co-authors? The extent and limits of collaborative citizen-professional journalism on newspaper comment threads', in J. Visnovsky and J. Radosinska (eds) *Journalism and Social Media: New Trends and Cultural Implications*, London: IntechOpen.

Moseley, T. (2013) 'Daily Mail front page on Mick Philpott provokes online storm', *www.huffingtonpost.co.uk*, 3 April, http://www.huffingtonpost.co.uk/2013/04/03/daily-mail-front-page-on-mick-philpott-provokes-online-storm_n_3003909.html, accessed 20 December 2017.

Mullan, K. (2016) 'State papers: RUC couldn't prove Provos' 10% "doing the double" tax', *Derry Journal*, 3 September, https://www.derryjournal.com/news/state-papers-ruc-couldn-t-prove-provos-10-doing-the-double-tax-1-7551165, accessed 22 December 2017.

Murden, J. (2006) '"City of change and challenge": Liverpool since 1945', in J. Belchem (ed.), *Liverpool 800, Culture, Character and History*, Liverpool: Liverpool University Press, pp.393–485.

Murray, C. (1990) 'Underclass', in C. Murray and F. Field *The Emerging British Underclass*, London: IEA Health and Welfare Unit.

Narain, J. (2016) 'Unemployed hero of the floods who helped save homeowners and their property has been rewarded with a host of job offers', *Mail Online*, 16 January, http://www.dailymail.co.uk/news/article-3402568/Unemployed-hero-floods-helped-save-homeowners-property-rewarded-host-job-offers.html, accessed 22 December 2017.

National Audit Office (2017) *A Short Guide to the Department for Work and Pensions*, https://www.nao.org.uk/wp-content/uploads/2017/09/11559-001-DWP-SG_6DP_final.pdf, accessed 21 December 2017.

Newman, J. (2005) 'Managerialism and social welfare', in G. Hughes and G. Lewis (eds.), *Unsettling Welfare: The Reconstruction of Social Policy*, London and New York: Routledge.

North Lanarkshire Council (2017) *The 10% Most Deprived Areas 2016*, https://www.northlanarkshire.gov.uk/index.aspx?articleid=32715, accessed 21 December 2017.

OECD (Organisation for Economic Co-operation and Development) (2001) *The Well-being of Nations: The Role of Human and Social Capital.* Paris: OECD Centre for Educational Research and Innovation.

Office for National Statistics (2013) *Internet Access – Households and Individuals: 2013*, https://www.ons.gov.uk/peoplepopulationandcommunity/householdcharacteristics/homeinternetandsocialmediausage/bulletins/internetaccesshouseholdsandindividuals/2013-08-08, accessed 23 January 2018.

Office for National Statistics (2017a) *Migration Statistics Quarterly Report: May 2016*, https://www.ons.gov.uk/peoplepopulationandcommunity/populationandmigration/internationalmigration/bulletins/migrationstatisticsquarterlyreport/may2016, accessed 22 December 2017.

Office for National Statistics (2017b) *UK Government Debt and Deficit as Reported to the European Commission: Jan to Mar 2017*, https://www.ons.gov.uk/economy/governmentpublicsectorandtaxes/publicspending/bulletins/ukgovernmentdebtanddeficitforeurostatmaast/jantomar2017, accessed 23 January 2018.

Office for National Statistics (2017c) *UK Labour Market: December 2017*,

https://www.ons.gov.uk/employmentandlabourmarket/peoplein
work/employmentandemployeetypes/bulletins/uklabourmarket/
latest, accessed 8 January 2018.

Osborne, G. (2008) 'Dependency culture' speech, 28 February, http://
conservative-speeches.sayit.mysociety.org/speech/599696,
accessed 10 January 2018.

Osborne, G. (2010a) Emergency Budget speech, 22 June, www.
theguardian.com/uk/2010/jun/22/emergency-budget-full-speech-
text, accessed 20 December 2017.

Osborne, G. (2010b) Comprehensive Spending Review speech, 20
October, http://www.bbc.co.uk/news/uk-politics-11585941,
accessed 20 December 2017.

Osborne, G. (2012) Speech to Conservative Party Conference, 8
October, https://www.newstatesman.com/blogs/politics/2012/10/
george-osbornes-speech-conservative-conference-full-text,
accessed 20 December 2017.

Osborne, G. (2013) Speech on benefits, 2 April, http://www.ukpol.
co.uk/george-osborne-2013-speech-on-benefits/, accessed 21
December 2017.

Osborne, G. and Duncan Smith, I. (2015) 'Our fight to make work pay
better than the dole has only just begun', *The Times*, 21 June, https://
www.thetimes.co.uk/article/our-fight-to-make-work-pay-better-
than-the-dole-has-only-just-begun-v03dw9tswx2, accessed 21
December 2017.

Oxford Dictionaries (2017a) 'Definition of bludger in English',
https://en.oxforddictionaries.com/definition/bludger, accessed 22
December 2017.

Oxford Dictionaries (2017b) 'Definition of scrounger in English',
https://en.oxforddictionaries.com/definition/scrounger, accessed
21 December 2017.

Oxford Dictionaries (2017c) 'Definition of shirk in English', https://
en.oxforddictionaries.com/definition/shirk, accessed 21 December
2017.

Oxford Dictionaries (2017d) 'Definition of social media in English',
https://en.oxforddictionaries.com/definition/social_media,
accessed 21 December 2017.

Patrick, R. (2017) 'Inaccurate, exploitative, and very popular: the problem with "Poverty Porn"', http://eprints.lse.ac.uk/76604/1/blogs.lse.ac.uk-Inaccurate%20exploitative%20and%20very%20popular%20the%20problem%20with%20Poverty%20Porn.pdf, accessed 22 May 2018.

Pearson, G. (1983) *Hooligan: a History of Respectable Fears*, London: Palgrave Macmillan.

Pedersen, S., Baxter, G., Burnett, S.M., Goker, A., Corney, D. and Martin, C. (2014) *Backchannel Chat: Peaks and Troughs in a Twitter Response to Three Televised Debates during the Scottish Independence Referendum campaign 2014*, Aberdeen: Aberdeen Business School Working Paper Series, 7(2).

Perkins, A. (2016) *The Welfare Trait: How State Benefits Affect Personality*, London: Palgrave Macmillan.

Pinney, T. (2004) *The Letters of Rudyard Kipling (Vol. 5): 1920–1930*, London: Palgrave.

Plunkett, J. (2014) 'Benefits Street adds nearly 1 million viewers for second episode', *The Guardian*, 14 January, https://www.theguardian.com/media/2014/jan/14/benefits-street-viewers-channel-4, accessed 22 May 2018.

Porter, A. (2008) 'David Cameron scraps Labour spending plan to avoid "borrowing bombshell"', *Daily Telegraph*, 18 November, http://www.telegraph.co.uk/news/politics/conservative/3477235/David-Cameron-scraps-Labour-spending-plan-to-avoid-borrowing-bombshell.html, accessed 20 December 2017.

Porter, A. and Winnett, R. (2010) 'Benefits shake-up: work-shy to lose benefits for three years', *Daily Telegraph*, 10 November, http://www.telegraph.co.uk/news/politics/conservative/8124769/Benefits-shake-up-work-shy-to-lose-benefits-for-three-years.html, accessed 17 January 2018.

Postans, A., 'Channel 5 is still baiting the unemployed with yet another show about benefits', *Daily Mirror*, 13 February, http://www.mirror.co.uk/tv/tv-reviews/channel-5-still-baiting-unemployed-7365341, accessed 22 December 2017.

Prior, D. and Paris. A. (2005) *Preventing Children's Involvement in Crime and Anti-social Behaviour: A Literature Review*, Birmingham: University of Birmingham.

Purnell, J. (2008a) Speech to Progress Challenge series, 19 June, http://www.progressonline.org.uk/2008/06/19/james-purnells-speech/, accessed 20 December 2017.

Purnell, J. (2008b) Introduction to *No One Written Off: Reforming Welfare to Reward Responsibility* public consultation, https://www.gov.uk/government/uploads/system/uploads/attachment_data/file/238741/7363.pdf, accessed 21 December 2017.

Rainie, L. and Smith, A. (2012) *Social Networking Sites and Politics*, Pew Research Center, 12 March, http://www.pewinternet.org/2012/03/12/main-findings-10/, accessed 9 January 2018.

Ransome, J. (2016) 'Dog poo found smeared over walls and windows after problem family evicted from Sutton Bridge council house', *Fenland Citizen*, 25 October.

Rayner, G., Farmer, B. and Boyle, D. (2016) 'Jo Cox "was victim of political killer who searched online for William Hague", court hears', 14 November, http://www.telegraph.co.uk/news/2016/11/14/jo-cox-murder-trial-prosecution-to-open-case-against-man-accused/, accessed 22 December 2017.

Ridge, S. (2014) 'White Dee interview: "What I really thought of Conservative Party Conference and all those Tories"', *Daily Telegraph*, 1 October, https://www.telegraph.co.uk/women/womens-life/11131506/White-Dee-interview-what-I-really-thought-of-Conservative-Party-conference-and-all-those-Tories.html, accessed 22 May 2018.

Roberts, E. (2016) 'Drunk single mother trashed an ambulance sent to help her after she was found sitting in the road at 7am after a night out', *Mail Online*, 13 July, http://www.dailymail.co.uk/news/article-3688087/Drunk-single-mother-trashed-ambulance-sent-help-sitting-road-7am-night-out.html, accessed 21 January 2018.

Robertson, A. (2016) 'Married father-of-five benefits cheat swindled £67,000 in disability payouts by claiming he could barely walk but managed to climb 10 flights of stairs at work and played cricket at the weekend', *Daily Mail*, 27 January, http://www.dailymail.co.uk/news/article-3418941/Married-father-five-benefits-cheat-swindled-67-000-disability-payouts-claiming-barely-walk-managed-climb-10-flights-stairs-work-played-cricket-weekend.html, accessed 23 December 2017.

Rodger, J. (2008) *Criminalising Social Policy: Antisocial Behaviour and Welfare in a De-civilised Society*, London: Willan Publishing.

Ross, T. (2013) 'Immigrants must live in Britain for a year before claiming benefits says welfare minister', *Daily Telegraph*, 17 February, http://www.telegraph.co.uk/news/uknews/immigration/9876143/Immigrants-must-live-in-Britain-for-a-year-before-claiming-benefits-says-welfare-minister.html, accessed 21 December 2017.

Rothstein, B. and Uslaner, E. (2005) 'All for all: equality, corruption and social trust', *World Politics* 58(1): 41–72.

Rowntree, B.S. and Lasker, B. (1911) *Unemployment, a Social Study*, London: Macmillan.

Rucki, A. (2016) 'Teenagers who robbed taxi drivers with machetes brought to justice – by their selfies', *Manchester Evening News*, 26 July, https://www.manchestereveningnews.co.uk/news/greater-manchester-news/machete-selfies-taxi-driver-robberies-11664435, accessed 21 January 2018.

Russell, J. (2008) 'We must dare to rethink the welfare that benefits no one', *The Guardian*, 21 November, https://www.theguardian.com/commentisfree/2008/nov/21/comment-welfare-child-protection, accessed 21 December 2017.

Russell, J. (2016) 'Let's think the unthinkable on the welfare trap', *The Times*, 3 March https://www.thetimes.co.uk/article/lets-think-the-unthinkable-on-the-welfare-trap-m9rdqzwjw, accessed 22 December 2017.

Rutter, M. and Madge, N. (1976) *Cycles of Disadvantage: a Review of Research (Vol. 1)*, London: Heinemann Educational Books.

Sabey, R. (2016) 'BRAKE POINT; Cam's bid to halt EU migrant cash', *The Sun*, 31 January, p.2.

Said, E. W. (1978) *Orientalism*, New York: Vintage Books.

Sackville, H. (1924) Introduction to Second Reading of Unemployment Insurance Bill, http://hansard.millbanksystems.com/lords/1924/feb/21/unemployment-insurance-bill, accessed 21 December 2017.

Saunders, C. (2016) 'Home rule bid by TV spongers', *Daily Star*, 14 March, p.6.

Scott, D. (2016) 'A good walk foiled – disability benefit cheat is caught playing golf', *Scottish Express*, 9 January, https://www.express.co.uk/

news/uk/633043/A-good-walk-foiled-disability-benefit-cheat-is-caught-playing-golf, accessed 23 December 2017.

Scott-Paul, A. (2013) 'Poverty porn? Who benefits from documentaries on Recession Britain?' [online]. Available from http://www.jrf.org.uk/blog/2013/08/poverty-porn-who-benefits-britain, accessed 22 May 2018.

Sharman, J. (2017) 'Department for Work and Pensions "has outrageous target" to reject 80% of benefits appeals', 17 May, http://www.independent.co.uk/news/uk/politics/dwp-benefit-appeals-target-reject-80-per-cent-outrageous-pip-jobseekers-allowance-department-work-a7740101.html, accessed 21 December 2017.

Shelter (2008) '"Work for housing" slammed', 1 May, http://m.england.shelter.org.uk/news/previous_years/2008/february_2008/work_for_housing_slammed, accessed 21 December 2017.

Shildrick, T., MacDonald, R. and Webster, C. (2012) *Poverty and Insecurity: Life in 'Low-Pay, No-Pay' Britain'*, Bristol: Policy Press.

Shipman, T. (2010) 'Cameron in benefits threat to the workshy as he declares: 'the free ride is over'', Daily Mail, 21 April, http://www.dailymail.co.uk/news/election/article-1267465/General-Election-2010-Cameron-benefits-threat-workshy-declares-The-free-ride-over.html, accessed 20 December 2017.

Shipman, T. (2016a) 'Cameron: I will bulldoze sink estates', *Sunday Times*, 10 January, https://www.thetimes.co.uk/article/cameron-i-will-bulldoze-sink-estates-2qzmgkgwlxn, accessed 21 January 2018.

Shipman, T. (2016b) 'Parenting class vouchers to help problem families', *Sunday Times*, 10 January, https://www.thetimes.co.uk/article/parenting-class-vouchers-to-help-problem-families-j6sh7ttmgrp, accessed 22 December 2017.

Sims, G.R. (1883) *How the Poor Live*, London: Chatto.

Sindall, R. (1987) 'The London garotting panics of 1856 and 1862', *Social History*, 12(3): 351–359.

Sinfield, A. (1981) *What Unemployment Means*, Oxford: Wiley-Blackwell.

Skeggs, B. (2004) *Class, Self, Culture*, Abingdon: Psychology Press.

Skeggs, B. (2005) 'The making of class and gender through visualizing moral subject formation', *Sociology*, 39(5): 965–982.

Slater, C. (2016) 'Footage shows police being pelted with bricks and petrol bombs by "angry mob"', *www.mirror.co.uk*, 1 April, https://www.mirror.co.uk/news/uk-news/footage-shows-police-being-pelted-7670513, accessed 21 January 2018.

Slater, T. (2014) 'The myth of "Broken Britain": welfare reform and the production of ignorance', *Antipode*, 46(4): 948–969.

Sloan, J. (2016) 'Government debt: Turnbull, Morrison can't delay budget repair', *The Australian*, 3 September, http://www.theaustralian.com.au/opinion/columnists/judith-sloan/government-debt-turnbull-morrison-cant-delay-budget-repair/news-story/2c8ad6f9b110bc-c62b03c8eebf154699, accessed 22 December 2017.

Smith, G. (2016) 'Mum of six locked up for £100k dole con', *The Sun*, 29 September, p.11.

Soothill, K. and Grover. C. (1997) 'A note on computer searches of newspapers', *Sociology*, 31(3): 591–596.

Spillett, R. (2016) 'Tail of filth left behind by "family from hell" as they are finally evicted after 20-year reign of terror over their neighbours', *Mail Online*, 12 August, http://www.dailymail.co.uk/news/article-3736053/Family-yobs-destroyed-council-house-ahead-eviction.html, accessed 21 January 2018.

Spours, K. (2015) *The Osborne Supremacy: Why Progressives have to Develop a Hegemonic Politics for the 21st Century*, London: Compass.

Squires, P. (2008) *ASBO Nation: the Criminalisation of Nuisance*, London: Policy Press.

Standing, G. (2014) *A Precariat Charter: From Denizens to Citizens*, London: A&C Black.

Standing, G. (2016) *The Precariat: The New Dangerous Class*, London: Bloomsbury Publishing.

StatsWales (2016) *Out-of-work Benefit Claimants by Welsh Economic Region, Variable and Statistical Group*, https://statswales.gov.wales/Catalogue/Business-Economy-and-Labour-Market/People-and-Work/Key-Benefit-Claimants/latestbenefitclaimants-by-welsh economicregion-statisticalgroup, accessed 21 January 2018.

Strauß, S. (2008) *Volunteering and Social Inclusion: Interrelations between Unemployment and Civic Engagement in Germany and Great Britain*, Berlin: Springer Science & Business Media.

The Sun (2016a) 'Dole in one', *The Sun*, 24 February, p.13.

The Sun (2016b) 'Bombers' £42k dole', *The Sun*, 6 August, p.33.

The Sun (2013) 'In the gutter', *The Sun*, 3 April, https://www.thesun. co.uk/archives/news/642197/in-the-gutter/, accessed 10 January 2018.

Sunday Express (2016) 'Turkey poll findings were flawed – clarification', *Sunday Express*, 20 June, https://www.express.co.uk/news/ clarifications-corrections/681097/Turkey-poll-findings-were-flawed-clarification, accessed 22 December 2017.

Taylor, G.P. (2016) 'A fair benefits system does not justify social housing for scroungers', *Yorkshire Post*, 14 September, https://www.york shirepost.co.uk/news/opinion/gp-taylor-a-fair-benefits-system-does-not-justify-social-housing-for-scroungers-1-8122985, accessed 22 December 2017.

Taylor, L. (2016) 'Welfare groups say job seekers are being demonised in budget lead-up', *The Guardian*, 26 April, https://www.theguardian. com/australia-news/2016/apr/27/welfare-groups-say-job-seekers-are-being-demonised-in-budget-lead-up, accessed 22 December 2017.

Taylor-Gooby, P. and Taylor, E. (2015) 'Benefits and welfare: long-term trends or short-term reactions?', in J. Curtice and R. Ormston (eds), *British Social Attitudes: The 32nd Report*, http://www.bsa.natcen. ac.uk/media/38977/bsa32_welfare.pdf, accessed 20 December 2017.

Tebbit, N. (1981) Speech to Conservative Party Conference, *Daily Telegraph*, 28 June 2010, http://www.telegraph.co.uk/news/news-video/7858570/Norman-Tebbit-my-father-got-on-his-bike-to-look-for-a-job.html, accessed 21 December 2017.

Teesside Evening Gazette (2016) 'House for homeless given a colour makeover', *Teesside Evening Gazette*, 2 July, https://www. thefreelibrary.com/House+for+homeless+given+a+makeover.-a0456757303, accessed 12 July 2018.

Thatcher, M. (1975) Speech to Young Conservative Conference, 8 February, http://www.margaretthatcher.org/document/102484, accessed 21 December 2017.

Thorp, A. and Kennedy, S. (2010) *The Problems of British Society*, http://www.parliament.uk/documents/commons/lib/research/key_issues/Key-Issues-The-problems-of-British-society.pdf, accessed 21 December 2017.

Tierney, B. (1959) *Medieval Poor Law: A Sketch of Canonical Theory and Its Application in England*. Berkeley: University of California Press.

Timmins, N. (2001) *The Five Giants: A Biography of the Welfare State*, London: HarperCollins.

Timms, S. (2008) Introduction of Employment and Support Allowance Regulations, 27 March, https://publications.parliament.uk/pa/cm200708/cmhansrd/cm080327/wmstext/80327m0002.htm, accessed 21 December 2017.

Tolj, B. (2016) '"I don't want to work my whole life and just die": Hundreds of thousands of young Australians don't work or study – and some vow to NEVER get a job', *Mail Online*, 14 September.

Tomlinson, S. and Dolan, A. (2013) 'Shameless to the bitter end: Philpott sticks up two fingers as cries of "Die, Mick, die" ring out from public gallery after judge sentences him to LIFE in prison for killing his six children in house blaze', *Daily Mail*, 4 April, http://www.dailymail.co.uk/news/article-2303851/Mick-Philpott-sentenced-LIFE-wife-Mairead-gets-17-years-Derby-house-plot.html, accessed 21 December 2017.

Tonkin, S. (2016) 'Jobless lotto couple who won £50,000 and then spent it all in eight months face eviction after being refused benefits', *Mail Online*, 7 January, http://www.dailymail.co.uk/news/article-3388359/Lotto-couple-won-50-000-spent-year-face-eviction-refused-benefits.html, accessed 9 January 2018.

Townsend, P. (1979) *Poverty in the United Kingdom: a Survey of Household Resources and Standards of Living*, Harmondsworth: Penguin Books.

Tuchman, G. (1972) 'Objectivity as strategic ritual: an examination of newsmen's notions of objectivity', in Tumber, H. (ed.) (1999) *News: A Reader*, Oxford: Oxford University Press, pp.297–307.

Twomey, J. (2016) 'Jailed: Scum who stole life-savings of aunt fighting cancer', *Daily Express*, 2 June, https://www.express.co.uk/news/

uk/676075/Jailed-scum-conman-Daniel-Money-stole-life-savings-aunt-Gillian-Kirk-fighting-cancer, accessed 21 January 2018.

Tyler, I. (2008) '"Chav mum chav scum" Class disgust in contemporary Britain', *Feminist Media Studies*, 8(1):17–34.

Tyler, I. (2013) *Revolting Subjects: Social Abjection and Resistance in Neoliberal Britain*, London: Zed Books Ltd.

Volmert, A., Gerstein Pineau, M. and Kendall-Taylor, N. (2016) 'Talking about poverty: how experts and the public understand poverty', in *Talking about Poverty,* https://www.jrf.org.uk/report/talking-about-poverty-how-experts-and-public-understand-uk-poverty, accessed 1 February 2018.

Waddington, S. (2016) 'Benefits scrounger wants to be next PM', *Plymouth Herald*, 29 June, p.6.

Waiton, S. (2008) *The Politics of Antisocial Behaviour: Amoral Panics*, London: Routledge.

Waiton, S. (2009) 'Policing after the crisis: crime, safety and the vulnerable public', *Punishment & Society*, 11(3): 359–376.

Wellman, A. (2016) 'Top Tory warns families on benefits to "find work now or risk impact of £6,000 welfare cut"', *www.mirror.co.uk*, 7 May, http://www.mirror.co.uk/news/uk-news/top-tory-warns-families-benefits-7917512, accessed 9 January 2018.

Welshman, J. (2007) *From Transmitted Deprivation to Social Exclusion: Policy, Poverty and Parenting*, Bristol: Policy Press.

Welshman, J. (2013) *Underclass: a History of the Excluded: 1880–2000*, London: Hambledon Continuum.

Wheeler, C. (2016) '12M TURKS SAY THEY'LL COME TO UK: Those planning to move are either unemployed or students according to shock poll', *Sunday Express*, 22 May, pp.1, 6–7.

White, R.B. (1971) 'Chaucer's Daun Piers and the rule of St. Benedict: The failure of an ideal', *The Journal of English and Germanic Philology*, 70(1): 13–30.

Wiggan, J. (2012) 'Telling stories of 21st century welfare: The UK Coalition government and the neo-liberal discourse of worklessness and dependency', *Critical Social Policy*, 32(3): 383–405.

Wilkinson, T. (2016) 'Benefits doctor "couldn't walk" ... but joined Army', *The Metro*, 19 January, p.7.

Williams, Z. (2013) 'Strivers and skivers: the argument that pollutes people's minds', *The Guardian*, 9 January, https://www.theguardian.com/politics/2013/jan/09/skivers-v-strivers-argument-pollutes, accessed 21 December 2017.

Wilson, A. (2013) 'Michael Philpott is a perfect parable for our age', *Daily Mail*, 2 April, http://www.dailymail.co.uk/debate/article-2303071/Mick-Philpotts-story-shows-pervasiveness-evil-born-welfare-dependency.html, accessed 15 January 2018.

Wilson, D. (2013) 'How Jeremy Kyle helped create Mick Philpott', *Daily Mail*, 3 April, http://www.dailymail.co.uk/debate/article-2303659/Mick-Philpott-Jeremy-Kyle-How-TV-helped-create-Shameless-Mick.html, accessed 20 December 2017.

Wintour, P. (2011) 'Cameron and Miliband clash over sickness benefit for cancer patients', *The Guardian*, 15 June, https://www.theguardian.com/politics/2011/jun/15/cameron-miliband-clash-benefits-for-cancer-patients, accessed 23 January 2018.

Wintour, P. (2015) 'Summer budget 2015 represents new centre of UK politics, says Osborne', *The Guardian*, 9 July, https://www.theguardian.com/uk-news/2015/jul/09/summer-budget-2015-working-tax-credits-cuts-work-penalty-labour-chris-leslie, accessed 8 January 2018.

Wodak, R. (2001) 'The discourse-historical approach', in R. Wodak and M. Meyer (eds) *Methods of Critical Discourse Analysis*, London: Sage, pp.63–94.

Woodhouse, C. (2014) 'Immigrants could be denied benefits in Labour crackdown', *Sun on Sunday*, 3 August, https://www.thesun.co.uk/archives/politics/1014313/immigrants-could-be-denied-benefits-in-labour-crackdown/, accessed 8 January 2018.

World Values Survey (2015) *World Values Survey 2015* [online], http://www.worldvaluessurvey.org/WVSDocumentationWV5.jsp.

Work and Pensions Committee (2014) 'The scale of fraud and error and the Government's response', in *Work and Pensions Committee: Sixth Report*, https://publications.parliament.uk/pa/cm201314/cmselect/cmworpen/1082/108205.htm, accessed 21 December 2017.

Wrigley, C. (2016) 'Gladstone and Labour', in R. Quinault, R. Swift, R. Clayton and Windscheffel (eds), *William Gladstone: New Studies and Perspectives*, Abingdon: Routledge, pp. 51–72.

www.belfasttelegraph.co.uk (2016a) 'Sink estates could be bulldozed in Cameron war on gang culture', *Belfast Telegraph*, 10 January, https://www.belfasttelegraph.co.uk/news/uk/sink-estates-could-be-bulldozed-in-david-cameron-war-on-gang-culture-34349845.html, accessed 21 January 2018.

www.belfasttelegraph.co.uk (2016b) 'Cameron: "Emergency brake" plan shows EU is taking on board my concerns', *Belfast Telegraph*, 28 January, https://www.belfasttelegraph.co.uk/news/uk/david-cameron-emergency-brake-plan-shows-eu-is-taking-on-board-my-concerns-34403634.html, accessed 22 December 2017.

www.change.org (2014) 'Channel 4 (@Channel4): Stop broadcasting Benefits Street and make a donation to a relevant charity for the harm caused', https://www.change.org/p/channel-4-channel4-stop-broadcasting-benefits-street-and-make-a-donation-to-a-relevant-charity-for-the-harm-caused, accessed 22 May 2018.

www.express.co.uk (2016) 'Turkey poll findings were flawed – clarification', 19 June, https://www.express.co.uk/news/clarifications-corrections/681097/Turkey-poll-findings-were-flawed-clarification, accessed 12 July 2018.

www.guardian.com (2013) 'Budget: cutting the poor adrift makes no economic sense', *The Guardian*, 24 March, https://www.theguardian.com/commentisfree/2013/mar/24/budget-osborne-cuts-poor-adrift, accessed 23 January 2018.

www.telegraph.co.uk (2016) 'Benefits Street star "Black Dee" jailed over drugs and bullets', *www.telegraph.co.uk*, 11 January, http://www.telegraph.co.uk/news/uknews/law-and-order/12093197/Benefits-Street-star-Black-Dee-jailed-over-drugs-and-bullets.html, accessed 9 January 2018.

Yorkshire Evening Post (2016) 'One in ten in Leeds struggling to heat homes', *Yorkshire Evening Post*, 15 December, https://www.yorkshireeveningpost.co.uk/news/one-in-ten-in-leeds-struggling-to-heat-homes-1-8290607, accessed 22 December 2017.

REFERENCES

Yorkshire Post (2016) 'YP: David Cameron's gimmicks fail troubled families', *Yorkshire Post*, 20 December, https://www.yorkshirepost.co.uk/news/opinion/yp-comment-david-cameron-s-gimmicks-fail-troubled-families-1-8297599, accessed 21 January 2018.

INDEX